Kinethic California

TITLES IN THE SERIES:

Kinethic California: Dancing Funk and Disco Era Kinships by Naomi Macalalad Bragin

Inhabiting the Impossible: Dance and Experimentation in Puerto Rico, edited by Susan Homar and Nibia Pastrana Santiago

The Body in Crisis: New Pathways and Short Circuits in Representation by Christine Greiner

Corporeal Politics: Dancing East Asia, edited by Katherine Mezur and Emily Wilcox

dance
studies
association

The Dance Studies Association (DSA) advances the field of dance studies through research, publication, performance, and outreach to audiences across the arts, humanities, and social sciences. As a constituent member of the American Council of Learned Societies, DSA holds annual conferences; publishes new scholarship through its book series, proceedings, and Conversations Across the Field of Dance Studies; collaborates regularly with peer institutions in the United States and abroad; and presents yearly awards for exemplary scholarship. A complete list of books in the series can be found on the University of Michigan website, www.press.umich.edu.

Kinethic California

DANCING FUNK & DISCO ERA KINSHIPS

NAOMI MACALALAD BRAGIN

University of Michigan Press
Ann Arbor

Published in the United States of America by the
University of Michigan Press
Printed and bound by CPI Group (UK) Ltd, Croydon, CR0 4YY

First published May 2024

A CIP catalog record for this book is available from the British Library.

Library of Congress Cataloging-in-Publication data has been applied for.

ISBN 978-0-472-07641-3 (hardcover : alk. paper)
ISBN 978-0-472-05641-5 (paper : alk. paper)
ISBN 978-0-472-90382-5 (open access ebook)

DOI: https://doi.org/10.3998/mpub.11950963

The University of Michigan Press's open access publishing program is made possible thanks to additional funding from the University of Michigan Office of the Provost and the generous support of contributing libraries.

for my parents

CONTENTS

Digital materials related to this title can be found on the Fulcrum platform via the following citable URL: https://doi.org/10.3998/mpub.11950963

THIS BOOK EMERGES from the movement of people with whom I have been dancing and the places where we dance together. Before dance, I learned to move by playing the violin, accompanied by my mother, a concert pianist. Music is her mother tongue, passed on to me through our extended collaboration which forms the deeper ground of the writing. I also grew up writing almost weekly to my father's parents, Jeanette Slotnick and Moses Bragin. Through these letters, my grandfather handed me his craft of writing, and our written conversations are stirred in the writing of this book.

The writing is very much inspired by the collective artistry of hip hop/streetdance culture and conversations with dancers who, over the course of this work, have become dancestors—Don Campbell, Deborah Johnson, Tyrone Proctor, Adolfo Quiñones, and Marjory Smarth. I appreciate ongoing conversations and various modes of dance study with Amanda Adams Louis, Emilio Austin, Niki Awandee, Jacque Barnes, Traci Bartlow, Jon Bayani, Eric Braflan, Junious Brickhouse, Martine Bruneau, Archie Burnett, Steffan Clemente, Samara Cohen, Sarah Crowell, Destiny Arts Center, Thelma Davis Martin, Sasha Dobos-Czarnocha, Dana Dorham, Deborah Dorzile, Moncell Durden, Jimmy Foster, Damita Jo Freeman, Leyda Garcia, Marquisa Gardner, Billy Goodson, Brian Green, Lonnie Green, Sabela Grimes, James Higgins, Kim Holmes, Abdiel Jacobsen, Natasha Jean-Bart, Flo Jenkins, Arnetta Johnson, Bryce Johnson, David Johnson, Kory Kato, Alexandra Landé, Reggie LaVince, Renée Lesley, Malonga Casquelord Center for the Arts, Viktor Manoel, Bruno Marignan, Thierry Martinvalet, Massive Monkees/The Beacon, Freddie Maxie, Boogie McClarin, Leah McKesey, Marie Medina, Ralph Montejo, Axelle Munezero, Sonia Mvondo, Lillian Nabaggala, Nubian Néné, Levant Obulie, Rashidi Omari, Jorgé Pabon, Rashaad Pearson, Lynn Pickens, Brian Polite, Rizqi Rachmat, Will Randolph, Margarita Reyna, Niels Robitzky, Sandra Sainte Rose Fanchine, Ana Sanchez, Caleaf Sellers, Timothy Solomon, Lenaya Straker, Kumari Suraj, Dani Tirrell, and Tommy Washington.

For all the folks who helped seed this book and kept it growing in various ways—opening their homes, co-writing on Zoom, supporting the writing in its various stages, reading drafts in their tenderest forms, sharing ideas with curiosity, care, kindness and wisdom, and joining together on dancefloors—love and thanks to Emily Arden, Holly Bass, Stephanie Batiste, Shannon Cram, Manuel Cuellar, Allison de Venter, Malkia Devich Cyril, Amanda Doxtater, Ugo Edu, Karla Etienne, Mary Fogarty, Nelson George, Ruth Goldstein, Jenna Grant, Sabela Grimes, Priscilla Guy, Romeo Guzmán, Judith Hamera, Vincenza Illiano, Imani Kai Johnson, Kareem Khubchandani, Kelley King, Katelyn Knox, LaTaSha Levy, Adrian Loving, Rahsaan Mahadeo, Angela Marino, Marco Mary, Marya McQuirter, Raquel Monroe, Meena Murugesan, Ọmọlará, Jessica Pabón-Colón, LaShawnDa Pittman, Jade Power Sotomayor, Heike Rafael Hernandez, Reico, José Rivera, Georgia Roberts, Omar Ricks, Doug Rosenberg, Micah Salkind, Marta Savigliano, Anna Scott, Sean Slusser, Shanté Smalls, Jen Soriano, Shannon Steen, Jasmine Syedullah, Sona Tatoyan, Tomi Tsunoda, Kathleen Woodward, Anida Yoeu Ali, Christina Zanfagna, and many others whose names escape this moment yet who I am no less grateful for.

I am indebted to mentors who have guided my multiple paths of study as a dancer, choreographer, teacher, ethnographer, and writer. Thank you to Brandi Catanese, Cheryl Cutler, Mickey Davidson, Tommy DeFrantz, SanSan Kwan, Susan Lourie, Juana Maria Rodriguez, Fred Moten, Ramón Rivera-Servera, and Darieck Scott. I appreciate the generous support of the entire faculty and staff of the School of Interdisciplinary Arts and Sciences at UW Bothell, and for their consistent advocacy, I thank Amaranth Borsuk, Bruce Burgett, Susan Harewood, Jeanne Heuving, Ted Hiebert, Brinda Sarathy and Wadiya Udell. Thank you for your outstanding developmental support, Emma Johnson and Cathy Hannabach at Ideas on Fire. Thank you for your commitment to this project, your editorial guidance, and tremendous patience with me, Clare Croft, LeAnn Fields, Jessica Hinds-Bond, Marcia LaBrenz and the entire staff at University of Michigan Press.

Research and writing of this book have been made possible by early institutional support from UC Berkeley's Program in Folklore, Department of Theater, Dance and Performance Studies, Center for Race and Gender, Women's and Gender Studies, Center for New Media, and Arts Research Center. I am grateful for funding from UC Berkeley's Mentored Research Fellowship, Dean's Doctoral Fellowship, University Fellowship, Graduate Division Block Fellowship, and a Eugene Cota Robles Fellowship. A University of California President's Postdoctoral Fellowship and support from the Harvard Book Workshop supported development of first drafts. University of Washington's Royalty Research Fellowship, Simpson Center for Humanities' Society of Scholars and First Book Fellowships, and National Endowment for the Humanities' Summer Stipend, all allowed me to deepen the writing significantly through mid-stage and final revisions. I appreciate the support of the NEH Open Book Award to publish an online version of the book that allows public access to and circulation of the writing.

For the ever-expanding gift of families, thanks and love to Michael Bragin, Melanie Heimbach, Hollis and Eloise Heimbach Bragin, Lisa Gloria, Rashonne Henderson, Anaya Dianne Simon and Semhar Yohannes, bashexo, Muna Muraisi, Milvia Pacheco Salvatierra and Akim Salvatierra. Bottomless love and gratitude for my parents and lifelong supporters, Joseph Bragin and Victoria Macalalad Bragin.

She steps up on the small platform rectangle lined with bulbs that glow like the ones glittering on the lettered sign fixed to the blue wall behind her. She's dressed in a black-and-yellow-pattern kimono, black shorts, and shiny black boots that hit her long legs midcalf. A single yellow ribbon sweeps back her natural.

His jaw drops slightly, a smile widening his face as he looks her way. She shimmies over, keeping time in rock-steady motion. Pausing his groove, he watches her move.

Clasping her hands together, she begins to dip and twist her hips, swinging her legs high in an up-down motion. Sharing the platform with them, the drummer kicks the beat forward alongside the guitarists' stabs and horn players' blasts. She fleshes out their driving rhythm, releasing wide pelvic rotations akin to a turntable's centripetal motion. He keeps watch, stepping to the side to tap out her groove in his heel.

Without stopping to rest she breaks into a machinelike bending of wrist and neck joints. Her limbs work acute angles, accenting the churning beat with a jerky flow appended with hip thrusts that jolt her backward and forward again. Suddenly she releases the staccato movement. A joyful smile plays across her face and his. Her spine lengthens. One leg floats skyward. She remixes the deceptively easeful leg extension into a funky développé, *reimagining her leg as a guitar fingerboard being majestically strummed by her hand.*

Next, she crosses the stage, throws her arms in the air, and halts, for a millisecond, before returning to her groove. She delivers a deft sequence of finger points and arm freezes. She shimmies her shoulders, inviting his emphatic response, "I got sooooouL. *I'm* super *bad."*

Raising and rolling her fist, she punctuates his verbal statement on cue. Their smiles meet each other in quiet agreement. She rounds out her dance with a recapitulation of robotic moves, and he, clutching the microphone until it tips in its stand, pounds one foot emphatically in time with the beat.

His voice shrills to a scream as the live broadcast cuts to a yellow screen, crisscrossed with a sketch of looping train tracks. The soooooooul train . . . *a voice calls in falsetto, following the animated mechanical movement of the black locomotive, winding through yellow hills and valleys, grooving into the distant horizon.*

DAMITA'S SOLO FLIGHT

It was February 10, 1973, when for a fleeting few minutes, nineteen-year-old Damita Jo Freeman stepped up off the film studio floor onto *Soul Train*'s music celebrity stage to dance with James Brown and his band.[1] Moving alongside and around Brown in an improvised riff off his number one R & B chart single "Super Bad," Damita joined the band's funk groove.

Her impromptu solo crowned the *Train*'s second season and forty-ninth episode of national broadcast syndication from the Southern California city of Los Angeles. Velvet-voiced host-creator-entrepreneur Don Cortez Cornelius had just moved the TV show from the city of his birth, Chicago, Illinois, to begin filming from Hollywood's Metromedia Square studios.[2] That was 1971, the same year Damita was spotted dancing at local Los Angeles club Climax by Pam Brown, the talent scout recruiting *Soul Train*'s everyday-extraordinary crowd of young audience participants—the *Soul Train* dancers.

There's multiple ways to talk about Damita's often-cited 1973 performance. Her unplanned solo (in response to Brown's urging that she dance with him onstage) challenged Don Cornelius's early attempts to control and limit interactions between paid musicians and unpaid dancers—a division of labor that remained inequitable. TV dance shows could designate dancers as "audience," freeing them of any legal obligation to pay dancers for their labor. During weekend-long tapings, often without breaks, *Soul Train* dancers were provided with a piece of fried chicken, one soda, and a drink of water. Dancers also resisted: Don Cornelius banned Damita's dance partner, Don Campbell, from *Soul Train* in 1973 for organizing dancers to fight for compensation.

The *Soul Train* dancers were young stars who gifted audiences tuning in with outrageous dance moves and clever fashion styles they often thrifted and hand crafted.[3] Significant jumps in viewer ratings after Damita's onstage appearances proved that interest in the show's nonprofessional dancers often upstaged the music celebrities.

Attention could also be given to the art of improvised partnership between music and dance, heralded by Damita's multiple unplanned stage solos, including two 1972 episodes with funk singer Joe Tex.[4] More than a relationality sustained solely among members of the live band, collective rhythm on *Soul Train* was generated in sonic-kinetic improvisations that included the dancers' power to reorient the band to movement, moving the medium of music forward along shared ritual grooves and into eclectic mixes of styles.[5]

The question of who's watching whom and from where, tuning in both within and beyond the United States, is another way to depart from the solo moment. Writer Hanif Abdurraqib asserts, "It's almost a myth to suggest that there was no white audience for the show." Journalist Ericka Blount Danois further recalls mimicking the moves of Cheryl Song, the Asian American dancer who first appeared on *Soul Train* in 1976 and danced through the 1980s.[6] *Soul Train* dancers in the performance group Something Special were touring the United States by 1973, and Japan, Mexico, the Philippines, Singapore, and Hong Kong by 1977. Martiniquan-born Paris streetdancer Sandra Sainte Rose Fanchine talked to me about watching *Soul Train* with her parents during broadcasts on Sunday afternoons in Abidjan, Côte d'Ivoire, in 1977.[7] Reception and circulation of popular dance among multiple *Soul Train* audiences, national and global, are key to a study of black social life that interanimates Damita's solo.

Returning to read between the lines of Damita's dance, I offer still another way to recall this moment—by tracing cultural histories of African American vernacular dance communities in California, emerging in the 1960s and '70s and enmeshing in her solo flight.

While "to the untuned-in observer it is audio-visual anarchy," as television studies scholar Christine Acham puts it, the "mostly unidentifiable Free-style Soul" to which offscreen audiences gravitated every Saturday was generated in common rhythms of black social and vernacular dances that the *Soul Train* dancers brought on set and onscreen—from their home environments.[8] Traced in Damita's solo improvising, these sensory-kinesthetic rhythms, commonly shared, informed the culturally specific emergence of local dance styles as well as an ongoing ethics-aesthetic of kinship reinvented in/as stylistic relation—the collective movement practices this book studies as kinethics.

With the jerky flow of bent-angled arms and neck, Damita gives recognition to a social dance called Robot.[9] Drawing on popular street mime and film animation yet danced to soul and funk, Robot has been emerging from the black vernacular in couple, solo, and group forms over the last decade. In South Central Los Angeles, several miles from *Soul Train*'s Hollywood film studio, dance couple Angela Robot Ann Johnson and Charles Robot Washington have been popularizing the dance in local party culture.[10] Going back to at least 1964 in the Northern California Bay Area city of Oakland, dancer John Murphy has been adopting robotic moves of sci-fi movie characters but adding fleshly rhythms of funk and soul. Both a social party dance and solo form, Robot reflects the sound of the times—soulful and funky, hard hitting and smooth—allowing dancers to experiment with feelings of rigidity and flow, resistance and release in the collective social body.

In 1972 John Murphy becomes a formative member of Oakland's Black Messengers (a.k.a. Mechanical Device), helping grow a local culture of Boogaloo style alongside groups like Black Resurgents, S.S. Enterprise, Derrick and Company, Pirate & The Easy Walkers, One Plus One, and Granny & Robotroid. By 1975, dancer Deborah Granny Johnson brings Robotroid west across the Bay Bridge, putting Oakland Boogalooing in dialogue with San Francisco groups to spark a movement that includes Live Incorporated, Demons of the Mind, and Close Encounters of the Funkiest Kind, who innovate Strutting style.[11] Simultaneously, Richmond Robotting emerges as a highly synchronized group form hailing from the northeast Bay Area epicenter of the same name and spawning more groups like Richmond Robots, Posing Puppets, Androids, Audionauts, Black Operators, Criminons, Saturn 5, Green Machine, and Lady Mechanical Robots. Robot's prolific styles incorporate Afrofuturist aesthetics that move dancers outside of linear space-time even as they articulate local practices of belonging-becoming embedded in the places where they are.

As dancers reinvent Robot, birthing interanimated styles informed by unique contexts, they grow cultural histories that are neither singular nor static. Robot kinship formation reflects dancers' intentional creative labor to shape dance lineages in motion, practicing a sociality of indebtedness that is central to the ethos of black social dance. The dance lineages they re-create are nonlinear and kinetic, allowing dancers to forge social bonds that move them dynamically within and across multiple locals.

Dancers have been growing a translocal network of movement vernaculars, enacting an effort of their collective social body to get in formation, in anticipation of Damita's 1973 solo. By routing dancing screened on *Soul Train* to offscreen contexts, I am also tracing dancers' entanglements with the cultural, historical, and political contexts where they live and move together. Dancers have been re-creating networks of affiliation that cross space and time, shaping dance lexicons and technical styles from which global contemporary hip hop/streetdance begins to emerge.

Next is the asymmetric dance punctuated by funky finger points and pauses, which Damita heralds by throwing her arms up in the air. Known as Locking, the dance emerged in 1970 from the freestyle movement artistry of Don Campbell, who not only partnered with Damita on *Soul Train* but also honed his unique style cutting up at dance contests throughout Los Angeles and the San Fernando Valley.[12] Damita's dip-and-twist move calls on the innovations of dancer Flukey Luke. Hitting the floors of Los Angeles clubs from Maverick's Flat to Summit on the Hill, he's been recreating a fast, high-flying swing they're calling the Which-a-Way, also part of Locking's common lexicon.[13] Flukey has been performing on entertainment stages with the Campbellockers, a group Don formed with his manager and dancer Toni Basil in 1973. Locking emerged at least a year before *Soul Train*'s first Los Angeles episode, moving through city neighborhoods of South Central, Compton, and Watts, birthing interrelated youth groups like the GoGo Brothers and Creative Generation, members of which are present in the dancing crowd just off the *Soul Train* stage.[14]

They join Damita in movement at a moment that defines Locking—not solely a dance of commercial entertainment stages but also a flow that's been moving locally through schools, community centers, around-the-way clubs, parks, and house parties. Where Locker Arnetta Nettabug Johnson, founder of the Toota Woota Sisters, gets down with her girlfriends Shelley Cepeda and Lorna Dune. Where *Soul Train* dancer Freddie Maxie parties, Tuesday to Sunday night: "I would just party, girl. We would party, party. Even when I went to Cal State. Then we go to after-hours. Maverick's Flat from two to six. We were really dancing. We would sweat our clothes. We used to eat and Lock. You ask any real Locker, they would eat and Lock at the same time."[15] Drawing on black social dances like the Robot Shuffle, Rock Steady, Funky Chicken, and Breakdown, Locking is a dance of the party and the street—cited in the neighborhood by people whose everyday gestures are entangled in the collective formation of the dance.[16]

By the 2000s, Locking will be an established technical style within global hip hop/streetdance culture, circulating a lexicon of steps and moves that dancers practice rigorously in studios, improvise in clubs, and perform competitively in dance battles. Touring internationally, Don Campbell would often stop classes to share with students his parable of invention, explaining how Locking emerged from his failed attempt to do a social dance called the Robot Shuffle. Declaring that he was socially awkward and could not dance, Don shifted focus away from individual genius or contrived artistry in his creative process, often concluding the lesson in reverse by telling students, "*Anyone* can dance." Don's stories located dance in the context of his everyday social interactions with people in offscreen spaces—clubs, a college cafeteria, living rooms—all of which inform the emergence of Locking style. Rather than utilizing choreographed routines and set moves, Don's dance pedagogy would mix storytelling with freestyle circles, emphasizing students' creative freedom in his affirmation: "Do me, but be you!"[17]

Dance scholar Jacqui Malone echoes this idea of the soloist's principled conversation with the dance community: "But creativity must be balanced between the artist's conception of what is good and the audience's idea of what is good. The point is to *add to* the tradition and extend it without straying too far from it."[18] Drawing on Zora Neale Hurston's study of black vernacular aesthetics, Malone underscores the "participatory nature of black performance," defined by resistance to "static reproductions of familiar patterns or imitations of someone else's hard-earned style."[19] Drawing on this idea of keeping with and adding to tradition, I am interested in the philosophy embedded in California dances that reorient dancers toward feeling kinship in movement. Their collective practices of continuity and survival re-create dance lineages as they innovate the dance.

The stories that populate *Kinethic California: Dancing Funk and Disco Era Kinships* attend to aesthetics of everyday movement, seen through the lens of young artists who were watching cartoons while their family's soul and funk records played on living room sound systems; watching bent-leg strolls and rhythmic handshakes of people moving through their neighborhoods; watching one another move at house parties, school gyms, and around-the-way social clubs. Their aesthetic sociality provided materials for collective study and creative play. Dancers were also traveling beyond their neighborhoods, curious to study one another's movement inventions, cutting up in local talent shows and dance contests. I attend to such multidirectional conversations between dancer, community, and tradition, by way of which California dance lineages emerge and take flight.

More than a spontaneous sharing between musician and dancer, Damita Jo's 1973 solo shows the Lady of Soul's intention to keep the spotlight on black dance. Though Damita Jo describes herself as a streetdancer, she also notes acquiring training in the ballet studio.[20] Damita's funky rendition of the *développé* gives a nod to her ballet training, nuancing her embodied citation of the contemporaneous social dances Robot and Locking. I reveal the *Soul Train* dancers' work in these moments, planned, improvised, and choreographed, asserting the vitality of the *Soul Train* dancers' cultural legacy.

When performance artist Nick Cave convened a 2020 panel on *Soul Train*, asking Damita Jo to reflect on the dancers' impact on black creativity, she responded, "I thought of a party . . . we used body. Our body expressed what we felt. That was my love for dance."[21] Pairing the plural pronoun *we* with singular noun *body*, Damita Jo describes her dance as the expression of a collective body. Her dance is a shared moving-feeling of "our body," a body that is not single. Her assertion resonates with Nick Cave's memory that watching *Soul Train* felt like a "collective coming together."[22] She performs the collective social body of black vernacular dancers in and on the One, arranging and designing their movement vocabularies as her solo flight.[23]

Damita's solo statement traces the collective making of black dance in the moment, over time and within different places where the "aesthetic sociality of blackness" moves.[24] What the solo also teaches is that within one version of history, multiple histories hide.[25] The 1970s dance Waacking/Punking is unseen yet anticipated by arms arcing in flight and freezes punctuated by funk sound. Felt in the underground life of dancers moving in Los Angeles's first black gay clubs and discos, the dance's cultural history emerges from the sounds of early disco mixing with funk, fostering a wild kinetic kinship of styles. The movement of the black vernacular embraces the expanding fullness, brokenness, and messiness of dance histories, holding a funky *we* who move on the One and four-on-the-floor.

What looks like a solo, feels like a party.

Introduction

Kinethic California: Dancing Funk and Disco Era Kinships looks to forms of social and vernacular dance, blooming in 1960s and 1970s California, that organize dancers in rhythm, embedding them in local cultural histories of place while connecting them to an emergent global contemporary culture of hip hop/streetdance.[1] I name their collective movement practices *kinethic* to bring attention to motion at the core of black aesthetics that generate dances as forms of kinship beyond blood relation. Kinethics reorient dancers toward kinetic kinship in ways that give continuity to black dance lineages under persistent conditions of disappearance and loss. As dancers engage kinethics, they reinvent gestural vocabularies that describe worlds they imagine into knowing-being.

Historical Background

Funk and disco era California dancing demonstrates a dynamic fluidity of stylistic boundaries, reflective of dancers' travels within and across neighborhoods, cities, and regions. By way of everyday people's movements of migration and dislocation, physical and imaginative wandering, vernacular dances trace circuitous routes, emerge from multiple centers, and proliferate in reinvented forms. The cultural histories of these dances challenge singular and linear origin narratives—an explosion of vernacular dancing interanimates locations touching Northern California's Bay Area cities of San Francisco, Oakland, and Richmond, the Central Valley city of Fresno, and, in the south, the Los Angeles neighborhoods of Watts, Compton, Baldwin Hills, and Leimert Park. In the north, dances were emerging in Sacramento and San Jose. In the south, dancers were traveling out to Orange County, Long Beach, and the San Fernando Valley. Connecting boogaloo style to popular dances of the 1960s and '70s, Oakland dancer and cultural worker Traci Bartlow rejoins, "It was a collective consciousness of blackness. It's something that came out of our black experience. It feels like it was all around the same time of black folks in California, on the West Coast, that had this style come out of them."[2] The California dances to which I turn have shaped global contemporary dance, spanning transnational competitions, battles and dance festivals, popular film and TV dance reality shows, TikTok and YouTube viral videos, private studio classes, university curricula, underground clubs and neighborhood gatherings.

New York is the birthplace of hip hop culture, yet dancers and scholars alike have noted its long-standing vital entanglement with California dance cultures. Widely respected hip hop dancers who research these histories have consistently acknowledged links between California and New York. Steffan Mr. Wiggles Clemente writes, "East Coast Hip Hop dancers met the West Coast Street Style dancers and exchanged styles. California had dances like POPPING and LOCKING. With this exchange came the acceptance of POPPING and LOCKING into Hip Hop dance."[3] Practitioner Jorge Popmaster Fabel Pabon asserts: "In order to properly report the history of hip-hop dance forms, one must journey both inside and outside of New York City. Although dance forms associated with hip-hop did develop in New York City, half of them (i.e. popping and locking) originated and developed on the west coast as part of a different cultural movement."[4] In his 1986 essay "Hip Hop 101," historian and cultural anthropologist Robert Farris Thompson similarly noted, "Hip hop is a tale of three cities. As I've said, breakdancing and the hip hop sound emerged in the Bronx, electric-boogaloo poppin' and tickin' moves arose in Fresno and Los Angeles (Watts, Long Beach, Crenshaw Heights)."[5]

While these statements connect the styles of hip hop, breaking, popping, and locking, as well as New York and Central and Southern California, dancers have also argued for inclusion of dance histories situated in Northern California's San Francisco Bay Area, citing styles of Oakland

Boogaloo, San Francisco Strutting, and Richmond Robotting.[6] The naming of dances for cities, neighborhoods, and areas is a familiar act of recognition by which dancers become embedded in place as a shared sociality and felt sense of being and belonging in movement. The Bay's distance from Los Angeles in the south (seven hours' drive) meant a whole network of local dance cultures could thrive without the direct impact of the Hollywood entertainment industrial complex. The influence of Bay Area dance histories on global hip hop/streetdance culture is still not widely narrated.[7]

To further complicate this mess of origins, Clemente makes the critical point that two popular films of 1984, *Breakin'* and *Beat Street*, "helped catapult Hip Hop to the mainstream audience."[8] New York Breaking appears alongside California Popping and Locking styles in *Breakin'* (filmed in California) and *Beat Street* (filmed in New York). One year earlier, popping appears alongside breaking in 1983's *Flashdance*, filmed in New York. In fact, popping (originally known among New York dancers as electric boogie) and locking appear in the underground hip hop classic *Wild Style*, a month before *Flashdance* was released. Waacking/punking, a style emerging in Los Angeles's first gay discos, makes fleeting appearances in *Breakin'* and its sequel, *Breakin' 2: Electric Boogaloo*.[9] While California dances were misrepresented as "breakdancing," a misnomer that circulated widely in mass media, the 1980s is nevertheless a key period in which the cultural kinship of styles becomes evident in mainstream media.[10]

Dancers in New York who were watching *Soul Train* and traveling themselves across regional, state, and national lines, were experimenting with movements innovated by California dancers, contributing to the growth of California styles alongside East Coast styles of breaking, rocking, and hip hop. As media representation continues to shape mainstream misconceptions of hip hop dance forms and histories, I attune to dancers' own intramural practices of affiliation, through which dances are born and reborn.

Dance lineages are not preconceived or immutable. They take shape and shift through dancers' practices of affiliation. During the early 1970s, the interrelated forms of breaking and rocking emerged in New York as dancers innovated styles that would become foundations of hip hop dance. With increasing mainstream media representation in the early 1980s, California street styles of popping and locking were embraced among dancers as dance kin of hip hop, while New York dancers were simultaneously birthing hip hop's golden era party dances like the Dougie, Running Man, Cabbage Patch, Reebok, and more. Acknowledging these cross-cultural translocations allows for more nuanced and dynamic conversations between dancers that don't reinscribe immobility and cultural stasis onto minoritized communities. What I am saying is that dance styles were in conversation because dancers were in conversation; they were not/are not producing culture in isolation.

Funk X Disco

Both funk and disco music were innovated as artists profusely mixed earlier genres, shaping forms with a dance orientation and an immersive sonic-kinetic feel. Funk artists, historiographer Tim Lawrence writes, "were more interested in generating a concentrated and constant rhythmic riff than a variable and undulating emotional journey."[11] Describing the emergence of funk in the late 1960s and early 1970s, music historian Rickey Vincent writes that live band artists—among them James Brown, Sly & the Family Stone, George Clinton/Parliament-Funkadelic, and Bootsy Collins—were "breaking formalized styles and generating a synthesis" of elements, mixing soul, R & B, gospel, rock, jazz, and blues.[12] Funk music's driving, dance-oriented feel, Vincent explains, centered rhythmic syncopation, sustained by collective improvisation among all members of the band. The genre brought a new focus to bass and electric guitarists, Tony Bolden writes, ensuing from "James Brown's rhythmic innovations [where] the drummer emphasized the first beat in a four-bar measure—generally known as the 'One.'"[13] By sustaining a pulsing anticipatory groove, the One supports funk's experiences of sensory immersion. Beyond musical genre, Bolden further emphasizes the spiritual element and "psychosomatic construct known as funk . . . as an alternative *form* of rationality."[14] LaMonda Horton-Stallings goes further to assert that funk is a practice of the erotic specific to black sexual cultures, examining it "as nonreproductive sex and transaesthetics of cultural art forms."[15]

While funk has widely been positioned in opposition to disco, Tavia Nyong'o nuances the politics of genre boundary keeping: "The unhappy hybridity of disco is still evinced in the uneasy status of its foremost cultural avatars—the Bee Gees and John Travolta, playing Tony Manero—white men occupying vocal registers and striking choreographic poses that usurp the disco diva and the gay man while at the same time infringing upon, even denaturing, the very white masculinity that such a colonizing move is supposed to secure."[16] Lawrence concurs, stating that "all sorts of protagonists had all sorts of problems with this highly politicized genre," which let go of the live band to focus on the producer and DJ's artistry, bringing extended dance tracks to the floors of new urban discotheques and underground parties alike.[17]

Early 1970s disco emerged from soul, funk, and jazz blendings, notable in Detroit Motown recordings of "Papa Was a Rollin' Stone" by the Undisputed Truth and the Temptations, Isaac Hayes's "Theme from Shaft," and Sly & the Family Stone's "Dance to the Music." Foundational to disco's development as a genre was the distinct sound shaped by Philadelphia producers like Gamble and Huff and extended by the New York-based Salsoul Records. Lawrence traces the disco beat to early innovations of the Philadelphia trio of musicians known as Baker-Harris-Young, soon brought to public attention by black entertainment entrepreneur Don Cornelius, who requested that Gamble and Huff create the theme song for his newly syndicated TV show *Soul Train*.[18] The result was the 1974 chart-topping hit "TSOP (The Sound of Philadelphia)" by Mother Father Sister Brother (MFSB).[19]

Troubling a potentially utopian division between early disco and an increasingly technologically mediated sound, Nyong'o hears a "genealogy of afrofuturism" in the musical range of Donna Summer's "I Feel Love," which he emphasizes "is the quintessential recording of a modulated aim, layering the sonic emblem of the 'disco diva' into a pulsating dance-floor scorcher built entirely out of the 'artifice' of synthesized sounds."[20] Disco innovated "a feeling-tone between the live and mediated," which, Nyong'o notes, immediately triggered a range of emotional responses, shaping an ambivalent politics of emerging dance music cultures.[21] Funk and disco genres emerged relationally, in ways that challenge conceptual hierarchies of live over mediated sound. Going beyond musical genre to consider psychosomatic aspects of funk and disco aesthetics, I follow the work of Nyong'o, Bolden, and Stallings, to articulate the ways 1970s dance music cultures continue to shape global contemporary hip hop/streetdance.

Hip Hop Dance X Streetdance

Hip hop, popping, locking, breaking, bonebreaking, boogaloo, strutting, turfing, tuttin', tickin', snaking, vibing, animating, robotting, gangsta walkin', jackin', jookin', jerkin', jittin', waacking, punking, voguing, house, lite feet, footwork, beat your feet (and on and on). Black vernacular style stays prolific, continuously reinventing self-described labels, unsettling predictable categories and wild styling genres. Style names are action oriented, giving instructions for how to move: *poppers'* muscles contract and explode; *lockers'* limbs click into place at the joints; *waackers'* arms strike out, cut through, stir up air.[22] Brenda Dixon Gottschild identifies this key principle of the Africanist aesthetic: "The movement of the action—is as important as getting it done, the static fact of the result or product."[23]

Umbrella uses of *hip hop* and *streetdance* are fraught. When I started writing this book, I was more convinced the terms were capacious enough to hold a body of wildly diverse styles and distinct cultural histories of dances emanating from Northern, Central, and Southern California, Chicago, and New York, among countless other areas. As my writing went deeper, I wondered about the helpfulness of both terms as umbrella references, knowing that *hip hop*, beyond its origins in Black and Latinx youth subcultures of 1970s and 1980s New York, continues to be used by mainstream media as a blanket term and by marketing industries as a brand. Similarly, *streetdance* comes specifically from a Los Angeles context associated with tensions between the entertainment industry and cultural styles that emerged from free-form social dancing in everyday spaces. I feel ambivalent toward the terms yet also understand their significance for articulating the interanimations of dancers' diverse cultural histories that this book studies.

As an umbrella term related to hip hop, *streetdance* is reflective less of a fixed collection of styles than of historical tensions between black vernacular and white establishment dance. Streetdancer James OG Skeeter Rabbit Higgins recalls that in 1970s Los Angeles, the label was used by entertainment industry dealers and dancers alike to "differen[tiate] between what was taught in the studios and what was taught in the streets. At first, we weren't welcome in the studios, until we became of value." Another dancer, Deputy, put it to me simply: "Locking was like dirt."[24] In the Los Angeles-specific context, *street* marked practitioners' ambivalent relations with (if not always total exclusion from) the Hollywood entertainment industry and white establishment dance.

The qualifier *street* became emphasized in dancers' discourse as industry promoters played an increasingly significant role in their access to commercial stage opportunities.[25] Streetdancers were hired as novelty entertainment acts (often recruited in local clubs via industry intermediaries). The first California dancers to perform and teach funk and disco era dances internationally had more consistent access to the professional dance and entertainment industry, either living in or traveling regularly to Los Angeles. The umbrella term *streetdance* became a reference point for the latest array of popular dances, improvised steps, and innovative movement expressions.

Yet within the everyday spaces of their schools, neighborhoods, and homes, they continued growing their cultural practices collectively and in artistic collaboration. This is to say, streetdance cannot be assumed a term of pure origin; rather, it was and is a discursive construction of practitioners' entanglement with a media-arts-entertainment power structure *and* their shaping of a self-determined artistry distinct from dominant-culture institutions.

Within rap and hip hop's subcultural value system, *street* is also a common marker of affiliation, signifying authenticity, credibility, rawness, realness, truth. In a contemporary context, *street* carries these inflections of hip hop authenticity and reflects the structural role of the US media-entertainment industrial complex in the global dissemination of dances that nonetheless maintain local histories that are culturally specific and distinct.

Streetdances have often been framed as "nontechnical" because methods of incorporating them into a dancer's repertoire are not always linear. Moving beyond the studio, there's often no regular schedule of classes to attend or predetermined levels of expertise to achieve. Practice time is open ended, woven intimately into the arbitrary time of everyday life: improvised in tight spaces of kitchens and living rooms; extended indefinitely through sleepless nights in bedrooms preparing for a talent show or club contest. Time is not bound to linear starting and ending points, nor is space delimited by studio walls or the proscenium theater stage. Practice can quickly turn to performance: jumping out the car to dance at a stoplight; gathering in a parking lot outside the after-hours club. Getting pushed before a crowd of adults at your momma's house party. Studying the off-balance stroll of a peg leg man who frequents your neighborhood store. Watching your mom get down to a nasty groove in her kitchen. On the porch. In sweaty jooks. This ethos of study animates hip hop/streetdance vernaculars, which encompass the sociality of dancing within unpredictable, everyday life flows—a protean movement that tends to embrace complexity and resist generalization.

Anthea Kraut has highlighted an implicit bias in the study of dance technique in a European-derived worldview.[26] Anthropologist Marcel Mauss expands a definition of "Techniques of the Body" to include everyday movements like walking and eating that "generate knowledge" through cultural tradition and social practice: "Learning and doing techniques takes place in a collective context; a context which forms and informs the social constitution of its practitioners."[27] In a similar vein, Marya McQuirter theorizes Malcolm X's autobiographical recounting "of moving from awkwardness to ballroom accomplishment," in order to flag a dearth of attention to how people learn to dance outside of formal or professional contexts, an overlooking that denies the cultural labor of learning processes people create and continue outside of institutions.[28] Streetdance involves collaborative and collective forms of creativity in contexts where boundaries blur between everyday life, artistic practice, study, and performance.

Streetdance techniques are deeply embedded in culture, and dancers access their philosophical principles as ways of moving through life. They play in unruly mixings of genre and persistent messiness of the vernacular. They refuse fixed location, traveling through streets, studios, stages, and cyberspaces. *Street* can describe geographic location, discursive space, ideology, political ontology. Street encompasses moving and being outside the studio, in ways that critique Eurocentric aesthetic hierarchy and white establishment dance.

Hip hop is now widely taught as a studio style, but the defining elements of hip hop technique are obscured by what's actually taught in any one hip hop class—appearing along a wide spectrum from freestyle movement to Broadway-style jazz dance. In tandem with vague definitions, the development of a choreo-centric model of transmission adjoins the dances' move onto entertainment stages from the early 1970s, to the release of the first hip hop films in the early 1980s, and another explosion of commercial dance films, industry competitions, and dance reality television since the 2000s. Choreography is now the most widespread approach to teaching hip hop in the studio. This is not to argue that choreography is an essentially inauthentic or incorrect approach to hip hop practice. I am arguing instead for attention to the function of choreography in a market system that relies on reproducing codes of black cool as a commodity relation to be owned and traded.[29]

The choreography/improvisation divide occupies a contentious space within hip hop/streetdance discourse, most evident in shifting labels arising over the last two decades that attempt to name performance practices as opposed to cultural-historical dances. Hip hop choreo, urban choreo, and lyrical choreo are terms that have gained traction with an increasing hybridization of dance styles. Though their usage and validity are contentious among practitioners, such terms more generally index the saturation of choreo-centric dancing in a neoliberal market driven by commodification of black culture and processes of professionalization.

Dance scholar Jonathan David Jackson's foundational study "Improvisation in African-American Vernacular Dancing" is key here: "My discussion is founded on the notion that improvisation in the dancing must be understood as a particular kind of choreographing enacted within the ritual moment of the actions. Black vernacular dance aesthetics force us to rethink dualistic Platonic-Cartesian notions and the sometimes ethnocentric divisions between improvisation and so-called set choreography."[30] Jackson's work details the improvisatory creative processes that black vernacular dancers engage in as they pass movement principles on, showing that innovation and tradition are always becoming entangled—the "new" emerging simultaneously to the recycling (the renewing) of the "old." Black aesthetics are sustained by black vernacular dancing's improvisatory drive. This is consequential for studying the kinds of evolving dance practices I am here calling choreo-centric, as such practices continue to adapt, distort, and erase black aesthetics.

Competition is a particularly prevalent force that structures social relations in present-day dance practices. Dance scholar Susan Leigh Foster summarizes a competition-oriented experience of dance that circulates in contemporary private studios and is driven by the imperative of neoliberal globalization: "all genres are embraced as the product of human diversity and valorized for their unique aesthetic contributions, even as the underlying standards of excellence, most closely associated with balletic virtuosity, prevail as the generalized standards for evaluation."[31] The question of standards pertains directly to the advent and mass popularity of TV dance reality shows, where judging is an ocular-centric operation that subjects the vernacular to whitening-cleansing processes (e.g., the rule of clean lines, transitions, and timing). Foster further highlights the bourgeois humanist subjectivity on which the business of training and teaching is premised: "a self that is in mastery over the world, where different genres simply provide technical challenges that one must overcome."[32]

While highly choreographed unison group dancing has been characteristic of the studio and transnational team competition performance circuit, a parallel circuit of battle dancing (which also offers dancers opportunities to travel as judges and master teachers) centers a culture of improvisation-based performance in which soloists and crews compete. Battling is a core way of demonstrating authenticity within global hip hop/streetdance culture, as Michele Byrd-Mcphee, director of dance organization Ladies of Hip Hop, suggests: "Anybody can do moves, it's how you live in them, it's how you feel in them, it's how people can connect to whatever you're trying to share . . . [a]nd vulnerability can be a catalyst."[33] In battles, dance is placed into categories and judged by style: breaking, hip hop, popping, locking, vogue, and, more recently, waacking and hybrid categories like all-styles and experimental. There is also an instability inherent to classification systems, which require dancers' ongoing assessment and evaluation of streetdance aesthetics.[34]

Contemporary dancers continue to use terms like *street* and *urban* to reference this cultural dance umbrella. I choose to avoid *urban* because of the ways the term circulates in political discourse as a euphemism for blackness. I find *street* to hold a critique of institutional power, as the term's use continues to align with the unsettled language of the vernacular. My purpose is not to reproduce false divides between street, studio, and stage, but to consider how streetdance interanimates these paradigmatic spaces, creating a metacritique of the hierarchical division of space and ideologies of value that maintain it. Streetdance holds a critically unstable relationship with institutions of cultural production, especially in connection with ideas of privacy, ownership, individualism, and property. Even as they teach and train in studios and on concert stages, streetdancers still insist on a politics of authenticity that aligns their dancing with an ideology of the streets, destabilizing the presumed standard of white establishment dance.[35] The studio is an important center for the transmission of dancers' embodied knowledge and dance histories. Yet *Kinethic California* decenters the studio as a historically privileged site of dance study to consider the multiply entangled places where dance training and study happen.

Streetdance affirms the informal, unprofessional study of dancing that remains unaccountable to linear methods of acquiring technique prevalent in a model of scheduled, level-based studio learning. The terminology continues to shift in response to changes in dancers' informal and everyday practices. I recycle the term *streetdance* to underscore the labor of dancers who still maintain an ethics of connection to cultural histories and lived experience embedded in the dance.

Kinethics

I build a framework of *kinethics* to emphasize the reinventive drive of African American social and vernacular dances that activate networks of relation and belonging. Kinethics riff on the words kinetic, kinesthetic, kinship, ethic, and aesthetic, bringing attention to cultural practices of kinship formation that mobilize dancers to collectively innovate hip hop/streetdance style. Kinethics define kinship as relationalities that are not premised on separability—the reduction of sociality to units premised on the individual. I am interested in collective movement practices that reorient dancers toward an ethic of kin relations, bearing on the ways dance styles emerge, interanimate, and transform.

Kinethics are inspired by Brazilian sociologist and political philosopher Denise Ferreira da Silva's call for a decolonial praxis of "Black Feminist Poethics," as she draws on the global social theory of Martiniquan philosopher and poet Édouard Glissant.[36] In his most widely known work, *Poetics of Relation*, Glissant departs from Western continental philosophy's hold on thinking as a distant activity, practiced in isolation, instead looking to ways of thinking embedded in the materials of artistic traditions and produced by people creatively reinventing themselves as a practice of relation.[37] Poetics and poethics allow me to study dance knowledges informing movement of a collective social body, situated in specific cultural contexts yet not rigidly rooted in monolithic communities of origin.

While Glissant's reformulation of rhizomatic relations in conversation with the philosophy of Gilles Deleuze and Félix Guattari is a direct critique of root identity that would seem to negate a theory of kinship, I am interested in ways kinship systems are made through dance, including dancers' creation of nonlinear lineages and nonbiological relations that emerge, move, shift, and transform. Kinethics bring attention to movement via routes traveled by dancers and dances across geographic, social, and cultural borders. Kinethics are rhizomatic not rooted, because they reorient dancers to practices of relationality in which multiplicity is inherent.

I am also thinking with Sylvia Wynter's argument for an "ethics-aesthetic" theory of cultural practices as I elucidate principles of black social dancing that drive the reinvention of kinship bonds as dance lineages.[38] In "Sambos and Minstrels," Wynter's sole publication from her manuscript "Black Metamorphosis," she argues that bourgeois humanist ethics are "born out of" relations of domination and reproduced through cultural performance to reinforce the ideology of normative white mastery and black exclusion.[39] Ethical concepts form the seeds of the slave relation—contained within its aesthetic codes—such that hegemonic culture must keep reproducing antiblackness as an ethical stance.

Silva draws on Wynter's work to assert that antiblackness does not require ethical justification; antiblackness creates humanism's ethics. For

Silva, whiteness is secured by and through ethical indifference to black life.[40] To indict this ethical relation, Wynter proposes that a "cultural process of INDIGENIZATION" arises from sustained acts of the enslaved to fashion a counterculture: "another collective identity whose coding and signification moved outside the framework of the dominant ideology . . . provides the basis for the theoretical formulations of the forms of revolution needed in America today."[41] Emerging through this cultural process of collective identity formation, black social dances offer ethics-aesthetic principles of practice that indict antiblackness.

Yet their forms are not unchanging. Dance scholar Anna Scott's theory of "tenaxis" challenges the attempt to reduce blackness to a monolithic cultural identity, weighing dancers' transcultural labor of tenaciously forming communities of practice that are interconnected through a material sense of place. Tenaxis differentiates dance as consumable product from dancing practices.[42] As dancers continue to reinvent black cultural forms into the present moment, tenaxis stores the codes of this indictment of antiblackness. The reinventive capacity of black social dancing, practiced in ethics-aesthetic principles of common rhythm sensing and improvisation, emerges in locally specific forms yet resists being bound to a static sense of position.

In "Rebellion/Invention/Groove," Katherine McKittrick converses with "Black Metamorphosis" to excavate cultural forms that carry the historical imprint of enslavement and insurgency. Applying principles for moving (like the groove), black social dancers sustain an ethical drive to reinvent form:

> Indeed, in sharing and grooving to music, histories are renarrated, kinships are reimagined, and a different mode of representation is performed, heard, repeated, enjoyed: this is a very different kind of initiation into humanness than a normative model that requires racial violence. . . . This opens up a meaningful way to think about how the politics of sound, and grooving to song, are assertions of black life that indict and subvert antiblackness and, at the same time, notice the inventive aspects of our collective and difficult plantocratic histories, traces, and memories: "The ethic is the aesthetic."[43]

Black social dancing's reinventive ethos is what allows robot styles to pop up in many different locations, taking on the culturally specific textures of their places of (re)emergence without losing a larger sense of what Wynter calls their aesthetic kin-relatedness. The ethos embedded in principles of collective movement practice subverts ethics of white domination and continues to seed a black consciousness. This sense of relation fosters historical continuity and a collective sense of knowing-being-becoming in the midst of change.

An ethos of reinvention is present in Damita Jo Freeman's 1973 *Soul Train* solo, as she activates a kinetic map of emergent dance lineages that will continue to be reinterpreted through collective movement practices of contemporary streetdancers in the 2000s. The work of dancers to name and organize these lineages is ongoing and contested. Yet reinvention of dance lineages gives continuity to dance histories and allows diverse dance communities to collectively participate in shaping these histories, even as the drive to be relevant (to resist stasis) spawns new dances.[44]

Black social dancing, specifically, shapes a collective sense of continuity and critically transformative possibility. The ethics-aesthetic principles carried in movement sustain the effort of a community reaching into the past to reinvent an ongoing present as a way to generate their emerging/becoming. These are neither idle fantasies nor, to borrow Saidiya Hartman's wording, "innocent amusements"; instead, such practice "endeavors to redress and nurture the broken body; it is a becoming together dedicated to establishing other terms of sociality."[45] Black social dancing's reinventive capacity allows dancers to adapt their movement in the moment—a practice that has always been of consequence for improvising black life under slavery and in its wake.[46]

Silva articulates the stakes of reinvented relations when she describes Black Feminist Poethics as a "radical praxis [that] acknowledges the creative capacity Blackness indexes, reclaims expropriated total value, and demands for nothing less than decolonization—that is, a reconstruction of the world, with the return of the total value without which capital would not have thrived and off of which it still lives."[47] Not reducible to money value alone, Black Feminist Poethics refuses the devaluation of social relations under racial capitalism. Kinethics, likewise, look to collective movement practices that reorient dancers' sense of kin relations, taking part in a larger commitment to build a sociality of care and indebtedness that is not premised on terms of the individual and ownership.

I began wondering about an ethics of relation as I noticed how often dancers would honor their dead through oral storytelling and dance performance. Because so much of my work came down to listening to stories of dance elders, I began to be curious about the kinds of lineages dancers create. I often felt a deluge of dance spirits in their stories, an intimacy and relationality that I could feel growing within my dance elders. I especially began to realize these are dances of mourning. I've witnessed dancers interrupt a studio class to embody their dancestors, showing students the ways they moved. I've also listened to their stories about dancers disappearing and suddenly resurfacing in the dance world. I've been in spaces dedicated to the memory of passed dancers, where those gathered practice mourning by celebrating with others in movement. I noticed prevailing themes of family and obligation, especially in practices of naming the progenitors of dance styles.

Many dancers I interviewed are now in their late sixties. They have lived with homelessness. Their living histories have moved in waves of death and incarceration in the wake of AIDS and the drug wars that swept 1980s Los Angeles, and ongoing displacement and gentrification in the San Francisco Bay Area. The names of dancers who have passed over the last decade, since 2010, thread through my writing: Greg Campbellock Jr. Pope, Deborah Granny Robotroid Johnson, Dallace Zeigler, Don Campbell, Tyrone Proctor, Adolfo Shabba Doo Quiñones. Bound up in loss as a collective condition and mourning as a collective call, their practices of belonging to others give a deeper valence to kinethics.

Playing off a cultural discourse of dancestors, *danscendance* is a mode of kinethics that shapes movement practices of collective loss and mourning. Danscendants practice an ethic of obligation to keep watch over one another's legacies.[48] Danscendance does not reify a notion of pure lineage from a single point of origin but rather suggests that kin belonging is a flexible practice dancers engage in by moving with their dancestors—those dancers who have passed on in the culture. Danscendance shows up in the stories that populate the book: locker Scoo B Doo's return to global streetdance after a decades-long disappearance; Bay Area dancers' creation of the interrelated styles of Oakland Boogaloo, Richmond Robotting, and San Francisco Strutting, dances embedded in local geographies of place, through cycles of gentrification and histories of displacement; performances of waacking/punking that reenact the movements of the dance's queer and trans* dancestors.[49] Danscendance thinks kinship as a complex and dynamic practice that emerges in the flow of dancers' life experience.

My study of California dance histories follows yet also goes beyond style categories to weigh dimensions of social life informing techniques such as locking, popping, and waacking/punking, which have become "kin" to hip hop dance. Silva, Glissant, and Wynter allow me to consider relationality emergent in hip hop/streetdance—not a static collection of technical styles but a collective artistic movement generated in the ethics-aesthetic practice of black social dancing. Style innovation is not an isolated individualistic endeavor but a collective processing and passing on of artistic traditions, which engage people in the activity of moving together.

The doing of kinship, or kinship in process, is emphasized in the ways dancers practice a common obligation to solidify social bonds as they innovate styles and flesh out networks of stylistic affiliation that shape their entanglements with one another's cultural histories and forms of collective artistry. In *Queer Kinship*, Elizabeth Freeman and Tyler Bradway put forth "kin-aesthetics as a core methodology for queer kinship theory," a method I similarly adopt by studying dance as practices of collective artistry through which dancers find themselves inhabiting movement materials of their dancestors, reinventing dancestries that are nonlinear and nonbiological. Kinethics converse with theories of queer kinship that take up "creative experimentation with relationality, and its ongoing imbrication with entrenched idioms of ancestry, descent, and family."[50] Yet kinethics bring the kinetic and aesthetics into focus around the question of ethics raised in the work of Glissant, Wynter, and Silva, considering how blackness repeatedly disrupts Enlightenment philosophical discourse of the individual body in relation to the other.

Kinethics as a framework for studying hip hop/streetdance converse with theories of blackness and black life that "demand for nothing less than . . . reconstruction of the world."[51] While black and blackness have been widely defined in terms of cultural identity, I am interested in reorienting a focus on black social and vernacular dance toward theories of blackness that move beyond what blackness represents to "what it *does* and *can do* . . . seeking [not to find] a black aesthetic but rather to understand blackness as aesthetics."[52] Black dance can be written about expansively, against the assertion of a singular monolithic identity onto dynamic assemblages of culture, ethnicity, and life experience. I am committed to the study of black culture and cultural identity insofar as such study takes shape around a radical critique of origins, relationality, being, becoming, and embodiment. Black and blackness materialize around an open set of questions concerned with motion, social life, and aesthetics, for which dance offers responses as a resource and imaginative worldbuilding practice of knowing-being, becoming, and belonging.

Regarding the question of whether to capitalize *black*, I follow the reflexive process articulated by the editors of the experimental literary journal *liquid blackness*, to "approach, while gently resisting, the complex task of committing the fluidity of blackness to the page . . . understand[ing] this is an issue of ontology that typography cannot resolve."[53] My use of the term *black* moves in the text in less clear ways than a push to capitalize by convention permits.[54] The framework of kinethics I build here follows critical theories of blackness, deliberately committing to black study in process, unfinished, and oriented toward ways of feeling-being-becoming unknown. As much as I write against a desire to lay claim to a definitive knowledge of black and blackness, I also move to expose the theory I write to necessary critique and failure.

Methodology

In hallways. Outside the club. In the parking lot. During a five-hour car ride. In late-night diners. These are all places where dance histories are told, which is to say where dancers remake history. There's always both a remaking and transmitting of history that dancers perform in these passing periods of improvised study. These are also places where my ethnographic study goes.

My formal ethnographic research spans the years 2008–22 and encompasses sixty in-person, phone, and online interviews. I spoke and moved with first-generation dancers who were part of California dancing cultures in the 1960s and 1970s. I also met with and learned from contemporary dancers who train, teach, judge, and compete in a range of global hip hop/streetdance styles associated with California funk and disco era dance cultures. Many of the first-generation dancers with whom I spoke were in their teens to midtwenties during that era. And though some of the better-known dancers moved on to teach in dance studios, I had to go into and beyond the studio to follow their dance histories.

I sat with dancers in their homes, they took me on neighborhood street tours, we gathered in restaurants and sat in hallways between classes. I danced in studio classes and informally in clubs, outdoor festivals, and dance reunions. I also followed hip hop/streetdance culture online, in dancers' moderated private and open Facebook groups, Instagram posts, and YouTube channels.

A big part of my method was to go into dance studios to watch how teachers teach. For teachers who have been with these movement practices for so long, I have found they have a fascinating capacity to convey the ethics-aesthetic through how they speak and move. This is not to say that the studio is a harm-free zone. Power dynamics infuse the structure and are cemented in its founding hierarchies, not least of which is the system of value set by Eurocentric standards of dance. I've tried to address some of those dynamics in cultural practice as well.

When I began writing about hip hop dance, I felt ethically committed to studying ways of knowing-being-becoming embedded in the movement aesthetics of black youth who shaped local cultural geographies that had become familiar to me as a dancer, artist, and youth worker. My experience of hip hop culture is connected strongly to youth activism in Oakland, where I lived and worked for over a decade. Yet my dancefloor studies extend to nightlife in both Los Angeles and New York, the latter city being key to my cultural knowledge of hip hop and streetdance styles. I sought out my training in nightclubs, dance classes, and community cultural events, on both east and west coasts, as well as traveling beyond the US to study dance in Cuba and Brazil. The circuitous routes I've chosen have brought me more closely in touch with the African Diasporic rhythms and improvisation-based practice of hip hop and streetdance, as a process of artistic self-redefinition.

I was raised artistically as a solo violinist within a highly competitive classical music world in Los Angeles, the city of my birth. Living in the wealthy, then majority-white suburb of San Marino, feeling the strong cultural influence of my father's Jewish ancestry, yet looking and sounding most like my Filipina pianist mother, my search for artistic identity was embattled by cultural elitism, cultural isolation and cultural assimilation. The experience moved me, once in the Bay Area, to focus on hip hop and streetdance as artistic forms that could build community and collectivity. While I noticed a large body of hip hop scholarship forming outside the United States, I chose to ground my research in conversation with local dance communities. I knew my focus needed to be on the kinds of collective artistry, artistic collaboration, and improvisation that catalyzed young people's innovation of dances emerging in the neighborhoods through which I traveled and where I found home.

A key way I studied these forms is by drawing on my own experience as a dancer training, teaching, choreographing, and performing African Diaspora dance forms since the early 1990s, primarily between the San Francisco Bay Area, Los Angeles, and New York City. While I have studied Caribbean, Brazilian, West African, hip hop, street, and club dances in studio classes, much of my training has happened in clubs, parties, and the many informal occasions where dancers gather, including in spaces outside the United States, most significantly in Brazil and Cuba. My writing on black social and vernacular dance is indebted to the people I've met and danced with in these contexts, extending the scope of this research beyond the formal parameters of academia to my lived experience of global hip hop, street, and club dance cultures.

While there are many possible locales and mappings for tracing histories of hip hop/street/club dances, this book is informed by the circuitous paths I've traveled through California, with a focus on Los Angeles and the San Francisco Bay Area, which have shaped my life in fundamental ways. Many locations cited by first-generation dancers in my study have held significance for me as a native Californian, yet doing critical research transformed my conceptual map of queer club, streetdance, and hip hop cultures. On my map I drive ten minutes down the street from the Kaiser hospital where I was born to reach Gino's, the queer nightlife club where dancestors of waacking/punking moved within the same time period. Five minutes east is Metromedia Square, where *Soul Train* began national syndication a few years earlier. Go another ten blocks and arrive at Arena, the gay Latinx nightclub where I often danced in the early 1990s, along with a string of clubs and underground parties—Bang the Drum, What, Does Your Mama Know, Sketch Pad, Club 1970. Moving to the Bay Area, I lived twice in the Fillmore district, in 1996 and again in 2005, and in neighborhoods of North and West Oakland through the 2000s, where dancers had been innovating boogaloo, strutting, and robotting styles since the 1960s. I taught dance from San Francisco's Bayview/Hunters Point to North Oakland's Destiny Arts Center and East Oakland's Youth UpRising, and co-organized the dance events Freestyle Fridays in West Oakland and Congregation in East Oakland, working with artists Rashad Pridgen and Hanifah Walidah. My writing is also a palimpsest of the places I have danced. Community, belonging, and family emerge as consistent themes in this work.

Because of the wide array of cultural spaces and training methods that make up my conceptual and experiential mappings of hip hop/streetdance culture, I have chosen a transmethodological approach, blending ethnography, oral history, poetry, creative nonfiction, and personal narrative, and using analytic tools of dance, performance, cultural, and media studies. I use my practiced knowledge of dance technique and culture to inform my writing, as well as the discourse of practitioners who shape dance histories through their pedagogies and training methods. I write to articulate what's at stake in the ways dancers move, as well as to locate my experience of the dances as ways of knowing that have come to be intimately part of me.

Chapter Map

Chapter 1, "*Soul Train* Locamotives," grounds my framework of kinethics in *black social dance* as a practice of shared rhythm-sensing that prepares dancers to collectively innovate style while sustaining connection with earlier forms. I use the animated image of a black locomotive train that opens and closes each televised episode of *Soul Train* to figure the generative power of black social dance, tracing an ethics-aesthetic principle I call *locamotivity*. Drawing on black aesthetics, anthropology of the senses, and theories of African retentions and syncretisms, I assert that an ethos of common rhythm consciousness generates black social dance practices cropping up in different locations while simultaneously building a shared sense capacity that moves dancers translocally.

Collective acts of watching, listening, and moving to music build dancers' shared sense of rhythm. When *Soul Train* moved to national broadcast syndication in the early 1970s, streets and blocks emptied as neighbors gathered in family homes to watch together. Through rituals of watching and listening (oftentimes dancing), audience-participants on- and offscreen could experience what Nick Cave expressed in conversation with Damita Jo as a "collective coming together" and a sense of moving as a collective social body joining across multiple locations at once. The show not only staged black music and dance but also extended locamotive practice as a principle embedded in black social dancing that trains dancers to feel familiarity in rhythm.

Locamotive practice creates bonds among dancers, who generate dance lineages, the nonlinear shifting patterns of relation through which dancers find and articulate familiarity with others. Dancers innovate form with a sense of obligation to sustain kinship with earlier dances. Whether a dancer is dancing solo or in a group, their sense of rhythm is interanimated with familiar patterns of moving that have emerged over time and grown in collective practice. Training in these dances, then, is not a simple means to an end—the acquisition of the dance as a product to own—but instead is a critical mode of survival through reinvention, continuing past traditions within an unfolding present.

The cartoon train also indexes *Soul Train* host/creator Don Cornelius's early work, producing traveling DJ dance parties that brought local black artists to high school lunchtime audiences, moving through the streets of his native Chicago. The mobile parties were part of Don's vision to reenact the vitality of dancers moving in the clubs—a vision he carried with him to Los Angeles. In the context of black social dancing on the *Soul Train* film set, early 1970s dancers were reenacting for the camera dances that had already been emerging locally in offscreen social spaces.

One of these dances was *locking*—an early global streetdance style connected to black social dances like the Breakdown and Robot Shuffle—melding the freestyle artistry of dancer Don Campbell with a collectivity of dancers who moved with him, adding to his dance. I listen to locking cultural history woven in dancers' stories that move on and beyond popular screens, into homes where young people danced, alone and together, and ending in the repeating loop of backward steps created by locker and *Soul Train* dancer Scoo B Doo, who disappears for over two decades before unexpectedly returning to the streetdance world in the 2000s. Danscendance is key to Scoo B Doo's story, activating locking's collective practice in ritual ways that exemplify Christina Sharpe's definition of "wake work," allowing dancers to shape kinship bonds, and articulating an ethic of obligation to mourn and keep watch over locking's open-ended dancestry.[55]

Chapter 2, "Popping and Other Dis/Appearing Acts," disrupts *Soul Train*'s Los Angeles emphasis to focus on an array of dances emerging in the mid-1960s through 1970s among dancers fascinated by robotic and animated movement, and moved by black vernacular rhythms of funk and soul. Dancers began to improvise an aesthetic that Will Randolph, member of Oakland's Black Resurgents, describes as a "stop-and-go approach" to mobility. Dancers' local cultures became affiliated with hip hop dance via the global streetdance popping, a style of contested origins in California's Central Valley city of Fresno and Northern California's San Francisco Bay Area.

Noting the aesthetic mess of multiple origin stories, I bring focus back to ethical principles embedded in collectively created techniques that share an aesthetic of polycentrism, described by dance scholar Brenda Dixon Gottschild in her naming of Africanist aesthetics in American performance.[56] The collective movement practices that articulate popping style trace an alternative mapping of *polycentric dance histories*, describing the improvisational force of black vernacular dancers who do not reify one universal center and marginalized cultures but instead decenter singular origin narratives.

Kinethics reorient dancers to dancing kinships that generate multiple centers of origin in the collective social body. They practice feeling-knowing-moving in common rhythms that articulate popping dancestries as a moving map of black vernacular cultural terrain: in the Bay Area alone, dancers have shaped interrelated lineages of Oakland Boogaloo, Richmond Robotting, and San Francisco Strutting. Polycentric dance histories also move hip hop dance—not only between New York and California but also within the California region itself, calling for more dance histories of Central, Northern, and Southern California, and beyond. Rather than presenting a tidy history of the dances, I note the ways their aesthetic sociality moves. Kinethics reorient dancers' felt sense of belonging to place from a location of displacement, as they improvise an open-ended sociality in flux.

Dance styles including but not limited to boogaloo, strutting, robotting, popping, and animation are fractal techniques that figure wider sociopolitical patterns of forced and interrupted movement, repeated in ethics-aesthetic principles of polycentrism, polyrhythm, isolation, muscle release, and contraction. Articulated in principles of dance technique, kinethics disrupt a racial capitalist logic of the individual and the body, attached to practices of gentrification, extraction, acquisition, and ownership.

I study an ethics-aesthetic that moves dancers from a location of displacement in the context of the gentrification of San Francisco's Fillmore district, where the eponymous dance called The Fillmore emerges to articulate San Francisco Strutting style. Ethics-aesthetics inform dancers' appropriation of stop-motion animation used in mid-twentieth-century sci-fi fantasy films. Reinventing camera technology as movement technique, dancers articulate animation style as a practice of becoming and shared embodiment that allow them to live otherworldly existences.

I extend my study to the pedagogy of Bronx, New York, hip hop dancer Steffan Mr. Wiggles Clemente, informed by a cultural history of popping from California's Central Valley city of Fresno. By opening my mapping beyond a purely California focus, I hope to show the ways hip hop/streetdance lineages entangle dancers across multiple locations, reimagining dancing kinships in the ways dancers move. Wiggles articulates an ethics-aesthetic principle of "zero," unsettling the hierarchy of seeing-as-knowing in a Western Enlightenment epistemology of the senses. Training in techniques of precise muscle contraction, dancers create the visual illusion of an appearing and disappearing "pop," shaping the energy of forces not held in rigid opposition but dynamically opening in rhythmic relation.

Ethics-aesthetic principles animate the practices of Bay Area innovators of synchronized group-style dance, who physically interconnect while in motion, entangling arms and legs, toppling over one another in domino falls, moving in close contact, and becoming temporally aligned. Their ethics-aesthetic practices of collective touch and breath disrupt the notion of an individual body as unit of relation, with consequences for the ways hip hop dance has become translated as a studio choreography form.

Following the improvisation-based aesthetics of popping style, the chapter experiments with ways of writing dance, interspersing sections of dance theory with poetry "innerludes" to mimic the "pop" as an opening of form.

Chapter 3, "The Rebirth of Waacking/Punking," shifts from relations of place to focus on queer kinships in the dance waacking/punking. Emerging in queer nightlife of 1970s Los Angeles and screened on *Soul Train* in the context of black social dance, waacking/punking experienced a rebirth into hip hop/streetdance in the early 2000s, accompanying women's increasing visibility within a global battle scene. The dance was not widely practiced in the 1980s and 1990s, as a wave of dancers vanished in the wake of AIDS, crack cocaine, militarism, and incarceration. Following a boom in transnational battles, dance competitions, dance reality shows, and films, waacking/punking rose to global prominence as a millennial technical style. Within hip hop/streetdance cultural history, waacking/punking is striking in its resurgence. The dance is included as a battle category, integrated into competition choreographies, screened on Hollywood TV and film, and taught in studio classes for children and adults.

I study the dance's travels through queer nightlife, onto *Soul Train*, and into the millennium, attending to ways queer kinships inform hip hop/streetdance, holding legacies of women and gender-nonconforming dancers, whose presence in dominant historical narratives is often hidden. Waacking/punking has put a spotlight on women in a cismale-dominant dance scene, fostering shifts in gendered power relations as dancers learn to connect with an expansive sense of power and freedom to move. Yet dancers in the 2000s also must navigate a neoliberal competition-oriented experience of dance and gender normative spaces that reinscribe binary gender assumptions of embodiment. More than a technical genre to be mastered, waacking/punking invites experiments with form.

I elaborate how kinethics of waacking/punking reorient dancers to queer kinship, as they reinvent hip hop/streetdance to reflect the culture's gender-expansive and transgressive lineages. I focus on spiritual and emotional dimensions of kinethics, emerging from loss, which dancers transform from private to collective experience through waacking/punking danscendances. I draw on black feminism, trans* feminism, and queer theory to describe danscendances as gifts of interpretation and kin labor through which danscendants resource the feminine, getting lost wildly in genre and gender to find themselves in queer history.

Streetdance Stories

Rather than tell history in a linear mode, I trace circuitous paths that I find more reflective of streetdance stories. Stories are fabulations. Fables incorporate fantastic characters and mythical experiences, making invention key to the story's power. Streetdancers often tell stories, beginning with dance names they use to highlight their unique movement styles. Stories are also part of the oral tradition of passing on cultural information, in conversation with dance techniques that improvise and reinvent characters of sci-fi, fantasy, and silent film worlds, blending fiction with everyday life.

In the approximation of writing to the moving languages that populate this book, my idea is to seek and translate stories of collective kinetic memory embedded in the techniques themselves. Dance may be most emphatic of the impossibility of translation, which is why I understand that between the language of movement and written words, this text is also a series of disappearing acts. I hope to write dance with an insight that Ronald A. T. Judy's words provide: "The most successful translation—the one that achieves not an identification of signification between two languages but the approximation of an affect articulated in one language that somehow is analogous to that of another—not only recalls the incommensurability of languages but also the incommensurability of language and experience."[57] I've chosen to focus on the story that I feel these dances have to tell collectively through practice.

A Note on Language

Throughout, I use the names by which practitioners self-identify in streetdance culture. When speaking of dancers in relation to their published writing, I use the convention of referencing the dancer's surname for publication. I write sections of the book in a nonacademic style, and dancers will sometimes appear without formal introduction. The dancers enter my writing fluidly like I came to know them, hiding and revealing who they are and were in ways that feel truer to how dance histories come to be told.

For consistency and ease of reading, I keep dance styles lowercase, except when quoting a dancer directly or when prefacing a style with the specific area with which it is affiliated, such as Oakland Boogaloo. I keep in uppercase black social dances, steps, and moves, such as the Breakdown and Robot Shuffle. I spell *streetdance* as one word throughout, to focus on interconnected histories of African American social and vernacular dances, rather than as reference to any general dancing done in the streets.

Illustration:
Contact Consciousness/Generative Lineages by d. sabela grimes

one
Soul Train Locamotives

THE BREAKDOWN

Honey baby, I been told. Von and Denee hunch down in a wide-leg squat. They're watching each other on the round platform that's lifting them—a foot off the TV studio floor. *I got to see for myself.* They rock, doubling time with ghost notes of guitar funk, a percussive scratch that's vibrating them steady on the One. Electric stabs inject their groove with staccato high pitches that move them—upward and back down. *Stop where you are, let your big hip rock. . . .*

The camera centers them in its eye while, nearby, another dancer moves with her partner, changing Denee's steady up-and-down grooving to a back-and-forth rocking that ricochets between her chest and hips. Horns blast their response. *It ain't the Funky Chicken.* Backdropping their dance, a set piece extends the painted railroad thread that's weaving under moving feet of the film studio crowd, but flips and multiplies the track to form a vertical grid up the wall, affixed with off-kilter signs pointing to cities on the freshly syndicated *Soul Train* Line: Saint Louis, Cleveland, Detroit, Birmingham, New York, Los Angeles, New Orleans, Washington, DC, Atlanta, San Francisco, Philadelphia, Baltimore. *Listen!*

It's the brand-new dance that's going around . . . cameras pan the floor, full of party people. Dancers change their facings. Couples fall into solos and groups. Rufus Thomas calls out: *Do the Breakdown chiiiillin! Break on down.*[1] Clasping her hands together, Denee mimics the music's churning groove. Her arms scoop backward to the left and then to the right like she's pulling an invisible oar. Von transfers her scoop-arm movement to his hips, adding a scooping rolling jaunt that rises up from pelvis to torso. They stay steady, rocking in the Breakdown's double-time bounce, held close in a rhythm with the dance floor crowd. Rufus's gritty uprising pitch punctuates their movement instructively. *Breakdown to the left! Breakdown to the right!* No one moves exactly the same, but following the groove they ring out a whole current of variations in synchronicity. The chugging-cycling motion carries Denee and Von in up-down loops, transporting the whole crowd together with their offscreen audience to *Soul Train*'s Chicago birthplace. *It's the brand-new dance that's goin around. It ain't the Funky Chicken. It's called the Breakdown.*

It's October 2, 1971. *Soul Train* is airing from the TV studio of Metromedia Square—5746 Sunset Boulevard, at the corner of Van Ness Avenue in Hollywood. Dance partners Denee Williams and Von Founder show the Breakdown, accompanied by Rufus Thomas's song of the same name. They take black music from audio to visual and kinetic. An electric vitality moves the dance floor crowd, all conducted in the baritone purr of *Soul Train*'s creator and host, Don Cornelius: "As dancing styles vary so much in different parts of the country, we like to feature dance couples from time to time in the various cities we serve. It gives you a chance to compare their style with the style of dancing in your area."[2] Party people watch one another from the places they are, all while listening to rhythms of funk and soul. Many join together to learn the movement. *Mama can do it, Papa too. Grandma, Grandpa, they're doing it too.* Don Cornelius signals his intention to connect *Soul Train* audiences translocally, prompting them to map their ways of moving in relation to the dancers they watch from home televisions.

Denee and Von explain they learned the Breakdown in their Chicago hometown, spotlighting the show's move from Chicago to Los Angeles for national syndication while reciting their debt to *Soul Train*'s midwestern origins.[3] Of the dancers, musician Questlove asserts, "They influenced how people felt on the other side of the TV. . . . I felt more like a participant than a spectator."[4] Journalist Ericka Blount Danois writes about getting dressed up with her sister, hoping their favorite fine celebrities could somehow see them there in the living room.[5] Anthropologist Laurence Ralph remembers, "waiting was part of the ritual, a crucial element of the viewing experience" that ultimately "became a way to solidify familial and communal bonds."[6] *Maaaama mama, just look at sis. She's in the backyard, Breakin down like this.* Early 1970s *Soul Train* dancer Tyrone Proctor recalls how his Philadelphia neighborhood block would empty when *Soul Train* came on—people gathering in living rooms of whichever families had a TV set.[7] Black social dances like the Breakdown reorient party people to kinship's funky possibilities, a multiply sensory being-belonging-becoming together in the rhythm of the dance.

I first learned the Breakdown in 2014 from Shabba Doo, also a Chicago native and *Soul Train* dancer, as well as a member of Don Campbell's original dance group, the Campbellockers.[8] During this time he was teaching weekend locking classes at the Performing Arts Center in Van Nuys, California.

"What's the 'Go' in the Stop-and-Go?"

We're a handful of students gathered to face ourselves in the mirror that runs adjacent to the studio's unrippled Marley floor. Shabb tests us.

I pause. I'm familiar with the Stop-and-Go: begin with a side-facing wide-leg squat, moving your hips in a double-time rock; step your back foot to meet the front while turning forward and throwing both arms up in the air; return to the squat/double-time hip rock again. Performing solo or facing a partner, lockers often loop the step, adding gestures of rhythmic agreement like finger pops, double-hand slaps, and wrist rolls as they step toward and away from each other. I can feel the accented force of the Stop, which punctuates my flow as I throw both arms up in the air. But where was the Go?

"I don't know?"

"The Go is the Breakdown." Shabb returns to the wide-leg stance, shifting his hips back and forth in a double-time groove. "I'm not teaching choreography," he tells us, while holding the groove. "These are assemblages to learn how the movements go together. Don't do moves but make it a fluid motion." We are learning how to speak the language of locking. Incorporated into locking's lexicon, the Breakdown sets the floor for the style's funky, full-body geometry of points, freezes, leaps, dives, and drops. Doing the Breakdown facilitates locking's flow, the sense of freedom at the core of the dance. So we can feel locking's groove in our body, the Breakdown generates a ritual rhythm connecting us to the social life of the dance.

Streetdance techniques emerge from black social dances. Locking has, over fifty years, evolved into a highly technical style establishing foundations of global hip hop/streetdance culture. The Breakdown tethers locking to black social dancing, as an inner rhythm of the Stop-and-Go. Black social dances set ritual grooves that anchor dancers in rhythm as they innovate form, heeding community values instilled in the dance. Dancers reinvent ways of moving that refer back to those grooves, such that the process of improvising allows "traditions, forms, and steps [to be] recycled at the same time that specific communities innovate their own adaptations of black vernacular dancing . . . a basic principle in the study of the dancing."[9] The grooves embedded in dance styles continue the social life of the dance, experienced as feeling in common rhythm.

The August 1971 screening of the Breakdown encapsulates the ways black social dancing connects dancers from place to place at the moment *Soul Train* moves from Chicago to Los Angeles for national syndication. "*Soul Train* Locamotives" moves from there, forward and backward in time, studying social dancers in Los Angeles prior to the show's syndication and the present-day formation of locking style in global streetdance culture. I combine oral histories of dancers from the show's first decade with ethnography of *Soul Train* reunion gatherings in local clubs and parks, streetdance classes and festivals, online forums, and interviews in dancers' homes. I follow black social dancing beyond the Hollywood film studio set into house parties, listening to stories of dance celebrities as well as dancers who moved on the edge of *Soul Train*'s spotlight yet also shared in streetdance's collective artistry.

In the book's introduction I laid out a framework of kinethics, drawing on Sylvia Wynter's description of ethics-aesthetic cultural practices, which, Katherine McKittrick argues, become reinvented as "assertions of black life" to collectively retell histories and reimagine kinship bonds.[10] I define a core movement principle of common rhythm-sensing that constitutes black social dance as ethics-aesthetic practice. This generative principle of black social dance practice trains rhythmic kinship among dancers who reinvent streetdance lineages. Black social dancing holds the capacity to generate funk kinships among dancers who feel in rhythmic relation, which this chapter explores through recursive practices of grooving and partying, watching and remembering, mourning and moving with loss.

To speak of kinship is not to say that envy, ire, enmity, and disregard are not of consequence among dancers. Kinethics acknowledge the complexities of dancers' relations. Kinship bonds fray, even as the practice of kinship is constituted by an obligation to create cultural continuity. I consider, for example, contributions of black girls and women, as well as noncelebrity, offstage, and amateur dancers, who often go unnoticed and unnamed in male-centric mass-mediated streetdance lineages. Bringing the idea of collective artistry back into streetdance histories helps tell a story of offscreen places where dancers' everyday practices come into play.

I focus on kinships reimagined through black social dancing as a practice that generates streetdance lineages, exemplified in the cultural history of locking in early 1970s Los Angeles. Don Campbell recalls how people often laughed at him, seeing his approach to the popular social dances of the day as strange, quirky, awkward. Nonetheless he was driven by what he describes as a practically obsessive impulse to create, guiding him to innovate a new style of dance that catalyzed a whole culture of locking throughout the area and quickly spread, by way of TV and film, nationally and globally. I note the ways *Soul Train* dancers' movement on entertainment stages entangles with social life in offscreen places where party people gather informally to dance—private social clubs, parks, grade school gyms, a college cafeteria, a studio apartment, backyards and kitchens of family houses. Locking was not only a high-visibility performance but, just as importantly, a dance of everyday life among school-age African American youth, who, finding inspiration in the dance's funk athleticism, helped shape a self-determined artistry distinct from dominant-culture institutions.

The chapter ends with a return to the idea of solo flight and collective practice through danscendance, the spiritual call of dancestors and dancestries recited in streetdance stories of Damita Jo's partner on *Soul Train*, dancer and locker Scoo B Doo. I study his story of locking practice over a period in which he moves from Northern to Southern California, from a studio apartment to Skid Row, disappearing from the streetdance world yet later returning to mourn the passing of his friend and fellow dancer Greg Campbellock Jr. Pope. Locking cultural histories also move under conditions of visibility and disappearance, mourning and loss, activating kinship bonds that tether dancers together in practice.

The ethics-aesthetic that generates black social dancing as an embodied practice of kinship formation informs all study of street-style dance. Black social dancing trains dancers to feel being-belonging-becoming together in the rhythms of the dance. This is the generative drive of black social dance as practice, figured in the animated image that precedes each televised episode—the Soul Train locomotive.

LOCAMOTIVE POWER

That Train is so memorable because when I see it moving?
I see it moving a whole people.
—AMY KELLEY

In various versions of the show's opening credits, the Soul Train travels across the screen in cartoon form: a black locomotive chugging through a city landscape, winding across yellow hills and valleys, dancing into outer space.[11] The animated image summons host-creator Don Cornelius's early years working in his Chicago hometown as a radio news reporter and producer. He helms a caravan of local soul artists like Curtis Mayfield and the Chi-Lites who travel from school to school, performing at lunchtime record hops.[12] The mobile DJ dance parties, Don would later remember, "felt like a train . . . moving around the city."[13] And, in fact, their caravan comes to be known as the Soul Train.

On August 17, 1970, Don begins working with Clinton Ghent, a local dancer. They gain permission to air *Soul Train* as a local show on WCIU-TV weekday afternoons. This early live version of *Soul Train* mirrors dance programs of the time that predominantly feature African American youth, including Chicago's *Red Hot and Blues* and *Kiddie-a-Go-Go*.[14] Ghent later described Don's impetus to relate dancing seen on the show to what was going on in black communal spaces: "Don was always checking out the dancers in the clubs and on the streets—he wanted to capture the same uninhibited, boisterous joy they exhibited dancing there and translate it to the show . . . to capture the real-life energy of a smoky, hole-in-the-wall club—a place where people came to dance until the sun rises . . . and sets again."[15] *Soul Train* becomes the vehicle for Don's vision to gather people as a whole in affective community (on- and offscreen).[16]

Once the show moves to Los Angeles, *Soul Train* dancers bring black social dances like the Breakdown onscreen, to national and international visibility. I find the Soul Train locomotive helpful as a figure and extended metaphor for black social dance, broadcast on the show and taking new forms in offscreen spaces during the years 1966–79.[17]

In this chapter, I define *black social dance* as a collective practice powered by the aesthetic principle of *locamotivity*, which trains dancers to feel a sense of being-becoming-belonging together in rhythm, guiding the generation of new dances from earlier forms. The locomotive is the self-propelled unit of the train, which transmits power, moving train and passengers from place to place. Locamotivity, likewise, builds dancers' collective capacity to find familiarity in rhythm, as dancers (and dances) move across and become embedded in different local contexts.

My interest in collective practices of black social dancing brings attention to the felt alchemy of multiple sensory phenomena activated in and as a rhythm-making social body. Anthropology of rhythm seeks to describe not only the patterning of sensory experience over time (durational) but also social experiences of rhythm acculturated through norms of everyday life and embodiment. Marcel Mauss proposed a study of social rhythm-making found in everyday techniques (walking, swimming, breathing) that are culturally constructed rather than innate.[18] Imani Kai-Johnson argues that aural kinesthesia (a simultaneous sensing of sound and motion) is a fundamental way that meaning is processed in social dance experiences, though "often overridden by the spectacle of dancing."[19] Sound-motion sensing does not preclude so much as decenter sight as a way of knowing within a Eurocentric hierarchy of the senses.

Funk, a black vernacular expression that unsettles boundaries of genre, further messes with sense categories, shaping what LaMonda Horton-Stallings calls "transaesthetics." Funk transaesthetics describe an alchemical feeling-sense that "disturb[s] forms" and categories of perception, encompassing the olfactory (smell) and, as Stallings' work shows, intuition and pleasure.[20] Rhythm-making in black social dance practice emphasizes ways of knowing that not only blend, disrupt, and remake sense categories but also don't make sense within the concept of an individual, self-possessed body.

Rhythm as a social sense capacity organizes dancers and dance lineages in motion, making funky kinships. Dance scholar Jacqui Malone suggests this capacity when she asserts "the power generated by rhythmical movement . . . as a unifying mechanism and a profound spiritual expression" present in African American vernacular dancing.[21] Situating New World expressive practices within the racial-political structure of transatlantic slavery, historian Saidiya Hartman frames cultural performances of community in ontological terms—ways of being and "becoming together" in the world "dedicated to establishing other terms of sociality."[22] A theory of black social dance practice does not assume sameness but attends to the ruptures and pressure points that define community, even as its members may continue to long for a sense of wholeness.

In his 1987 study of black nationalist thought, Sterling Stuckey argues that slave culture fused together African-derived principles of "rhythm consciousness," exemplified in the performative structure of the Ring Shout, a counterclockwise circle dance ritual functioning to organize "different ethnic groups, on the plantations of the South, [who] began moving toward unity almost before being aware." For Stuckey, the Ring Shout could foster collectivity among enslaved Africans taking action to forge "a common consciousness and ethos" that was vitally of one people.[23] While circle practices are certainly reflective of hip hop culture's core, I extend Stuckey's argument to notice rhythm-sensing in black social dance practices as an organizing principle emerging from this common ethos.[24]

The principle of common rhythm consciousness, I'm proposing, acts as a grammatical structure for sustaining relational dialogue. Choreographer Camille Brown asserts that African American social dance is about finding a common language in the process of which the enslaved "got around the slave owners' ban on drumming, improvising complex rhythms . . . keeping cultural traditions alive and retaining a sense of inner freedom under captivity."[25] Shared rhythm-sensing folds Stuckey's "common consciousness and ethos" into sense perception, expressed outwardly in the material production of new dances and cultivated among groups of dancers who move together. Not a subjective sense, the capacity to freedom-sense is built by a dancer's intention to feel familiarity through the movement of the group.

Nuancing the discourse of African retentions, dance scholar Anna Scott argues that the black aesthetic is not universal, offering the term *tenaxis* to describe the purposeful labor of dancers to continuously modify other forms, allowing dances to move across cultural borders yet become reinvented as they reroot in new contexts among dynamic collectivities of dancers. While a dance's cultural codes can be read across contexts, the process of tenaxis by which dancers unfix the codes is critical: "the new dance move is, in fact, the old as well as the not-yet-new."[26] Tenaxis helps me bring attention to black social dance practices underlying the innovative artistry of dancers who move with the old while generating the "not-yet-new." Black social dances are flexible and adaptive, taking the shape of what's culturally relevant for dancers who come together in the moment to practice.

Locamotivity takes up the relationship between the local and translocal in the historical emergence of streetdance techniques from black social dance practice, allowing dancers to embed themselves in cultural histories of place yet keep a sense of place in motion. Dancers with whom I spoke often emphasized their interest in learning one another's dances, impelling them to travel not just to different neighborhoods and cities but also across social boundaries. Crossing gay/straight club borders, dancers in Los Angeles's early disco scene helped grow the global streetdance style waacking/punking. The West Coast Relays in California's Central Valley city of Fresno were a key factor in the cross-pollination of dances entangled under the umbrella term *popping*.[27] Dance contests and talent shows were a major motivator for dancers to travel beyond their local area, for some providing a key source of financial income.

Don Campbell honed his innovative artistry in just this way. While he was also a celebrated *Soul Train* dancer, his movement through offscreen spaces critically informed locking. Decades later, in studio classes, Don would tell stories. He was an awkward dancer who could never get the popular social dances of the time right. He tried to dance the Robot Shuffle and accidentally ended up inventing the Campbellock. He created locking's lexicon of freezes and points when he used the characteristic gestures in quick rejoinder to a girl who was pointing at him and laughing, mocking his strange dancing.[28] These gestures of acknowledgment are irreducibly social, rhythmically repeated in locking's signature hand slaps—called "giving fives"—which can be performed with another dancer, for oneself, or to the floor. Don portrayed locking as a conversation emerging from his interactions with people in everyday situations.

Seen another way, Don's story serves as a critique of natural ability in favor of immanent creative potential. Malcolm X tells a similar story in his autobiography, where he links dance ability directly with black identity.[29] Whereas Malcolm initially feels shame for his awkwardness, Don turns the tables on those who ridicule him, turning to point back at them and incorporating their gestures into his dance. His story suggests that the ability to dance is not bound by social belief but realized in self-connection and creative courage. He resources a perceived social awkwardness, leading him to innovate a whole new style of dance.

By prefacing his creation story with a negative proposition that he proceeds to overturn by the story's end, Don underscores a guiding philosophy: dance is simply the creative potential to move, inherent in life. Don's philosophy guided his pedagogy, which focused on improvising within locking, rather than copying steps. In this way, Don was always already giving away his dance: "I want you to take my dance and make it yours."[30]

Don's stories take place in the Los Angeles Trade-Technical College cafeteria, where he is dancing with friends around a jukebox, preparing for a club dance contest at Maverick's Flat. For him, locking was a way to access a freestyle spirit of moving—an active social process inspired by coming together with everyday people in everyday places. Located in emergent rhythms of black social dances like the Robot Shuffle and Breakdown, locking takes root in Don's signature Campbellock dance, growing as his aesthetic innovations find kinship with those of the many dancers who move with him.[31]

The "local" in locamotive points off the *Soul Train* screen and beyond the camera's gaze to dancers, known and unknown, whose translocal travels set the foundations for global streetdance. Place is not a static concept but is shaped by dancers intent on traveling. In the process, dance communities change composition. Dancers grow their cultural histories in dialogue. Place moves; meaning dances do not emerge from a place as petrified cultural objects isolated in space and time. Yet, dancers follow the ethics-aesthetic of black social dance practice, re-creating kinship bonds by continuously adapting rhythms in new contexts so that familiar patterns cohere, are affirmed and sustained, yet resist predictable replication of moves. In this way dance lineages emerge, form, transform. Translocal lineages of hip hop/streetdance cultural histories allow for this messiness, tethering dancers to an ethics-aesthetic of kinship that generates dance styles as movements in and of relation.

Locamotive power requires a nuanced approach to dance training too. The dance studio can't account for all the ways that dancers study as they travel from place to place. Dance study is not solely determined by preset time schedules, spaces reserved for dance alone, or linear pathways to achievement that establish the dance studio as a proprietary institution of artistic creation. Malone states, "formal dance studios are usually years behind the real source of America's major social dances: the black community." She goes on to clarify a different approach to training in black vernacular dance cultures: "Training in this context is a matter of conditioning. It is informal but it is training nevertheless. Because the training is so subtle, the outcome often seems like second nature."[32] Enfolded in Malone's critique of black people's assumed inborn sense of rhythm and (super)natural physical ability is a critique of clock time. Locamotivity thinks about training beyond the linear accounting of time or enclosed sense of space that are conventions of studio-trained dance. Locamotive power extends training to dancers whose everyday practices don't need to be measured by terms of value set by the studio.

With the idea of locamotive power, I am asserting that black social dancing sustains a common consciousness that not only resists an ideological power structure upheld by white establishment dance (which reproduces relations built on an account of the individual subject) but also resources dancers with an alternative system of value through which to shape a sense of being-belonging-becoming together. Locamotivity embeds these ideas of common power and translocal movement in the image of the animated Soul Train, showing that dancers don't just stay in place, they travel. It is often in less visible places that dancers practice the transmission of collective dance knowledges—as locker Arnetta Johnson recalls when I ask her about making up dances at parties at her house: "We all knew. It wasn't one person. So, that's how it became. That was the good part about it. That's just what we did. It was the goal of the party."[33]

Soul Train was a high visibility platform for the transmission of black social dances, helping establish the first styles of hip hop/streetdance to be recognized on a global scale. Streetdancers continue to access *Soul Train* videos in the 2000s as methods of dance research and training.[34] Yet, the animated train also suggests travel beyond the screen. In Northern California's San Francisco Bay Area, for example, dancers with whom I spoke explained they did not primarily draw on *Soul Train* for inspiration as they watched and moved together, growing their local cultural styles.[35] Hip hop/streetdance emerges from these formations and reformations of cultural kinship. Locamotive power generates local and translocal lineages, touching on all the ways dancers innovate. Locamotivity keeps the offscreen artistry of dancers, known and unknown, in play.

AT NETTA'S HOUSE[36]*

"I am the first woman locker," Netta quietly proclaims. Her declaration holds weight—but not because I'm seeking an incontrovertible truth. Certainly it's possible to contest such a telling. Yet, I'm drawn in by her humility and patience with me, over eight years of our intermittent conversations (by phone, by text, online, and at her house). I've become touched by her memories of the dance.

The power of Netta's statement is built in the frame her words make possible, opening a door for those who have not yet been visible to come through. Locating Netta's house as a center (among multiple centers) of locking culture—beyond the *Soul Train* screen and celebrity clubs—means allowing many dancers, yet unnamed and unknown, to enter dance history so that we don't lose them.

For a young black girl growing up in Compton, navigating male-centric performance culture, a white dance establishment, and exploitative entertainment industry, the common fact is Netta's unnoticed place in locking history. "Don Cornelius did offer me a contract to be a *Soul Train* dancer. To travel around and all that. Like we did with James Brown. When he gave it to me, I gave it to my mom. My mom took it to my uncle who was a producer. He said, 'No. He's takin most of your money.'"[37]

I pause to let her words sink in.

Me, Netta, and Skeet, her longtime dance partner, huddle around her kitchen table, a single ceiling lamp casting our faces in its bare glow. Albert and Thelma Johnson's Carson family home is the kind of place that welcomes you in and holds you close. Ten miles directly south of East 103rd Street, off Charcoal Alley at Watts Writers Workshop, where Netta used to make up dance routines with her all-girls group the Toota Woota Sisters and the youth performance group Creative Generation.[38] Ten minutes' drive south of the campus that used to be the Regina Caeli Catholic girls' school in Compton, which she attended as a teen.

I've become familiar with Netta's soft drawl and unadorned delivery, unusual in a dance world that leans more toward animated boasting. She also remembers the non-invitations. "I already knew it was a guy's game. Everybody had formed their groups. They didn't want no woman in it." What set her apart, Netta matter-of-factly explains, was her training in ballet, jazz, tap, and gymnastics at Willie Covan's South Central Los Angeles dance studio.[39] She could memorize a routine instantly by counting out the steps in her head. "Whether Skeet 'nem didn't wanna show me, I could count out the moves.[40] You let me see it once and I had it. I wasn't afraid a hoppin up in the air, landing on my knees. They don't want someone to come in and outdance them. I could keep up."

"Arnetta was one of the few females who could really lock," *Soul Train* dancer Eddie Cole confirms. "She locked like Don and Scoo B Doo. She hit the floor. She did the dive. She did all of that."[41] Overlooking the on-par athleticism of black women and girls, the social spotlight most often shined on men, Hollywood-pretty women, and celebrity entertainers. Agendas of dancers and industry producers alike were shaped by race, colorism, gender, and industry status.

House parties recover certain intimacies of social dance practice not captured televisually or felt in the male-dominant competitive atmosphere of clubs and school dances. Netta's house was an everyday place for dance study where they assembled for after-school hangouts, pool parties, late-night gatherings, sleepovers. If, as dancer-choreographer Ron Gatsby observes, "hip hop dance [is] how black people have always danced at home," then parties at Netta's house are core to locking's locamotive practice and affiliation with the hip hop canon.[42]

At Netta's house, the goal is fun. If it was after school a couple of friends might come by to hang out. "We sat right here in this li'l room and we'd make our step up. Okay, let's do. We'd be joking and all of a sudden Greg'll run through the room and hop." *Greg Pope's suddenly spread-eagle leaping over my head—airborn.*[43]

I eye the path between the opposite wall and the kitchen counter's edge, wary. No more than twenty feet long and ten feet wide. The low ceiling wasn't adding but another eight feet up. I imagine dancers forty years ago, still here. Locking's outstretched gestures could have felt miraculous in such a tight place.

"We say okay that's a movement right there," Netta interrupts my reverie. "It was a move that we all incorporated. You know, she's giving a party this weekend. Let me sit up here and make up something." Describing a regular scene of parties—friends' houses, friends' brothers' and sisters' houses—Netta elaborates the party as the destination for invention. The move "we all incorporated" is a way that locking's collective social body has become reinvented and renewed.

"Picnics. And pool parties," Skeet adds. "I think a lot of times stuff was made up diving off the side of the pool. We'd go out in the garage and dance, or in the backyard."

Netta's house was also the party after the party. If the club gets out at two, they're at the house by four in the morning. "They'd find a place to sleep—here or in the living room," Netta explains. It didn't matter where you slept except for upstairs. Then in the morning her dad would come down to make breakfast for everyone. Netta remembers one time Fred Berry (affectionately called Penguin) rubbing lard in her face and them getting into a food fight, running all around the room laughing. "We were all just having fun."

"After the prom, guess where we came? They knew my parents was cool. They'd say, 'hey let's go back to Netta's house!'"

When they come through the front door, they walk straight down the narrow hall into the kitchen that opens up onto the family room. They move aside tables and chairs. Someone turns the radio on. Sly & the Family Stone. Earth, Wind & Fire. Parliament. Another jumps up and shows a step. The room packs up with young people.

Netta shows me, raising her shoulders to her ears as if she's squeezed in on all sides. *Make my funk the P-Funk.*

"A lot of it was watching," she recollects. "Watching other dancers and not imitating but grooving with them. Like oh yeah, you can do that. Like oh yeah, I feel that groove. I feel that rhythm and then you all get down."

"What's that step called?" I'm watching Netta's kitchen dancing—a double-time bounce performed from the chair where she's seated.

"That's why my knees are bad now," she responds, kicking one leg out while stepping the other foot to the floor in time with her vocal beat—*umm dum dah dum dumm*. She pauses the looping step, closes her eyes. Dropping her head in her hands, she laughs. "Oh I can't remember!" Names matter less at the moment. *Someone puts the needle on a record.* She keeps the rhythm going, talking as she moves from her chair, interjecting her words with sharp hand claps and rapid exhales.

"The whole room might be doing this together *hmm* and then I call out, 'Two times! *Huh! Skeeter Rabbit* two times.' I might be watching someone else and jump up. *Clap!* To let everybody know, 'Okay, let's go back.' *Ah.* And we all knew. If the record stopped, and everybody was in the groove, the whole party would stop . . ."

"*FREEZE.*"

"and everybody Freeze. Then somebody would say,"

"Hey!"

"Tchooka tchooka tchook ba boom boom! *Scoo B Doo*, hey!" Netta's speech flows with Skeet's staccato interjections. They verbalize the rhythms of the dance together, as names of steps—*Skeeter Rabbit, Scoo B Doo*—come back to her. They recall the movement of the party in vernacular speech, reenacting a common rhythm-sensing I'm describing as the locamotive organizing principle at the core of black social dance.

"We would start almost to put choreography together just by hollering out steps," Skeet observes.

"*SWITCH!* We knew we spin. And he's over there."

"I'd go that way, and she would go this way."

"I'd go this way. You knew and you just waited. It didn't make a difference, somebody called it out."

Verbal speech interanimates locking movement—an aural-kinesthetic practice operating at a register below the televisual broadcast. Skeet explains, "A lot of times what they took back to Hollywood came out of houses just like this, house parties like this, dances just like this." Embedded in the social dance of locking, Netta and Skeet reenact a black vernacular practice of the party that *Soul Train*'s controlled camera frame can't fully capture. "Everybody would just fall in. It was part of a whole movement." *They're falling together.* Locking emerges in rhythm-sensing, knowledges moving through the collective social body of the dance.

Netta laughs, "And we all knew. It wasn't one person. So, that's how it became. That was the good part about it. That's just what we did. It was the goal of the party."

ALL THE WAYS WE DANCE BACKWARDS

Locking . . . is a freestyle dance where you are free to move to the music, returning to 'The Lock' as a place to start over, pause/end or where you let the music guide your movements somewhere else.

—DON CAMPBELL

She watches as he shoots his hands up overhead, elbows bent and shoulders tensed, back locked at attention.[44] His hands curl into fists. In contrast to the clench of his shoulders and puffed-up chest, the thumbs soften over the other fingers, leaving a small hollow inside. On beat, he releases the lock. His arms shoot down, as he bends his knees in a funky plié. The next sequence of gestures unfolds in rhythmic time: right biceps curl, kick out, scoop jump. He presents one foot forward as his opposing arm punctuates the downbeat, completing the step with a final biceps curl.

What's that? Lock-kick-step. *Show it again.* She follows, keeping close watch. Lock-kick-step. They move in rhythm together. Lock-kick-step. *Hey, that's a move right there.* Lock-kick-step. *I'm a call that the Scoo B Doo.*

This is a story about a dance that was created on a stairway. But first I'm going to preface it by saying: hip hop is site-specific dance. Not because any hip hop dancer said, "I'm going to go create a dance on a stairway! Because no one's ever done that before." This dance wasn't created because going off the concert stage was novel. Or because dancing on a stairway would offer a social critique of upward mobility. Or perhaps, in another version, because dancing on a stairway would deconstruct the binary of down and up, progress and decline. But this dance also just so happens to do all that.

This is simply a story of a dance stupendously created on a stairway because the building manager said, "*Stop* sliding down the banister!" And so there had to be a way to get up and down those stairs that was fresher than walking.

Part 1

Amid rumors of Jimmy Scoo B Doo Foster's passing since the 1980s, lockers in the 2000s have been studying the lock-kick-step—extending his living memory, fleshed out in the steps of his dance. The Scoo B Doo step incorporates Don Campbell's Lock and often pairs with other movements of locking's lexicon, among them, a quick back-and-forth step called the Stop-and-Go and a scoop-up double-kick-clap called the Scoobot.

In 2011, shortly after his unpredicted return, Bay Area funk dance film crew Funk'd Up TV posted an interview with Scoo B Doo. Instead of traditional locker attire (apple caps, striped shirts, knickers, suspenders, knee socks) he dresses simply in black pants, T-shirt, and a solid black cap on which is centered one white question mark. Scoo B Doo begins to tell the story of how the step named after him came to be:

> At the place where I was living, I kept sliding down the banister all the time. Sliding down, sliding down. The manager would say, *his tone turning crackly and strident*, "You gotta quit sliding down the banister, why don't you walk like everybody else!" And I said, "Well I'm a dancer." "Well then dance up it!" So I said OK. I started dancing up it, and I was doing what is now the Scoo B Doo. I just started stepping up there. Backwards. . . . I put Don's Lock, with that step. It's Lock, Scoo B Doo. That I didn't name. Damita named it. She said, "Well I'm a call that the Scoo B Doo."[45]

Scoo B Doo's story possesses all the best elements of streetdance legend. He capriciously undermines the structural authority of banisters and building managers, sliding between the world of dance and mundane ways of walking. Sliding down the banister (he tells me later, "I'd be flying!") and stepping backward and up, he transforms the stairway into a movement experiment—a material catalyst for improvising other ways to get down.[46] Stairs become a way to move the dance of locking forward, just as Scoo B Doo uses his locking practice as a way to upend convention. Like Don Campbell's story of how he accidentally invented locking style because he couldn't dance right, Scoo B Doo's story emphasizes the creative friction between walking properly and finding fresh ways to move. Their dance parables revel in streetdance's ethic of reinvention.

Repeating over time, Scoo B Doo's up-and-down movement takes the form of a backward loop, an experiment with flights of ascent and descent that delay the necessity of arrival on the stairway landing. Going with music scholar Jason King's phrasing, this "terminally ambivalent" movement animates Scoo B Doo's study—an open-ended invitation to take flight between landings, it shifts the structure's straightforward orientation, allowing him to question, *which way is down?*[47]

Sociologist Rahsaan Mahadeo observes the ways black youth "funk the clock," breaking with Western clock time to create temporalities that make their worldviews relevant.[48] Funking with time, Scoo B Doo's step orients him to the whimsical possibilities of stairways that mess with a teleology of progress toward the next landing. Funking with the stairway's spatial orientation, he simultaneously funks with the logic of moving bodies forward in time, luxuriating in funk'd up possibilities of looping back again. Repeating this backward-forward motion, Scoo-B-Doo establishes his unique groove, the goal of reaching a landing deferred.

Streetdance practice also brings Scoo B Doo inward, into a deeper inhabitation of his groove. A Eurocentric philosophy of progress portrays repetition in black culture as backwardness.[49] Yet Scoo B Doo's story underscores the backward movement of his dance, which moves locking tradition forward, spotlighting a streetdance worldview.[50]

Calling more dancers into his story, Scoo B Doo returns listeners to the collective locamotive practice that generates the dance locking. While his staircase study is performed as a solo, his act of invention is not purely individualistic but rather emerges in company with others. He articulates the movement sequence—Lock, Scoo B Doo—elaborating that his backwards step follows Don Campbell's Lock. Damita Jo, who partnered with both him and Don on *Soul Train*, enters the story next: "I just know I liked doing the step. There was no name. After doing it almost nine months, Damita said to me, well I'm a call that the Scoo B Doo."[51] Her act of naming the step is not oriented toward ownership; the name is borne in the social life of the dance they share.

Scoo B Doo's indebtedness to Don and Damita for giving him the Scoo B Doo step holds weight—a bond of kinship that invokes the many, moving in and on the One. Their artistic practice includes dancing in partnership as they watch and follow one another over the nine-month period of the dance's gestation. Watching and following in partnership are practices I notice, thinking with Christina Sharpe's description of "wake work," as acts of lateral care "in the register of the intramural, in a different relation than" state modes of surveilling the black body.[52] Their wake work, performed repeatedly as an ethic of obligation to keep watch over and follow one another, allows Damita to become familiar with how Scoo B Doo moves, moving her to name the step that immortalizes her dance partner in locking history.

Returning to Funk'd Up's interview, Scoo B Doo goes on to tell another creation story, now about the step called the Stop-and-Go. He recollects how he and fellow locker Greg Pope are preparing for a show in the apartment where they both are living at the time.[53] Greg, who suffers from asthma, is resting on the bed to catch his breath. Meantime, Scoo B Doo has been dancing the Breakdown. As he turns back to see if Greg is going to get up, Greg suddenly notices the step.

Wait, what's that?

Greg tells him to do it again. Repeating the move, he turns around as if to leave, pauses, then comes back around again. Greg gets up, and they try the step together: "Break*down*, turn and back, Breakdown, turn and back. That's how the Stop-and-Go was created."[54]

Scoo B Doo's story describes yet another step that loops around and back again, returning listeners to the ethics-aesthetic practice of watching and following. Wake work is what Greg performs as he watches Scoo B Doo improvise. What is becoming the Stop-and-Go emerges from the Breakdown's visual-kinetic groove and unfurls in Scoo B Doo's dance. They watch and follow each other, feeling-fleshing their sense of the step's emergent rhythm together. Their locamotive home study shapes a funky kinship—a collective being-belonging-becoming in the movement of the dance.

The ways Damita and Greg keep close watch over Scoo B Doo's dance resound in earlier stories he tells to me, of keeping watch, over and over, in his journey to becoming a dancer. From childhood, growing up in Northern California at his mother's house, 2707 Yreka Avenue in Sacramento, he has been watching, not dancing. In the 1950s, his neighborhood was residential, a mix of mostly Mexican, Indian, and Jewish families. They'd often go to visit his grandmother, he remembers, who lived in one of those classic Victorian houses in the Fillmore neighborhood of San Francisco.

> "*All* family. *All* family. All my cousins and everybody would come over there. A lot of us would get together, and I would sit there and watch them. Party time. At my grandmother's house. My cousin was crazy. He was the best dancer in the whole world. The reason why we didn't dance, 'cause he was so good. I *know* I watched. I can see myself watching."[55]

Not yet seeing himself as a dancer, Scoo B Doo nonetheless communicates his fascination with the dancing happening all around him as he sits and watches. His wake work is elaborated in his recursive phrasing—"I can see myself watching."

By 1968 he has moved to stay with his father in Los Angeles and attend Fremont High School, living at his other grandmother's house on 126th Street in Compton. Her family had migrated from the South and owned several houses in the neighborhood. He's in eleventh grade when a friend takes him to a noon dance party at the Fremont gym. The lights are dim, the room filled with dancing. The music is upbeat—James Brown, the Temptations. He watches the dancers, over and over. His fascination soon leads him to 4225 South Crenshaw Boulevard, the now-historic nightclub called Maverick's Flat. It's 1970, and he's about to graduate.

> When I walked in that day, I'd seen a dancer and I'm saying, *what the hell is he doin?*
>
> He's the best. I sat down and I just watched him. I think I watched him from nine thirty until two o'clock. I'd never seen anybody dance like that before. And I'd never been to a place where they partied like that. Every week. I went back. Every every every single week. Watching him, tryin to learn what he was doin. I would watch. I'd take it home, and I'd have to wait a whole week to see what I was practicing was what *he* was doin. *Oh well, I gotta go back again. It ain't look good.* We didn't have no cell phones. Couldn't record it. Always remembering.[56]

Like the up-down stairway loop that leads him to re-create the Scoo B Doo step, watching Don Campbell improvise is a collective act he performs solo—sitting at the club, going home to his one-room studio to remember Don's moves, waiting to return to the club to watch again. Sharpe elaborates the ritual process of wake work that, in Scoo B Doo's memory of a four-hour vigil at Maverick's Flat, prepares him to take what he remembers home, where he goes to practice in solitude, after the party.[57] Home is where he fleshes out his dance, inhabiting Don's movement materials, which have not yet become known as locking style. Watching Don dance over and over becomes a study of what come to be Scoo B Doo's steps, adding to the dance, emerging from remembering how Don moves. Remembering is not replicating but allowing Don's dance to be entangled in how he moves. In remembering he gives continuity to the dance, following Don while finding his way.

Scoo B Doo's vigil is wake work, a practice of return. "Every week. I went back." The ethic is embedded in the aesthetics of practice. Remembering is wrapped up in the ethics-aesthetic of return. Following Don's move with his backwards step is not only collective artistry, emergent in Scoo B Doo's solo stairway flight, but also the way Scoo B Doo elaborates the choreography of wake work—designed to keep returning to Don's dance so we don't lose him.

Part 2

Stop-n-Go, ONE time, TWO time. Lock shake it. Scoo B DOO. Skeeter Rabbit. UPlock hop Scoo B DOO. Skeeter Rabbit TWO times. Scoo BOT. Scoo BOT hop kick. Leo walk.

The steps are not counted, they are called. It's spring 2014, and I'm back in locking class with Shabba Doo. Shabb calls the steps, and we respond, attempting to remember the gestural sequences that go with each step he's taught, all while keeping in time with the rhythms of his speech. Opting out of the studio's conventional language of eight-counts—"one-two-three-four-five-six-seven-eight"—Shabb uses the cultural names of the steps to mark time, accenting our routine with nuanced vocal rhythms that simultaneously help us recall dancers in locking history: Scoo B Doo, Skeeter Rabbit, Leo Fluky Luke Williamson.[58] We repeat the ways they move, over and over, feeling out our knowledge of locking lineages.

Like Scoo B Doo's repurposed stairway, lines of ascent and descent are nonlinear and unfinished. Names are left out, not least of which are women lockers like Arnetta Johnson, Freddie Maxie, Janet Lock . . . plus countless more everyday people who all share locking dancestries. Their names return in cyberspace through the ongoing work of dancers who maintain streetdance archives on sites like Skeeter Rabbit's Locker Legends.[59] The steps we dance are ciphers, codes that carry knowledges shared by many dancers in locking's hidden histories.

Cultural contexts of dance study are important too, where dancers go to recollect one another through stories told in the between-spaces of rest that surround practice time: hallway water breaks, parking lot smokes, diner runs. Dancers coming from different social locations don't just learn but also reinterpret the steps, deciphering the codes in shifting contexts as the dance travels beyond sites of its emergence. In processes of circulating the dance, an entangled web of relations is continuously re-created—kinship formations remain open ended and undone.

Reinterpreting Scoo B Doo's stories, I am also creating a cipher that connects him with his cousin, Greg Pope, and Don Campbell, who inspired him to feel out his dance. This cipher extends to Damita Jo, whose act of naming allows his flesh memory to be passed on in the Scoo B Doo step. Yet other dancers fall out of this cipher, leaving silences in the history.[60] This cipher is simultaneously a work of celebration and of mourning.

Part 3

In the early 2000s, Scoo B Doo returned. In a 2010 interview with *Soul Train* dancer and journalist Stephen McMillian, he described his decades-long absence from the dance world as a kind of death:

> "Around 1986. I did die emotionally and spiritually. I gave up on life. I was homeless and had little odd jobs here and there. I was living in and out of hotels and was hanging on Skid Row for seven years. I began to go over in my mind how locking came to be. . . . From 1993 to 2006, I was still psychologically studying and analyzing the movement and foundation of locking."[61]

Scoo B Doo's story observes multiple waves of loss. Spiritual death and homelessness become entangled, as he describes a shift in his locking practice from *Soul Train*'s celebrity stage spotlight to a solo movement inward: "I didn't lock for anybody. I didn't really practice. But every once in a while I just wanted to see if I could lock. Damn. I used to lock. It was like that." I ask him whether the dance was still there in his spirit. "Oh yeah, 100 percent."[62] It so happens the last episode of *Soul Train* aired in 2006, the same year that closes a phase of Scoo B Doo's spiritual quest through locking. Ambivalent attempts to air archived episodes and in some form revive the show failed. Scoo B Doo's recollection of his journey through a kind of death feels prescient. Locking's social life is given as much in the *Soul Train* dancers' collective celebration of coming together as in the solitude that comes after the party falls apart.

Scoo B Doo's story intimates psychosomatic and biopolitical dimensions of locking's ethics-aesthetic practice.[63] The uncertain ending of the Scoo B Doo step's backward loop also animates life on Skid Row, keeping Scoo B Doo returning to locking, knowing that "in the event of a fall . . . dance always already implies movement, rather than immobility, as political possibility."[64] Alicia Garza likewise writes about falling apart as a paradigm for political change, without which emergent strategies for organizing people's movements cannot grow.[65] For Joshua Chambers-Letson, the party (in both political and social senses) is an experimental, ambiguous formation defined not solely by ways people gather together but, also, by the experience of loss that follows after. He asserts that every failure or falling opens up social imagination to rearranging forms of relation that make more life possible.[66] All together they suggest that the party is useful less as an unchanging formation than as a process of experimenting with form and its dissolution. Falling apart prepares us for coming together—an invitation to experiment with open-ended movement, physical and political.

In the early 1970s of locking's emergence, the party was simultaneously coming together and falling apart. *Soul Train* dancers got black people moving together in their homes and onscreen with the locamotive power of black social dance, just as black political movements like the Black Panther Party (BPP) were getting systematically dismantled in the wake of the civil rights era and the ratcheting up of state surveillance of black life.[67] Their collective movement experiments are embedded in locking as an ethics-aesthetic assertion of black life that returns in Scoo B Doo's story of loss and mourning:

> In January 2010, my wife Gina typed my nickname into the Internet search engines and came up with all kinds of things about me and my influence on dance. One of the things that came up was the webpage lockerlegends.net, stating that my very close and dear friend Greg Pope passed away. I was so hurt by his death and I wanted to express my condolences. Gina went to the Locker Legends website and typed a message stating something like, "My name is Jimmy Scoo B Doo Foster and I want to express my condolences over the passing of Greg Pope."[68]

By way of Gina Foster's search, Scoo B Doo reaches out, expressing his grief over Greg's loss in a gesture of mourning that has already been becoming embedded in the practice of locking. See, up until his death, Greg had been teaching locking to students internationally. Lockers have been calling Scoo B Doo's steps, practicing the world over. Calling his name over and over. In Scoo B Doo's absence, over the decades-long course of his extended fall from locking, his steps were continuing to animate Greg's dance, fleshed in the rhythm of a displacement that goes by the name of Scoo B Doo. And also Scoobot. And also Stop-and-Go. And also Skid Row. And also.

Greg and Scoo B Doo's kinship bond is practiced in danscendance, a mode of kinethics through which dancers mourn, transforming loss from a private to collective experience. Danscendance is a spiritual call of kinship that extends an obligation to the dancer to keep watch over dance legacies as a ritual practice of return:

> "One of the moderators of that site, Skeeter Higgins, another good friend of mine from years ago, replied and got in touch with her. We reunited and he posted photos of him and me on the Locker Legends website along with a story that I was very much alive."[69]

Scoo B Doo and Greg "insist life and being into the wake" by refusing to deny their collective loss and the ongoing entangled practice of their mourning.[70] In Scoo B Doo's story, mourning and celebration are not easily separated and even anticipate a kind of rebirth, as he ends up explaining how Gina helped him open a Facebook account that filled up with dancers the world over on the same day. Since then he has been traveling internationally to teach, judge, and perform locking.

Scoo B Doo's rebirth in global streetdance after a kind of death is animated by an ethics-aesthetic of return that remains terminally ambivalent, embedded in Scoo B Doo's repetition and reinvention of steps that loop backward. Not the same as repair or reconciliation, danscendance keeps the past in the present. And like the political possibility of the party as an experimental formation, danscendance is always in the process of falling apart. Scoo B Doo keeps moving forward by returning to remember the passed, mourning Don Campbell and Greg Pope as he also recites his debts to them for their mutual acts of sharing the dance.

What often goes unstated by streetdancers is that you learn to live by dancing and that dancing gives you resources for how to live. Ethics-aesthetics hold these resources, shaping ways of knowing how to be. A backwards step that Scoo B Doo reinvents makes sense as a repeating figure for his life experience, bringing him back to the streetdance world after a period of mourning that is ongoing. In my reinterpretation of his story, danscendance becomes a practice of return that does not resolve collective loss yet continues to generate the movement of locking.

Illustration:
Down for the Fade: Twisting Reinvention by d. sabela grimes

two
Popping & Other Dis/Appearing Acts

flesh surfaces riPPle
exOskeleTal disTurbulenT
TwisT-O-flexx
regisTerr
sysTem
a Tic
jiT
Ter
y
ness
concenTraTed
exPlOsions jOlt bOnes
sending flesh riPPle
Pulsing
thru scalP
necktorsOshhOulderelbOwwristfingerwristelbOwshhOulder
chestbelly
pelviswOrld
swivel funkK
juT hip
in
two
knees
cOllaPse
agiTaTing ground
lose structurewhOle integrity
shimmer uP
bodyquakes
surfaces
riPPle
floats
flesh

POLYCENTRIC DANCE HISTORIES

That *popping* has messy origins creates an opening through which to study the dance's kinship with multiple "other" styles, appearing and disappearing in genealogies of hip hop dance. Dancers challenge the use of popping in global hip hop/streetdance culture as an umbrella reference and shorthand for a wide variety of styles that have been emerging from diverse local histories of place and form. Northern California Bay Area dancers explain that *boogaloo* was the umbrella term in their cities before popping became popularized in the discourse of younger generations of dancers through the 1980s and 1990s. Oakland cultural worker and dancer Traci Bartlow reflects on the emergence as a key "opportunity for [dancers] to come together and see each other . . . they were taking the popular dances from the '60s and the early '70s and fusing it into their own style."[1] My research shows an interanimation of styles via the popular social party dance of the 1960s and '70s called the Robot, danced to soul and emerging funk music. This chapter acknowledges popping's hidden histories and lesser-known innovators, taking up common aesthetics and kinship of styles that become entangled in dancers' everyday practices.

Commenting on Bay Area dance histories, Will Randolph, who cofounded the Oakland dance group Black Resurgents in 1971, describes the emergence of local styles from black social dance:

> My aunt and my mom took me to a New Year's Eve party. December 31st, 1966. I was in third or fourth grade. The song by Wicked Wilson Pickett—*down on Broadway, there's a street*—the funky "Funky Broadway" was the song that was playin. I was doin' my James Brown. I hit the splits, did a li'l Jerk, did the Camel Walk, and here come Lester and Duck out of the hallway, doin' a duck move with their heads. Lester got out on the floor, he's rollin' his chest and jumped to the side. *Blam!* Pose. I stopped. I had never seen anybody up close and personal do what I saw. For me, that's how boogalooing was born. It wasn't a continuous flow of movement of the body. It was a use of space with your body in a stop-go formula that changed how I perceived dancing to be done.[2]

In his story, Will inhabits James Brown's dance artistry, articulating a sense of belonging that's animated by the Jerk and Camel Walk, black social dances that generate improvised solo dancing of the party, urged on by the grown-ups in the room: "Oh he can dance! Let me see! Who can get down?" Will cites the party as "up close" creative space to show out and invent, corresponding with Netta's story in chapter 1 of family house parties that harbor locking's locamotive practice. "For me" is a subtle but important qualifier, allowing Will to locate the collective creation of Oakland Boogaloo in his lived experience. Following the aesthetic principle of locamotivity, local styles emerge from black social dancing, as dancers embed themselves in cultural histories of place: here, Will links the emergence of Oakland Boogaloo to the dancers Lester and Duck.[3]

Besides bringing visibility to Bay Area dance histories, the concept of *dis/appearing* also leans into the ways popular histories of hip hop dance are created and transmitted. "Popping & Other Dis/Appearing Acts" shows that dancers weave intricate webs of kinship among styles, through which their dance histories become visible. In the process of making kinship bonds, dancers also shape what I call *polycentric dance histories*, ways of telling history that activate the multiple locations from which dancers move. Defined by the multiple centers a dancer activates simultaneously—spiraling hips, shoulders, torso, and neck, in different directions that coalesce in rhythm as they improvise these funk styles—polycentrism is an Africanist aesthetic philosophy, fitting dance histories that refuse to be erased by a Eurocentric worldview that constructs one culture and history as singular center and vertical line of origin.[4] Just as boogaloo and popping styles train dancers in the art of the off-center lean, the inventiveness of vernacular dance lineages challenges a top-down hierarchy and conventional modes of telling history.

Interanimated dances of Oakland Boogaloo, San Francisco Strutting, and Richmond Robotting exemplify the aesthetic-cultural enmeshment of polycentric dance histories, mapping routes traveled by dancers in and across the three major cities of the region.[5] By the mid- to late 1960s, Bay Area dancers were experimenting with robotic movement, incorporating rhythms of soul and funk music to innovate the velvet gestures and hard-hitting muscle contractions characteristic of popping styles today. Watching Lester and Duck, Will notices the groove established by their rhythmic duck-neck isolation flowing into a rolling action of the chest, juxtaposed with a jump and sudden stop, called up in his vocal punctuation—*Blam!* He emphasizes the aesthetic relationship between movement flow and its sudden interruption at the core of Oakland Boogaloo style.

Funk era dances in the Northern California Bay Area tell a history of place in movement. Oakland's Black Messengers and Black Resurgents are progenitors of Bay Area hip hop dance, explain Boogaloo Dana and Fayzo, who have been dancing since the early 1970s. Both initially danced with San

Francisco's Demons of the Mind before forming the group Medea Sirkas (pronounced "media circus") in 1991. Dana describes a cross-fertilization of movements that he experienced in creating his unique style: "In Oakland, where I'm originally from, Boogalooing is an umbrella name to describe many other styles, substyles. Robots was one of 'em. I had all kind of multidifferent styles. In Boogaloo, you could Sinbad, you could Dinosaur, you could Robot, you could Vibrate."[6] Fayzo, who first began dancing with Demons of the Mind in 1978, remembers, "In San Francisco, where I'm from, it was all about doing the Robot, initially. Strutting came later."[7] The Northeast bay city of Richmond was known for a practice of synchronized Robottin', which produced local dance groups like the Richmond Robots and Lady Mechanical Robots. Robot, the popular social/party dance of the day, was becoming embedded in their neighborhood vernaculars.

Abundant shifts in terminology tell a dynamic cultural process of translocation and reinvention as dancers traveled across locales, rerouting their histories within different contexts. Naming these dances of neighborhood and street is an ethical call to care for dancers' local work of aesthetic reinvention and highlights an intimate sociality that gives dancers a sense of embeddedness in the places where they are.

Yet also, the dynamic circulation of vernacular dance style resists defining place in any singular or static sense. Dana describes a brief encounter with Fayzo in 1982, a year before they began dancing together: "It wasn't serious enemies. It was more like metaphoric dance enemies in the dance game. What happened was [Demons of the Mind] were popular in San Francisco and [Criminons] were popular in Richmond, even though I wasn't from Richmond. We ran into them at Oakland Technical High School."[8] Dana's recollection exemplifies the intertwined circuitries of dancers' travels (especially for youth who grew of age in the late 1970s) through the Bay Area cities of Oakland, Richmond, and San Francisco. A steady shifting of group members and changing of group names continued to inform the growth of the dances themselves, seeding a common culture of artistic collaboration.

The material of Robot is reinvented in the locally embedded movements of Oakland Boogaloo, Richmond Robotting, and San Francisco Strutting. For dancers with living knowledge of the history, cross-fertilization of movements did not reduce or erase local difference but instead, as Dana emphasizes, allowed varieties of style to become highly nuanced:

> What a lot of people don't know is there's over a thousand varieties of different Robot you could do from the human perspective. Richmond had

> their own perspective. I call it the inside-outside Robot or the spontaneous Robot. Boogalooing [in Oakland] is done on "the One" in the music. But [Richmond's] Robot was done on the "and," and "the One." Seventy-five percent of their stuff is a torso straight and hand movement. *Dana intersperses dancing as he talks.* That's their trademark. That's what separates them from all the other groups.[9]

In the Bay Area, dance styles became affiliated on the basis of ties between local dancers and shifting composition of dance crews. Bay Area promoter Jay Payton, host of Oakland's *Soul Is* variety show on KEMO-TV, gave youth groups a chance to perform and see themselves screened, bringing routines crafted for high school assembly and community center talent show stages into the film studio. Following *Soul Train*'s 1971 syndication, these shows circulating within local black-owned networks spotlighted their area's dance cultures. Describing the emergence of a whole dance culture centering the Bay, dancers with whom I spoke explained that, for them, *Soul Train* was not a main inspiration for their innovations of local styles.

Cultural histories of popping are also indebted to the rich dance history of California's Central Valley city of Fresno.[10] Located almost halfway between the major West Coast cities of San Francisco to the north and Los Angeles to the south, Fresno surfaces as a less-expected center of hip hop dance history beyond New York.[11] The West Coast Relays, an annual track-and-field event held at Ratcliffe Stadium, drew world record-setting athletes to Fresno and were crucial for sprouting a translocal culture of California dance. Young people gathered at relay after-parties where they could show and hone their dance skills informally, watching and studying together. The relays supported a dynamic dispersal of dances, further nuancing the reinvention process. Bay Area dancers cite the relays as a primary way they circulated their local dances to Fresno, helping foster what came to be known as the dance popping. In 1979, Fresno dancers the Electric Boogaloos appeared on *Soul Train*, performing boogaloo and popping styles that incorporated influences from Bay Area dance culture into their routines. In the 1980s, New York-based hip hop dancers began to incorporate popping into their style of electric boogie.[12] As key innovators of popping style, the Electric Boogaloos became widely influential from the early decades of the dance's global circulation—as they still are today.

Overlooked in mass media representations of hip hop culture, hidden histories of these dances have been appearing over the last two decades, a result of dancers' labor to document their local cultures. To cite Fresno cultural historian Sean Slusser, "These stories are too often ignored or drowned out by stories coming from bigger cities or from well-funded archives."[13] Vernacular dancers continued the process of rerouting and reinvention within their home contexts, where new forms took shape as dancers embedded themselves locally in their travels from place to place. Yet there was not a unidirectional line of creation from one center dispersed out—dancers kept traveling back and forth, always with the possibility of opening new paths of influence. Dancers' travels sparked multidirectional networks that entangled styles in practice, even as they simultaneously reinvented dances embedded with the stamp of their neighborhoods and areas. By asserting kinship of styles, I am saying that the cultural specificity of dancers' local histories does not disprove but rather emphasizes their place in hip hop's capacious inheritance.

Importantly, San Francisco Strutter Lonnie Pop Tart Green complicates the quick use of "hip hop dancer" as an identity label because it hides West Coast lineages:

> "Everybody started identifying everything with hip hop and calling us hip hop dancers. That became a distraction for us. It's no knocking the East Coast, but we know what we do. My response was what is a hip hop dancer? We Strutters out here. We have Boogaloos here too. It's our world, you know what I'm saying. The children, the mothers, the grandmothers, the uncles, the aunties, they all did it and can still do it. It's our lifestyle. Where we're from."[14]

In his national role as Hip Hop Congress cultural education director, Pop Tart highlights distinct local histories while also recognizing the importance of creating global dance networks of relation.[15] Bay Area vernaculars of boogaloo, robotting, and strutting belong to hip hop/streetdance history, yet blanket labeling of dance genres hides situated cultural contexts of style. His statement suggests that hip hop/streetdancestries can simultaneously protect and obscure dance histories, meaning that the work of collective identity formation and belonging remains unfinished.

Mothers, grandmothers, and aunties play central roles in Pop Tart's listing of many unnamed women in Bay Area dance history, and he often credits Deborah Granny Robotroid Johnson—founder of the San Francisco-based group Granny & Robotroid—for raising him up in strutting culture. Granny & Robotroid was a "family group," Granny explained, telling me how she named Ezra, her two-year-old foster child, Baby Robotroid and took on the name Granny for herself as an entertainment industry entrepreneur in her twenties at a time when women weren't supposed to be dancing without a male partner: "My grandmother told me I couldn't do anything because I had kids. So I said, 'well I'll be Granny,' that way no matter how old I get, I can always do something. I had no idea how Granny was gonna look. I didn't have a picture. Granny & Robotroid created theyself."[16] Under cover of Granny, bespectacled with gray wig and matronly sartorial style, Deborah Johnson choreographed her central role in Bay Area dance history.

Pop Tart calls deeper attention to these dances as practices of kinetic kinship—a moving sense of their rootedness births a world of extended family relations, those who know the dance as a place "where we're from" because they live the dance together. Creating a sense of familiarity in movement, dancers deliberately enact their dancestries as creative resources for practicing cultural and historical continuity. Pop Tart's way of locating San Francisco Strutting in familiar social bonds is an ethos at the core of the aesthetic practices this chapter studies: to dance *where* we are from means, also, to reinvent kinship bonds that derive from displacement.

As collective practices embedded with ethics-aesthetic principles, the dance techniques studied in this chapter figure wider sociopolitical patterns of forced and interrupted movement, conditioned by what Christina Sharpe calls "the il/logic of Black life in the wake" of slavery.[17] Vital to this aesthetic grouping of robotic-style dances are the repeated actions of rhythmic isolation, release, and contraction of various muscle groups, anchoring dancers' exploration of the relationship between stopping and moving. The dances also share a common interest in animated and mechanical movement as skilled dancers perform visual illusions, making the human body appear to transform into something other than real. Drawing on critical theories of geography, film, literature, dance, performance, and philosophy, I assert that the dances' kinethics revise dominant ethics-aesthetic codes of antiblackness upheld by a racial capitalist logic of the individual and attendant practices of gentrification, acquisition, ownership, and removal.

I follow an ethics-aesthetic of place and displacement in a dance called The Fillmore, embedded in the San Francisco neighborhood of the same name. I move to consider how the cinematic technique of stop-motion animation shapes a practice of being-becoming Shiva-Kali for Bay Area dancer Boogaloo Dana. I pause to study the principle of "zero" in the dance pedagogy of Bronx, New York, dancer Steffan Mr. Wiggles Clemente, carefully informed by dancestries of popping from the California Central Valley city of Fresno. I go to the East Bay Area city of Richmond, where all-girls group the Lady Mechanical Robots once danced their local style of Richmond Robotting, interlocking limbs to create highly synchronized unison movement. I listen to stories of the members of dance group Medea Sirkas, who have danced together for over forty years, representing their style of San Francisco Strutting. Drawing on ethics-aesthetic practices of touch and breath, both the Lady Mechanical Robots and Medea Sirkas build a sense of shared embodiment that solidifies their kinship bonds in tight spaces they make into moving place.

My approach to dance theory and history follows experimental routes, moving with various styles and practices of dancers who travel. My focus grows out of conversations, spoken and danced, with dancers who generously shared their practices and stories with me, from 2008, as I was finding a common entryway into writing the aesthetic philosophy of hip hop/streetdances. It is beyond the scope of my study to discuss other stylistic threads, although they certainly exist and are vast.

I do not claim to present a neat, universal, or final history of these dances—their aesthetic sociality moves. In so moving, they perform disappearing acts that escape rigid categories, shift out of static positions, and re-create dancestries. The chapter's title poses the possibility that the dance popping exists in moving relation with other disappearing acts—dances named and unnamed whose hidden histories are being retold and reinterpreted, showing the abundant ongoingness of dancers' cultural work. The dances are practices of relation and belonging with others, work that remains undone.

This chapter also experiments with creative ways of writing dance. The flow of sections is interrupted by pauses, short "innerludes" that shape a poetics of the dances, mimicking through the chapter structure the aesthetics of the collective styles. The pause is also meant to create an opening—an invitation to breathe and shift into different rhythms of reading. Likewise, this chapter is less an arrival and more a departure that's open ended. What I do present is a dance study with edges unfinished. The stories I tell are partial. I imagine I've left visible threads hanging in my telling. They can be picked up or discarded, pulled out or left hanging, allowing many more possibilities for histories to be told.

a marionette starts to dance
two feet faltering
appendage irrupting

in all directions
in one
sloping
forward
tipping

on edge
of
loose limbs
surrendering a body
into softness *syncopated*
buckle and sag
still
invisible strings pull
the doll recollects
reassembles
this dance of suspension

anticipating
impossible positions

WHAT'S POPPIN'?

Linguistically, the verbal noun *popping* functions as an ideophone—the word sonically imitates the dance's visual aesthetics of miniature fleshly explosions that animate the dancer from inside. In its naming, popping signifies the sensory blending of sight, sound, and motion at the core of a popper's technical practice. Sounded out in the "pop" and informed by electrical charges of motor neurons, these concentrations of energy move isolated muscles of neck, torso, pelvis, and limbs in polyrhythmic and syncopated sensory-rhythmic feel. Poppers shape a kind of spectacular body moved by the little blasts that funk with their flow—sharp spasms that appear to disappear, paradoxically breaking apart while enhancing a visual feel of rhythmic smoothness and wholeness expressed as dance style.[18]

The aesthetic of muscle contraction plays with halting the continuous flow of movement through the popping body in a range of ways, such as highly concentrated, rhythmic muscle contraction (popping and hitting), protracted muscle contraction (animation and robot styles), and culminating muscle contraction (dime-stopping). Subtle differentiations between types of muscle contractions and rhythmic approaches point to the high level of expertise trained in a popper's demonstration of style, with the community expectation that poppers draw on a shared vocabulary by studying subtleties of multiple stylistic techniques.

Unconcerned with upholding a presumed "proper" anatomical position that fixes alignment symmetrically on a plumb line (still widely taught as proper dance alignment and standard orientation to ground), poppers experiment with asymmetry and cultivate a decentered sense of spatial orientation. Katrina Hazzard-Gordon (later Hazzard-Donald) explains that in this "African esthetic, balance is achieved through the combination of opposites. . . . This principle of asymmetry as balance" allows poppers to delight in the play of suspending from multiple centers, rotating joints in opposition to produce awkward positions.[19] Turning hip joints inward, they collapse in a knock-kneed drop before sliding back to their feet sideways. Twisting torso and neck, they look over their shoulder backward while torquing hips to step forward. It could be said, poppers practice an aesthetic preoccupation with "trying to figure out which way is up" while refusing straightforward ways of moving.[20]

Shape-shifting is inherent to popping styles, a show of bodily pliability. Depending on the quality of the visual illusion, dancers build a sense of being animated by involuntary impulses: a machine rigidly motorized by internal sensors, a doll jerking on a puppeteer's invisible strings. Lack of bodily agency is thematically reflected in the names of popping's affiliate styles, like puppet, skarekrow, robot. All the while, poppers build intimate sensory connection to the beat (traditionally, rhythms of funk, and later, electro and hip hop).[21] Popping aesthetics transform form to imagine and perform otherworldly being in ways that challenge the viewer's perception of the human body and bodily agency.

At the same time, these improvisation-based styles do the most with minimal use of space. Robots make incremental adjustments of position, a spectacle of movement in miniature.[22] Borrowing Michel Foucault's "practices of freedom," dance scholar Danielle Goldman puts Houston Baker's literary critique of "tight places" in conversation with improvised social dance forms that work through limitation, challenging an idealized notion of freedom as release from all boundaries and constraints.[23] Such practices shape their ethics-aesthetic philosophy through style vocabularies and technical grammars situated by "social and historical positions in the world [that] affect one's mobility."[24] Generated from the ethos of black social dance practice and drawing on themes of outer space and fantasy, popping styles invite dancers to improvise otherwise worlds in tight places that imaginatively expand their sense of being-becoming beyond human existence.

Again, this is not to say that limitations don't exist. Rather, dancers invent mobilities by working with physical restraint and constraint. Robotter Renée Lesley points out this making do with limitation in the dance of Richmond icon Riley Rally Moe Moore: "Riley couldn't play sports because of his legs. He used that to his advantage. I used to love watching Riley. People would laugh at him. When he started Robottin he used those legs. He Skarekrowed. He did things with his arms, his body, his head. It was like he was detaching his body from his legs. He just started doing things that were unbelievable. He created a whole new style. His mom didn't get him the corrective shoes so he was stuck."[25] Riley's inventive skarekrow style improvises from the social location of "stuck" mobility, upending presumptions of a "correct" mobility fashioned from shoes his mom can't afford. Riley's now-legendary skarekrow performs an extraordinary orientation to ground, challenging conventional expectations of sport masculinity and fitting with Rizvana Bradley's theory of black cinematic gesture: "experimental black dance forms that oscillate between contradictory affects—aspiration and refusal, desire and aversion, perfection and failure."[26] Renée offers an exemplary description of the experimentalism embedded in these technology-inspired movement practices.

"Otherwise movements" of black social dance, Ashon Crawley writes, constitute a force of excess that presents a critique of the normative.[27] Otherwise movements activate a temporality in which all that precedes a movement always already gives meaning to its present iteration as new—as the potential for change. By opening up otherwise world possibilities of center, position, and orientation, popping styles define mobility and physical ableness expansively, more so than limiting which bodies can participate in the dance. Dancers work within these styles to build stylistic literacies, drawing on tradition embedded as abstract principles that they access in the improvisatory moment they transform form.

the body steels itself
Robot appears on edge
a blank gaze
into space
mechanical attachments
fuse
rotating joints
in isolation
they perform
machinic dislocations
of pelviselbowskneeswrists
steel turns liquid
the body morphs
an empty mass
of animated
clay
mass fragments
losing hold of bits of its
self
in halting attempts
to seize
it
self
back

DANCING THE FILLMORE ON THE GROUND OF DISPLACEMENT

With minimal use of space, the dance's angular architecture combines slanting lines and smoothed out curves to reveal The Fillmore's distinctive rhythmic design. The solo dancer steps tightly forward and backward into place, showing the influence of precision stepping carried over from high school Army ROTC drills. He carves the space around him with animated mechanical revolutions of arms, legs, torso, neck—in a moment the elliptical shapes dissolve into undulating waves. His limbs segment, elongate, lean and snake around one another in repeating patterns that loop and effortlessly unravel.[28]

Embedded in Northern California's San Francisco Bay Area, the dance called The Fillmore is agitated by the ground of displacement—a racial ontology of forced movement that conditions people's struggles with growth and development in the dance's eponymous neighborhood, the Fillmore district, known at one time as the Harlem of the West.[29]

From 1940 to 1945, San Francisco's black population increased by 600 percent, largely representing new residents from the South migrating west to follow the promise of liberal inclusion: a California of plentiful jobs and less-segregated living conditions. Yet, new black residents to the Western Addition/Fillmore often moved into homes emptied by the forced internment of Japanese residents. The naval shipyards in San Francisco's Bayview/Hunters Point neighborhood and Kaiser Shipyards in the East Bay Area city of Richmond drew migrants looking for plentiful wartime industry jobs. In Fillmore's twenty-square-block area, black businesses bloomed, supporting a lively street life where "you could always pay later" and people knew one another by name.[30] Such acts of reciprocity characterized the informal social mixing of low- and middle-class residents who created the district's tightly woven social fabric.[31] Nightclubs like the New Orleans Swing Club, Club Alabam, Jackson's Nook, California Theater Club, Can-Do Club, Jack's, and Bop City brought cultural vitality to Fillmore through the 1950s.[32]

The 1949 Housing Act opened the door for major, still-reverberating shifts in the Bay Area's demographics and social life. The San Francisco Redevelopment Agency targeted black neighborhoods for urban "renewal," demolition and renovation projects that translated as removal of black residents. Neglecting the Fillmore's cultural vitality, city planners labeled whole neighborhoods as slums and leveraged powers of eminent domain to raze homes and raise prices on "rehabilitated" housing. By 1970, the region's black population had peaked, and by 1974 the naval shipyards closed, leaving eight thousand people out of work and without retraining in the midst of disappearing job opportunities.

Writing in 2012, Jasmine Johnson and Sean Ossei-Owusu note that San Francisco's African American demographic decreased 50 percent between 1970 and 2010, "represent[ing] one of the biggest decreases in a major city's black population."[33] In their chapter "From Fillmore to No More," they state: "Only two remaining neighborhoods have a semblance of a salient black community, the Fillmore and Bayview-Hunters Point, the former standing as the last majority African-American community in the city."[34] The Fillmore (both dance and place) holds a history of forced movement and disappearance. Different from the violence of property acquisition (counting land as static units), The Fillmore embeds dancers in place as they move, a way to reimagine a condition of being displaced that persists in slavery's afterlife.[35] Dancing The Fillmore on the ground of displacement, dancers institute a different set and sense of relations to place.

I'm not proposing dancing The Fillmore be considered a political act of resistance to gentrification, or even political in any sense of politics proper. Instead, The Fillmore institutes black San Francisco's kinetic memory, embedding dancers in place as an ethic, a way to be—a movement that's felt differently from the selective appreciation of Fillmore history in urban "renewal" projects like the city government-established jazz district. Such institutional establishments, Johnson and Ossei-Owusu argue, often function to depoliticize local people's struggles with cycles of gentrification as well as the forced removal of blackness. In the same funk breath dancers improvise an aesthetic remaking of social bonds: The Fillmore kinethics reorient dancers to feeling-knowing belonging to place. Dancing The Fillmore, San Francisco Strutters move from a location of displacement, therein moving place "from noun to verb"; they articulate an ethics-aesthetic that unsettles and transforms static place in the dance's isolated gestures, bold salutes, smooth stepping, and precise hits.[36]

Although the idea that place moves could be seen as a romance with fluidity that depoliticizes displacement, I insist The Fillmore is a practice of embeddedness that does not collude with antiblackness. Black feminist geographer Katherine McKittrick extends Édouard Glissant's "poetics of landscape" to assert the "sayability" of geography. She puts forth ways of naming and claiming place that participate in the *unfin-*

ished work of belonging, and emphasizes that such acts "should not be naturally followed by material ownership and black repossession but rather by a grammar of liberation, through which ethical *human-geographies* can be recognized and expressed."[37] In naming The Fillmore, dancers show these sayings of space and place can be danced. I borrow from McKittrick and Glissant to consider The Fillmore and its affiliated local style of San Francisco Strutting as "expressive method and technique . . . of inevitable black geographic presence."[38] The Fillmore's movement from a location of displacement embeds a feel of neighborhood, generating kinships among dancers who get together to dance The Fillmore's rhythmic language.

In their study of gentrification in San Francisco leading up to the housing bubble of the early 2000s, Nikki Jones and Christina Jackson describe a social practice of "discursive redlining" that extends redlining beyond institutional lending laws to a raced and classed language of ghettoization, made popular in people's casual conversations, behaviors, and attitudes. Identifying a shift in the use of *ghetto* from noun to adjective, they explain that the ghetto is defined no longer by geographic boundaries but by people's existence—the question of who *is* ghetto and the impact of *those people*'s values on perceptions of crime and violence.[39] Their study suggests two possible ways of defining value: financial investments for profit and "interpersonal investments." They argue that discursive redlining attenuates the latter, transforming the fabric of everyday sociality of the neighborhood. Citing numerous comments of Yelp reviewers describing where to go and where (who) to avoid in the Fillmore district, they aptly show the consequences of discursive redlining, affectively *felt* in the tenuous quality of people's social relations. It's about how black people feel they're "seen"—a tangled dynamic of oversight and disappearance, as this dialectic captures those who are literally "out there" on the block. The Fillmore moves on and beyond these same blocks, calling and claiming a counterpractice of belonging to place, and carrying resources for differently valuing neighborhood life.

The Fillmore's form of recognition emerges in the wake of displacement's historically specific violence. Not the same as but related to displacement, cycles of gentrification and land ownership have in part depended on a mythology of vacant space/no people measured by static units of property to be counted, securing the logic of acquisition. The history of blackness has been held in this violent accounting, for which the blueprint is the accumulation of no-bodies as objects.

In a related operation that I encounter in the final section of this chapter, competition and industry dance choreography, pervasive in online representations and contemporary practices of hip hop/streetdance, utilizes a studio-derived practice of eight-counting that involves separating movement into units on a linear timeline. Like flipping houses for a gentrified urban market, flipping vernacular dance for a neoliberal dance market is accelerated when the messiness of movement cultures is reduced to replicable moves, making the dance more widely accessible but also vulnerable to commodification. Cleaning up the funk is a function of racial capital, extracting movement for commercial distribution, consumption, and exchange. Vernacular dancers also choreograph and perform set routines using less visible collective practices of breath and touch that build kinship bonds through shared embodiment—feeling-knowing as one in rhythms that escape translation into counts.

The Fillmore is a familiar rhythm-gesture of mutual affirmation and recognition that makes the neighborhood "a place where everyone said hello and was accounted for."[40] The temporality of the dance extends the past in the present moment of dancing, beyond the physical geography of the Fillmore district, articulating what Jasmine Johnson calls the present perfect tense of black mourning. Ensconced in her phrasing "sorrow's swing," this temporal poetics alliterates a dialectic of mourning and joy born in and by black dance.[41] It is through the work of improvising place in motion that The Fillmore, "escaping anticipations of its next move . . . thus embodies one rhythm of blackness: that black time is both of the past and ongoing."[42] Counting practices bely The Fillmore kinethics, which can't be stilled.

The Fillmore re/moves those who dance on the ground of displacement, unsettling the terms of acquisition which see the Fillmore as empty void. They dance the 'Moe as a place of felt dislocation that undoes static positions and shifts single points of origin.[43] Displacement conditions The Fillmore's "aesthetic sociality"—a sociality that moves place and belonging in practice, unfinished and always in flux.[44]

In a feature interview with Medea Sirkas for Sway's Universe, cohost Mike Muse remarks:

MIKE MUSE: I love origin stories . . . I'm curious about the *naming* of the dances. You call it "The Fillmore." Was there a collective? Were you guys at a park and you guys all said, at the same time, we're going to call this The Fillmore?

FAYZO: Names were organic. You didn't say, "I'm going to call that the so and so." In San Francisco, there was this guy named Ben James. Ben, he lived in Kansas City. He moved out to the Bay. I think he moved to Oakland and moved to San Francisco, back to Oakland, and then back to San Francisco. He lived in San Francisco in the Fillmore district. *He* was doing that dance that you just saw me do. Moving his hands, shuffling his feet, moving from side to side. We just started calling it The Fillmore. We all lived in Fillmore. It was just a name that stuck with what he was doing. He was the one that brought that dance over. It didn't have a name. The dancers named it.[45]

Fayzo's creation story shows how dancing together can be a practice of becoming embedded in place. His story allows for a certain messiness of origins, suggesting that The Fillmore's rootedness is defined not by rigid attachment to place but through routes of travel—a sense of place that's in motion. Tracing Ben's travels from Kansas City to Oakland to San Francisco, Fayzo also maps black migrations to and within California, especially significant given the Fillmore district's historical context. Ben's solo artistry—moving his hands, shuffling his feet—is always already danced as an ensemble movement: "The dancers named it." Naming The Fillmore initiates a way of moving that is inseparable from the social life of the dance. If we add on Pop Tart's statement that opens this chapter, The Fillmore creates the world "where we're from."

Formations of identity in The Fillmore as a dance of the street trace paths of migration through the San Francisco Bay Area and well beyond California, encoding experiences of movement both forced and emergent. Danced from the location of displacement, these embedded movements are consequential as The Fillmore continues to travel across borders of district, city, state and nation. Rather than making purely territorial claims or erasing the complexity of polycentric dance histories, dancers of the street embed their collective social body in The Fillmore—they offer ways of being in movement that are simultaneously in flux and undone. At stake is a dance that unsettles the ethics that require indifference to the disappearing of a neighborhood, holding and moving them all in its name.

an acephalous skeleton
a hyperflexible
moving
head
a
Gumby-like
neck bone
sideways
head glances
pelvic revolving
following
sneak slinking in
the body
transforms

recomposing self
torso twisting around
axis detached
left
float
skeletons
cartoon
levitating
in one
in the other
legs
peculiar cadence
creep away
form

STOP-MOTION DANCE

It's almost like a self-hypnosis. I go blank. I become the character of the movie. Shiva: God of Dance, God of Death. When I'm dancing, I'm really Shiva at the moment. I'm actually living her.

—BOOGALOO DANA

The fierce god lifts her arm, gripping all her muscles to trace a staggered arc through the air.[46] The animation dancer sustains a full-arm muscle contraction for the duration of the movement, then punctuates her gesture, applying a staccato arm-pop that interrupts her already interrupted movement flow.

Dancers of *animation* style embody the cinematographic technique of stop-motion animation, isolating limbs, torso, and pelvis into parts that move and stop independently, while organized in improvisatory rhythmic relation to produce an overall funk technological effect. Funk sensibility derives from a dancer's ability to orchestrate all elements of shape, flow, rhythm, and force, building a graceful rhythmic feel without detracting from but instead highlighting the aesthetics of awkward angularity and broken flow. Popping styles in general are premised on breaking up the body's symmetry and disrupting the free flow of movement, without losing the characteristic smoothness of funk. Animation, however, is striking for its extremely nuanced visual effect, as the dancer makes such minuscule adjustments of body position that they stretch out the duration of the dance's phrasing and flow, producing the sense of time slowing down.[47]

Though imitation is part of the process by which dancers appropriate gestures of stop-motion film characters, they are not interested in simply reenacting the films' narrative content. Becoming the stop-motion creature is the animation dancer's aim. Animation dancers are "actually living," as Boogaloo Dana expresses in the section epigraph, the beyond-human being. As animation dancers transfer the illusion of a still object that moves into the context of live performance, they flip stop-motion technology's intention to appear real, seeking instead to improvise forms of embodiment that appear unreal.

Building on my primary framework of kinethics, I describe animation dance as an ethics-aesthetic practice that emerged from dancers' collective artistic interest to reinvent stop-motion technology as dance technique. While dancers were crafting a rigorous technique, drawing on the core principle of interrupting movement flow, they were also practicing improvising animation dance as open-ended form. Dancing to funk music, animation dancers revised the "backward" technological medium of stop-motion animation (and more generally cinema's structure of captured movement) toward a philosophy of being-becoming otherworldly. Moving in their everyday life worlds, dancers were seeding a *funk*-a-mentally black consciousness—undoing boundaries of the individual body and likewise unsettling racial-gender divisions of self/other subjectivity and human/nonhuman being.[48]

Animation style emerged from dancers' common interest in animated characters of popular mid-twentieth-century television and film. Dancers were inspired by cartoons and sci-fi and fantasy films, and consistently cite characters brought to life by stop-motion innovator Ray Harryhausen. To train animation's illusionary style, dancers studied and mimicked movement dynamics of Harryhausen's clay models. Representative characters are the giant cyclops and cobra woman in the 1958 *The 7th Voyage of Sinbad*, the first color stop-motion film, as well as the skeleton army in *Jason and the Argonauts* and the goddess Kali in *The Golden Voyage of Sinbad*.[49]

Animation dances, while collectively forged from the materials of cinematic screen technology itself, were primarily practiced and performed offscreen, in home and neighborhood living spaces, which became impromptu stages for dancers experimenting with their styles as young as grade-school age. Scholar-dancer Jo Read's in-depth study of sophisticated approaches to musicality among popping and animation dancers cites the style's significance, observing, "Animators frequently discuss the importance of dance and choreography in their practice, yet few scholars discuss the impact of animated film techniques on the live dancing body."[50] Dance scholarship has largely approached the screen in terms of how dances and solo artists "function within the filmic apparatus" when they transition onto screens, therein negotiating screen as context and representational structure.[51] Animation dance, however, centered young dancers' artistic curiosity to appropriate and inhabit (and be inhabited by) the materials of stop-motion otherworlds, taking film content and form beyond the screen for their everyday cultural use.[52]

Funk music provided a critical sonic context for dancers' early improvisations of stop-motion dance, emerging in the 1960s and early '70s. While popular funk artists rarely expressed direct political demands, Tony Bolden asserts, "fundamental rebellion . . . was encoded in funk music."[53] Bolden describes embodied ways of knowing black power, which, he argues, bring dancers to the center of funk aesthetics "as organic intellectuals in black vernacular culture."[54] Animation dancers are twenty years younger than their funk era and Black Arts contemporaries, yet they are key, if less heralded, participants in cocreating funk ways of knowing-feeling-being.

Dancers stretched animation film technology and content to fit a function of black consciousness it was never meant to serve, and they did so by applying their knowledge of black power as a funk sensibility. I'm not saying that dancers' intentions were to articulate overt messages of black power in their dances. Rather, drawing on Bolden, I am saying they were sensing the discourse of black power embedded in embodied funk philosophy. In the process of reinventing stop-motion technique as funk dance, they were also reinventing vocabularies and grammars of cinematic gesture that could describe worlds they were imagining into being.

Read notes, "The troubled historical relationship between animated film and race . . . demands rethinking when animation is transferred to real bodies."[55] If animation dancing played a central function within black vernacular cultures, how were dancers incorporating and transforming the fraught racial dynamics of stop-motion cinema? What are the implications of transferring the apparatus of cinematic capture (with all the repercussions of the white gaze) to live performance as a technique of black embodiment?

In this section's epigraph, dancer Boogaloo Dana references *The Golden Voyage of Sinbad* (1973), the second film of the Sinbad Hollywood trilogy, which began with *The 7th Voyage of Sinbad* and concluded with *Sinbad and the Eye of the Tiger* (1977). Played by different white American actors in each film, Sinbad takes on the hero's quest as he voyages through regions vaguely suggestive of ancient Greece and the Middle East, encountering and battling fantasy creatures and morally suspect humans. The trilogy constitutes a Hollywood retelling of *Arabian Nights*, itself a Eurocentric translation of the Arabic folktale cycle *One Thousand and One Nights*. Reifying an orientalist worldview, the Sinbad character stereotype remains in global circulation via popular literature, TV, and film, amplifying the entangled history of antiblackness with anti-Arab and Islamophobic sentiment. At the same time, Sinbad stories within Arabic literary history were also perceived as low culture, popular entertainment, and childish fantasy. Therein, the tales' reception in popular culture is mired in intersecting dynamics of race, gender, age, and religion. Given Gregory E. Rutledge's statement that "Diasporic Africans have been the subjects of a protracted science fiction, or insidious fantasy, against which the slave narratives were some of the first counter-briefs," African American youths' innovative appropriation of stop-motion sci-fi fantasy films as dance is consequential.[56]

In its inception at the start of the twentieth century, stop-motion animation was regarded as an unsophisticated trick that underutilized the video camera's perceived technological supremacy. Relying on a basic but labor-intensive principle, the animation team takes numerous snapshots and repositions the object each time, a technique easily performed by a handheld camera.[57] Ray Harryhausen developed his branded Dynamation style of stop-motion as a technique for filming scenes where the hand-sculpted creatures could appear to interact in live-action environments with real-life actors. Dynamation's procedure of "blacking out" the animated character in subsequent takes effected the sense that "two worlds [have] collided"—the world of live humans and that of animated otherness.[58]

In terms of the Sinbad film plots and cinematic effects, stop-motion's "backward" medium paradoxically signals technology's potential to eclipse humanity. Oversize, otherworldly beings antagonize and bewitch the plot's human actors, threatening to eradicate civilization and make insignificant its live human architects, who are cinematically rendered in miniature. Viewers' suspension of disbelief is thereby predicated on seeing the animated character as real; the clay models' spasmodic movement style becomes an inherent property of their own. They possess the onscreen illusion of life, while the hands of the animator as puppet master remain invisible.

Homologous to stop-motion's play between intentional self-animation and the illusion of being animated is the way stop-motion produces a double effect of self-representation and being represented by another. In the film studio, the clay megamonsters are made to move via the touch of the animator's unseen hands. Within the taleworld, the events of plot and characters' actions possess their own internal logic. Spectacular, brashly colored bodies push the screen's visual bounds with exaggerated physicality—limbs hyperextend, organs stretch and swell, eyes bulge out. They call attention to the body's pliancy and materiality. At the same time, animated bodies falter, producing unnerving strobe-like effects. The animated body seems to constantly check itself, frustrating the easy flow of movement. Outside the taleworld, the animator chooses each minute detail of the clay's movement, literally molding its representation for the camera. In the animator's perceived absence, the onscreen objects appear to animate and represent themselves, creating a taleworld with an ontological status distinct from the real world, where the animator carefully constructs their every movement.

Stop-motion is a slightly misleading term, as Harryhausen stresses, "The pauses are most difficult, because you can't just have 'em stop. You have to have just a slight movement, so that it doesn't look like a dead puppet." Because the object's appearance of liveliness is premised on the need to always appear in motion, the labor-intensive demands of stop-motion capture intensify at the moments when the object appears to stop moving, requiring the animator to capture the object in ever more minute shifts of position.

For the animation dancer, interrupted movement—the sign of stop-motion's "failure" to perform the object's capacity to move on its own—becomes the founding principle of the dance technique. To return to chapter 1, the discourse of accident, failure, awkwardness, and backward movement that links Don Campbell's and Scoo B Doo's parables of inventing the dance locking and the Scoo B Doo step, respectively, also undergirds techniques of animation dance.[59] The stop-motion effect, once transferred to the dance as a technique of muscle release-contraction, is no longer a sign of imperfect mobility but rather a carefully practiced mobility that uses what would be perceived as awkwardness as material for performances of funk flow.

Halting movement, no longer a sign of the object's lack of agency, is now an index of the dancer's rigorous attention to practice—the fastidious muscular control that grounds her technical performance—utilizing an array of tools for improvising within the form. The dancer crafts a spectacular performance by activating and shifting between various combinations of muscle contraction to replicate the cinematic effect. She practices nuanced movement dynamics, adjusting speed, duration, scale, and force of the muscle release-contraction. She does all this while sustaining her groove, improvising a fluid rhythmic relationship with the sounds and beats of the music. Improvisation in black vernacular dancing serves a key function to present open-ended possibilities for the dancer as she adheres to principles of the dance style.[60] As she deliberately crafts her unique interpretation of the dance, the technique foregrounds the "stop," not as a total stilling of movement but rather as a catalyst for improvising within the form.

Like the cinematic technique, the dancer's intention is to keep moving despite the challenge to flow that interrupted movement presents. Each muscle contraction breaks the movement up, yet the dancer sustains a sense of flow. André Lepecki argues that "being-in-flow" is dance's standard identity within modernity, such that "any disrupting of dance's flow . . . performs a critical act of deep ontological impact."[61] Revising stop-motion's technology of capture as a funk approach to stopping moving, animation dance presents an improvised critique of "a body and subjectivity fit to perform this unstoppable motility."[62] Insomuch as the dance technique is premised on a "backward" technology, animation dancers incorporate the "stop" into their sense of flow to improvise a "backward" sense of freedom to move.[63] Dancers improvise on a failure to move freely (the animated object's inability to possess free will), using the aesthetic as a resource to reinvent ways of moving expansively. Animation dance fleshes out this ethics-aesthetic of captured movement, revising cinema's technology of capture into a modality of funk imagination.

Transporting creatures of stop-motion worlds offscreen, animation dancers are not focused on the film character's representation in terms of fidelity to details of plot and narrative. Animation dancer JRock Nelson details the dancer's intention to look unreal, not by imitating the animated character but through maintaining a "focus on becoming."[64] While Harryhausen's stop-motion animation plays with clay form to make the unreal appear real, dancers play with technical form for precisely the reverse aim: to make the real appear unreal, dancing the animated being as a practice of feeling-becoming otherworldly. Dancers deliberately use the films, then, in two interrelated ways: to reinvent stop-motion technology as an improvisation-based dance technique; and to reinvent themself through their appropriation of the films' content. In both ways, stop-motion style allows dancers to access "unreal" forms of fleshly being.

Boogaloo Dana invokes the entity Shiva to reference the character Kali in *The Golden Voyage of Sinbad*. As he enfleshes the animated figure in his dance, Shiva-Kali become bound as aesthetic principle, way of knowing, and life force. In some interpretations of Hindu mythology, Shiva and Kali are variously portrayed as husband-wife, father-daughter, and son-mother, opening up possibilities for imagining multiple and fluid forms of kin relation through Dana's dance. Kali also carries associations with time, blackness, death, fertility, sexuality, and fierceness, echoing Dana's description.

While it's beyond the scope of my abridged study of animation dance, Dana's dancing Shiva-Kali makes possible an expansive discussion of blackness that considers multiple entanglements of coloniality, modernity, and the human.[65] That being said, I have been building a framework of kinethics as ethics-aesthetic practices drawing on Sylvia Wynter's "Black Metamorphosis," in which she puts forth an indigenizing process of collective identity formation that overturns the ethics of the slave relation.[66] In this respect, the ethos that makes Dana's becoming Shiva-Kali possible unsettles the grammar of diametric opposites on which the slave relation relies.

Dana names Shiva using the feminine pronoun to describe how, in the moment of dancing, "I'm living her," evoking the fluidly gendered sense of relation that LaMonda Horton-Stallings locates in funk transaesthetics.[67] Horton-Stallings defines funk as force, rather than power, emphasizing the erotic charge of communal creative expressions that generate more-than-human intimacies of embodiment—"not seen but felt by everyone all at once."[68] She argues that this sense of sacred connection exists outside state power and reorganizes human relations, especially normative sexualities and sexual relations. Dancing Shiva-Kali, Dana relates funk ways of knowing-feeling-being that shift out of a strict cisgender binary. Animation also deconstructs a nature/technology binary by reorienting Dana's sense of embodiment through the practice of becoming simultaneously goddess and animated clay figure in the moment of dance.[69] He reinvents himself, improvising Shiva-Kali in a form of shared embodiment that undoes normative relations, funking with gender, sexuality, and the human.

Animation dance kinethics take him deeper still, for the practice of becoming Shiva-Kali reorients Dana to their multiply entangled relations of kin belonging—husband-wife, father-daughter, son-mother. Animation dancers access shared embodiment as "otherwise possibilities" of feeling-knowing-moving, fashioned outside a Eurocentric subject/object distinction and beyond stop-motion cinematography's representational logic.[70] Rizvana Bradley's theory of black cinematic gesture "as open-ended form, and as an open-ended challenge to . . . gesture" expands Lepecki's critique of modernity to show the antichoreographic and migratory potential of gestures that escape attempts to be captured in a subject/object relation.[71] The disciplining choreographic apparatus of state power is mirrored in the structure of cinematic capture; in both cases, institutional power determines who is in/invisible or whose lives are meaningful.

Reinventing materials of otherness that the white cinematic gaze frames as a threat, Dana's dance moves beyond the structure of representation. While the camera captures the object in position to feign its motion, the dancer imitates the technology to feel a sense of becoming the character, living the other who is no longer other in the dance's philosophy. The dance critiques the structure of visuality not by opposing it but by appropriating the technology as a resource for imagining otherworlds. Embodying the Claymation figure, the dancer transforms onscreen representations of nonhumanness into a practice Dana describes as living Shiva. He inhabits the materials of Hollywood film representation to become inhabited by her/them. He is not representing Shiva-Kali; rather, he's living all of them, deconstructing human/nonhuman, nature/technology, and self/other binary relations of the subject.

Black cinematic gesture, for Bradley, remains intimately social and kinesthetically contagious, tethering dancers to "the violent historical interdiction of black movement," yet thwarting possession by the individual subject.[72] Dancing Shiva-Kali animation style, Dana practices being-becoming entangled in ways that release him from the political construct of the individual body and relations that reduce intimacy to oppositional categories. Insomuch as animation reorients dancers to funk transaesthetics "not seen but felt by everyone all at once," the technique shapes a sensory-kinesthetic critique of ways of looking that secure racial difference.[73]

Kinethics reorient dancers to intimacies of shared embodiment as different ways to be in relation. Animation dancers appropriate stop-motion technology and animated representations to improvise otherwise world possibilities they become in the moment of dancing. Their stretchy sideways vibratory motions exemplify irruptions of black cinematic gesture: "placed within the historical context of the biopolitical exclusion and containment of black social life . . . the scene of their fits and starts, of psychophysical outbreak, marks a breaking out of the body, a release from the normative ontology of movement."[74] Yet these dances do not redress the conditions of historical violence under which they continue to operate. They improvise other intimacies, practices of being-becoming entangled existences that imagine worlds undone.

pause
become still
listen
with your breath
see if you can follow
the small spaces
breath moves
you come to rest where
you soften where
you slow where
you feel
spine twist
belly soften
chest hollow
where is your breath now?
re/move
out of place
rotate
neck
flex
feet
swivel
shoulders
lift
collapse
breathing is not easy always or
the only way
to ground

ZERO ( ) IS WHERE WE DANCE

Each One contains the kernel of its own explosion.
—CALVIN WARREN

I'm studying a video uploaded in 2009 to the now-defunct site West Coast Poppin, a once-popular internet forum for dancers.[75] A feeling of familiarity arises as I replay the short clip. Before the internet was a primary source of information, dancers often traded VHS tapes, then MiniDVs and CDs, animatedly discussing aspects of technique, cultural history, social relationships, and personal style. Through the 2000s, dancers have circulated footage of first-generation hip hop/streetdance culture practitioners and dance innovators on social media as a form of study.

Centered in the clip's small, slightly dim frame, Wiggles stands in three-quarter profile with his back to a mirrored wall. He speaks to a quiet, off-camera audience. I notice his slow-paced, carefully articulated speech and abundant use of hand gestures, suggesting a non-English-speaking audience outside the United States. Checking the clip's post date, I guess the location—possibly a dance studio somewhere in East Asia.[76] I imagine an attentive cluster of students facing their mirror reflections, some standing, some crouched or cross-legged on the floor. Long pauses are common in classes where prominent dancers often put technique in cultural, social, and historical contexts, underscoring streetdance culture's mode of oral transmission and even taking over time given to dancing itself. As teachers illustrate technical skills they reveal the dance's capacity, Joseph Schloss notes, "to make abstract statements about things that are important to [practitioners]."[77] It's not uncommon for poppers to talk philosophy, as the intricate array of popping techniques invites deeper, interwoven reflections on practice.

A South Bronx native of Puerto Rican descent, Wiggles is a member of the Bronx's Rock Steady Crew and Fresno's Electric Boogaloos.[78] His dance repertoire embodies a lineage of popping that acknowledges first-generation innovator Boogaloo Sam and links the New York City borough of the Bronx with California's Central Valley city of Fresno, activating the strong kinship between New York hip hop and California streetdance. The Fresno, a base move of popping performed by shifting side to side while raising alternating arms, is also a practice of displacement that prepares the popper to groove, in dialogue with such eponymously named dances as The Fillmore. While beyond the limited scope of my research, popping's polycentric history follows Fresno stories of Boogaloo Sam watching Baptist church ladies vibrate in ceremony and friends William Tick'n Will Green and Ricky Darnell McDowell watching the peg-legged swivel of an old man stepping through the street. What's common in their stories is a meditation on kinethics, the collective movement practices that generate the dance popping.

Embodied knowledge, relayed in Wiggles's teaching, carries the charge of these specific historical paths of the dance's circulation (local, translocal, global), which he activates in practice. Such dancestries are neither static nor linear; dancers are constantly participating in the creation of lineages as they study, challenge, and revise hip hop/streetdance histories. Shaped by dance lineages, these histories are polycentric—interanimating the multiple locations from which dancers move.

Now I turn a close focus to the repeated act of muscle release and contraction at the core of popping practice. I put Wiggles's popping pedagogy of the "zero . . . where we dance" in conversation with black cultural theorist Kevin Quashie's poetics of aliveness and quiet, to articulate an ethics-aesthetic philosophy of popping as improvisation-based dance. Wiggles and Quashie help me move beyond an overemphasis on the stopping of motion, to describe popping as a dance of forces in relation that works creatively with muscle tension to increase movement flow. These relational forces produce fractal patterns recurring in electrochemical interactions and nervous system activity, tracing material inner workings of muscles, bones, and neurons. Ultimately I locate popping within a framework of kinethics to elaborate blackness as an ethics-aesthetic articulated in Wiggles's pedagogy as ways of seeing-knowing-moving that disrupt a Western colonial mode of knowledge production.

Speaking as he moves, Wiggles shows two different approaches to popping that define the relationship between viewer and the dancer who performs the illusion of little jolts surfacing and disappearing into flesh.[79]

> You don't want to see. *Pauses, pointing to his eyes.* Where the pop comes from. That's the illusion. I don't know where it comes from. It's coming from *in-side*. That's popping . . . when we pop? People think we're here. *Wiggles lifts his shoulders and arms, stiffening and freezing Frankenstein-style.* No. *His voice softens, lowers.* We're here. *His shoulders relax, hands wobbling at wrist joints.* We're here.[80]

At one level, Wiggles refers to a common misapprehension of how poppers move. Trying to imitate the visual spectacle of the pop's irruptive force, uninitiated dancers rigidly hold tension in their muscles. On the other hand, dancers drawn to the funk rhythm and kinetic liveliness of the dance often try to imitate the body's visual form by jerking stiffly back and forth between flexion and extension. They move "from the bones" and begin to lock out their joints without actively engaging their muscles. For example, a dancer might try to mimic an arm pop by jerking their shoulders up, rather than relaxing the shoulder joint and pulsing biceps and triceps. Another confusion is the initiation point of the contraction, which is not always the same as the muscle group that appears to "pop." For example, chest poppin' activates contractions of the abdominals and diaphragm, not simply the pectorals. Pointing to his eyes and shaking his head, then relaxing into full-body movement, Wiggles performs the transition from sight-centered to kinesthetic knowledge of popping.

Watching the video I remember traveling in 2002 with a group of dancers in my company to attend Illadelph Legends Dance Festival. After a couple of days training with Wiggles, one dancer had developed pain in her knees, serious enough that she couldn't continue class. Overlooking the use of her leg muscles to support the repeated loose jerking movements of the dance had caused overuse and hyperextension in her knee joints. Moving too loosely causes hyperextension. Too much muscle tension decreases blood flow. We learned to practice leg-pops by keeping our knees slightly bent while applying the contraction in the quadriceps muscles of the thighs. Practiced correctly, popping's stop-and-go cycling of nervous impulses grooves neural pathways that build muscle memory and increase blood flow, giving spongy support to the joints.[81]

The softening that Wiggles mirrors in his posture and vocal tone is key. Though "hitting hard" is a common aim for dancers who have refined their style, popping requires softness in the joints, which, perhaps counterintuitively, takes muscular work.[82] Whereas a dancer may appear to be hitting hard, the pop's function in practice is to assist relaxation, flow, and joint support. Muscle training is especially vital for poppers as they improvise flow between the extreme off-center body positions that characterize the dance.

Next, Wiggles goes deeper to describe the unseen place where popping comes from—"in-side."

> Zero. No energy. This is where we dance. We groove. *Wiggles's arms, torso, and legs wobble. His feet rock rhythmically back and forth between heels and toes.* No energy. *He suddenly freezes.* The pop! is for only one second. One fraction of every beat. We pop. *Clenching fists* . . . and let it go. *His fists release and fingers stretch open as the studio door slams shut, an unexpectedly loud vibrating sound that punctuates his words.*[83]

Wiggles demonstrates the rhythmic actions of muscle relaxation and contraction by clapping his hands, figuring dynamics of the pop in the space that closes () and opens ( ) as the palms of his hands touch and move apart. Here, I use closed () and open ( ) parentheses to represent the moments when Wiggles interrupts his spoken explanation with handclaps, visually sounding out the lesson:

> We don't pop like this ()()() *his hands stiffen and he jerks his head back and forth, mirroring the forceful clapping* No. We pop like this ( ) ( ) ( ) *he claps again, now widening the space between palms that flutter and vibrate* ((( ))) *shifting rhythmic emphasis to the silent opening.* 'Cause when you pop like this? ((( ))) You're relaxed. This is the dance popping. Now you can groove. When you pop like this? () No groove, no funk. ((( ))) let it go ((( ))) let it go ((( ))) let it go . . . this is the beat? *His finger traces an invisible circle on the studio mirror.* That's the outside. Inner side. *He traces concentric circles smaller and smaller inside of each other toward a center point.* Inside. Inside.[84]

At first Wiggles rigidly forces his hands open and closed, placing rhythmic emphasis on the sound of palms slamming together: ()()(). Then he shifts to rhythmically accent *the silence between* handclaps, transforming the movement's energetic feel: ( ) ( ) ( ). He flutters his hands lightly on each opening accent ((( ))) to visualize a magnetic shimmering tension between palms, suggesting a vital energy of elastic force. As he transitions into the second way of clapping, I can hear the rhythmic movement as syncopation—a temporary displacement of the regular beat, made possible by accenting the silence of palms opening. This movement of suspension and syncopation produces a visible-audible sense of anticipation in the *dance* popping. Moving with this vibrant quality, Wiggles teaches aural kinesthetics of muscle contraction embedded in popping technique.[85]

At the same time, this rhythm of displacement from the regular beat generates funk capacities that are mirrored in popping's polycentric ethics-aesthetic. Circling back by way of Crawley to my earlier description of popping, we find that these otherwise world possibilities of center, position, and orientation are trained as dance technique, allowing dancers to flesh out deliberate movements of displacement—rotating hips, chest, shoulder girdle, neck, knees, ankles to generate multiple centers spinning in rhythmic relation.[86]

I dwell with this interpretation of popping to deepen attention to the dance's ethics-aesthetic philosophy, which Wiggles's lesson nuances as a *rhythmic movement-of-relation*: more than a singular focus on contraction figured as forces in rigid, static opposition, the pop encapsulates constantly shifting patterns of dynamic release and contraction that generate open-ended energy, driving the dancer to move. Too visual a focus on form detaches the dancer from this vibrant inner-rhythmic feel. Building a capacity to move energetic forces, the ethics-aesthetic practice disorients acts of looking that center desire to capture the pop as object of the gaze.

The disappearing pop is not achieved by holding, freezing, stopping energy. Instead, the pop is playfully moved (and removed) in a springy funk articulation of rhythm Wiggles improvises as the *dance* popping: "zero, no energy." Zero is an indicator of the aliveness that encompasses the dancer's moment-to-moment return to openness as they improvise under repeated constraint, anticipating the pop's interruption of movement flow. I find Quashie's language especially helpful for describing the kind of improvisation process inherent to popping: "aliveness is constituted in repetition and therefore is unfurling, an experience one encounters rather than possesses"; aliveness is "not an enclosure but an opening."[87] The pop does not simply freeze or stop movement but generates movement—"its exclamation of force and openness . . . framed as a question."[88] Popping invites an infinite play of form emerging into/out of formlessness, which dancers access by navigating their relation to the "zero . . . where we dance." Attuning to this sense of aliveness, poppers activate their imaginative capacity to shift forms and states of being.

Dropping to the level of electrochemical energy and nervous system communications, the zero resonates again, not as a total interdiction of motion, so much as a relational movement. During the cellular event of muscle relaxation, firing of motor neurons stops and electrical impulses to muscle fibers cease their transmissions, moving the chemical charge in the cell away from zero (more negative). The muscle lengthens, relaxes. "Stopping," then, is a process of little modulations of electrical states, when the nervous system signal transmits and when it is no longer present. Zero describes not stasis but relation between more positively or negatively charged chemical states within the cell membrane. In this respect, the stop is more than the force of muscle contraction; it's the ceasing of nervous signals in the event of relaxation and the movement away from zero toward a more negative charge of the muscle cell.

These infinitesimal movements of relation set the stage for the pop's jolting effect. In practice, poppers repeatedly return their energy to its lowest state, under constraint of firing neurons. For the onlooker, the force of contraction may visibly seem to disrupt the dancer's free flow of movement. Yet the dancer's capacity to flow is made possible by maintaining this no-energy, zero feel of the dance popping, practiced as the muscles keep on rebalancing energy in relation to chemical reactions in the cell.

In useful conversation with Wiggles's teaching, modern dancer-choreographer Martha Graham describes the contraction that is a signature element of Graham technique: "The contraction is not a position. It is a movement into something. It is like a pebble thrown into the water, which makes rippling circles when it hits the water. The contraction moves."[89] In a manner akin to popping philosophy, Graham distinguishes between a technique based on rigid positions and the principle of power as moving energy/energies. Graham's pebble thrown in water creates ripples similar to Wiggles's vibrating hands, which show energy release in relation to contracting force. The intention of both techniques of contraction is to move (though in popping, moving is always already rhythmically defined by grooving and funk). Like the circles Wiggles traces on the dance studio mirror to end the lesson, as he repeats the words "inner side . . . inside," Graham's contraction creates "rippling circles" on the water's reflective surface.[90] Like the dancer, the water seeks its lowest energy state before the pebble is thrown. The throw creates energy, causing ripples as water always finds its way back to the smallest energy state possible—the zero.

Let's return to Wiggles's initial statement: "You don't want to see. Where the pop comes from. That's the illusion. I don't know where it comes from. It's coming from *in-side*. That's popping . . . when we pop? People think we're here. No. We're here. We're here." Wiggles defines the function of illusion in popping as creating a visual play between two states of being—a state of rigidly held tension that viewers think they see and a deeper "here" where the dancer actually is. This place is akin to quiet, in the sense that Quashie uses the word to trace a less publicly apparent aesthetic in black cultural production. Shifting away from a dominant perspective of resistance in black culture, often constituted by "the imperative to represent," Quashie beautifully gives attention to different ways of looking that include the capacity to wonder and wander through an interior terrain of the human.[91] For Quashie, "quiet is the capacity and quality of the interior, of the inner life . . . a manner of being that is deep within us, a being that is not always exactly quiet—it can be raging and wild," and a "practice of knowing that is incomplete . . . its beat is insistent lurching, pulsing, but its agency is not only resistance."[92] An ethics-aesthetic of quiet is useful for noticing how Wiggles softens and lowers his voice, how his stance also softens, transforming into a loosely held gesture of release and openness. The quiet of palms opening anticipates the sharp sound of palms striking closed; a disappearing of form into formlessness, sensed as a disappearing of sound into quiet.

Remember, though, that the dance popping is driven by funk's hard-hitting beat, meaning that this potential quiet "here," which Wiggles invites students to access in the dance, also moves with the rhythmic beat of quiet, its "insistent lurching, pulsing" edge. This unfinished way of seeking fits a speculative leaning, I've noticed when poppers study the dance, toward the style's metaphysical dimensions. Studying Wiggles's zero as an open-ended rhythmic movement-of-relation, I conclude that popping is best described as a dance not of rigid stopping or chaotic disarticulation (both of which might cause painfully ruptured joints) but of dynamically held dislocation; not of purely oppositional force but of springy, spongy mobility and, following Quashie, of capacious quiet.

The dancer's capacity to navigate this sensory-somatic relationship to zero is the *dance* popping. Wiggles underscores the difference between this way of dancing and dancing senselessly—lacking a deeper knowing of groove and funk. Likewise, Jon Bionic Bayani teaches his students to practice relaxing *before* tensing their muscles, describing the technique with similar language: "A lot of the time popping is being relaxed. Right away. That way you don't see the hit. People think you have to be tense and in class they're always like that. That's why I'm telling the class, 'Just relax. Zero to one hundred.'"[93] Again, Bionic highlights the idea of moving between two states—returning to zero and accelerating to one hundred. The zero can also be described as a slowing that changes the quality of force exerted in muscle contraction. The dancer learns to control their precise application of force, opening up possibilities for improvising within the dance form—a way to encounter their inner sense of groove and funk, which is the spiritual terrain of the dance popping.

Going deeper with popping's metaphysics, Wiggles's lesson moves between the languages of seeing and knowing. I find his shift in words curious, since the illusion he's teaching would seem to primarily be concerned with the former—how to hide the kinetic trick of popping from the viewer's sight. Yet, popping's illusionary acts go beyond a play of appearances to critically speculate on the nature of knowledge and reality. The relationship between not wanting to see and not knowing has a deeper resonance, considering the dominance of visuality within Western modernity's sensorial episteme. European Enlightenment thought of the seventeenth and eighteenth centuries constructed a cultural hierarchy of the senses, elevating sight over other senses. Resting on René Descartes's philosophy of mind-body dualism, sight as the seat of rational knowledge was bound to notions of property and the white male bourgeois subject. Enlightenment Man possessed dominant power over (his) Others as affectable objects of rational knowledge, possessed by his gaze.[94] Man's command of vision included the powers of reason and free will, subjecting the Other to his rights of possession. Possessive individualism is the basis for modernity's liberal subject, determining one's ability to see and to know. In this regard, the individual subject *I* is coconstituted through the gaze, the dominant power assumed by the "eye" to grasp and control knowledge of Man's Others. Following Wiggles's use of pronouns in the lesson it's possible to learn something about what the I/eye can see and know by reorienting to popping kinethics.

Wiggles uses the first-person plural *we* to clearly include himself in the group of initiated poppers, although it's less clear whether the listening students are included in that address or might be in the more distant position of "people"—the uninitiated viewers who think poppers are in one place (when they're really in another). The *you* works in the lesson as a similarly indirect form of address; the "you" who doesn't want to see where the pop comes from could be the expert creating the illusion of popping or the uninitiated students who are still learning how popping works, or both at once. Wiggles's indirect address here opens up the possibility for the listening students to figure out where *they* are in relationship to the practice.

In contrast, his use of the *I* is significant in its placement in the lesson. In a momentary shift into the first-person singular pronoun, Wiggles clearly positions himself in the role of the one who *doesn't know*, suggesting that the not-knowing of this *I* is different from the kind of knowing necessary for the expert popper to do the dance. Here, Wiggles makes a distinction between knowledge he's dropping in his lesson and another kind of knowledge—the "I don't know" that is directly connected to the illusion of popping, an impossible position of seeing-knowing where the pop comes from. Yet it's also possible to hear his statement differently: "eye don't know where it comes from." In this transposition, the individual *I* becomes the object of critique—the uninitiated liberal subject who wants to see, yet, within popping epistemology, doesn't know. Actually, Wiggles posits an unknowing that issues from the history of coloniality, which, I offer, affirms with difference the sense of Quashie's incomplete practice of knowing.[95] In fact, Quashie makes clear that quiet's "subjectivity of the 'one'" is not the same as individualism.[96] By positioning the *I* in relation to seeing-knowing, Wiggles emphasizes the idea that the dance popping is based less on a dancer's visual grasp of the dance than on their inward-turning surrender to feeling—a knowing that hides from sight yet may be glimpsed through popping's ethics-aesthetic philosophy.

Popping kinethics embed the "eye/I don't know" in popping's dis/appearing act, extending in their collective movement practice Denise Ferreira da Silva's speculation on Black Feminist Poethics: "Because without Desire, the object, the other, and the commodity dissolve . . . the World is emancipated from universal reason, and other possible ways of knowing and doing can be contemplated without the charge of irrationality, mysticism, or idle fantasy."[97] The "eye/I don't know" suggests that the individual self-possessed subject is also a kind of fiction, unable to locate the pop on Enlightenment's ocular-centric epistemological map. Popping isn't hard to see for the ones who don't lack insight.

In this regard, Wiggles's zero is in conversation with the empty set or void set of mathematics, figured as {}. Calvin Warren argues, by way of Alain Badiou, that the empty set figures "the point of departure of the whole construction" of ontology, the branch of Western continental philosophy addressing questions of existence and being.[98] The empty set is something that contains nothing and so is not the same thing as nothing. Likewise, "emptying the bag" is an exercise the Flooridians battle dance crew teach in their class on freestyle dance, their premise being that in order to access the freestyle state a dancer has to gradually discard their preconceived or set, predictable ways of dancing. At the start of their class, they go through several quick rounds of freestyle dancing, telling everyone to push their dance to physical exhaustion: "you can't fill a cup that's full, you have to empty the cup in order to fill it up."[99] The freestyle state can be described as the dancer's connection to their most expansive creative potential, once they've let go of static, formulaic, habitual ways of moving: "from within this emptiness, change and newness can emerge."[100] While Warren argues that destroying both form and matter is required as a critique of the notion of value that sustains antiblackness, I am interested in drawing attention to popping practice as a repeated cyclical movement between destruction and creation that Wiggles emphasizes in the practice of zero.

Popping's "inner side" shapes an ethic of practice that includes the experimental, playful, and unprecedented, and that calls the student to an inner encounter with psychic-spiritual systems beyond the replication of codified steps and moves.[101] In the next and final section, I consider how studio-derived counting practices, heard in the "five-six-seven-eight" vocal cue often used in teaching commercial dance choreography, can promote surface ways of knowing, linked to relations of property ownership that extract movement in order to neatly package and consume dance as linear, replicable sequences of moves. Decentering the dominance of sight in their learning process, the dancer accesses popping as a visual-aural-kinesthetic way of knowing, whereas learning the dance as a static lexicon of moves and steps facilitates quick exchange of the dance form (and formulaic dancing), without a commitment to deeper practice. Apprenticeship asks a different commitment of students, who gradually build long-term relationships with virtuosic dancers, expanding their study to learn the dance's philosophy and social and cultural history. Revolving around the fundamental idea that the pop can't be visually found, Wiggles's lesson questions the idea that dance can be apprehended by distanced ways of looking. The teaching calls dancers to go deeper with their practice, to access their insight through a spiritual sense of funk and groove.

The "inner side," Wiggles suggests, is a deeper place of seeing-knowing-moving than popping's surface form. When the visual register is no longer dominant, this inner feeling of motion registers in the dancer's capacity to groove, to funk. Being inside the beat is a way of allowing the rhythm to move you rather than controlling the rhythm as if it is a separate object to be grasped onto. Seen as a movement not of opposition but of relation—the force of contraction moving in concert with practiced softening—the pop interrupts movement flow to bring dancers into a deeper state of release that Wiggles describes as "zero . . . where we dance." The inner side of the beat is the way the dancer is not remaining separate from the rhythm but folding and unfolding into the rhythm. Popping is an ongoing returning to quiet—the zero-space antecedent to muscle contraction.

limbs fold
snake at angles
sharply anteversion
flesh surfaces stretch
fuse they form break
a row of knees wave
brrrrdah! pop up
then fall apart fold back
together then feel and
domino-like they fall…
topple over inside
one another

flexing wrists
palms slap joint
collapse remaking
making their body
Robot work a synergy of rhythms
they jump together apart
reverse back rejoin the corps
seeing touch

BREATH TOUCH

This section explores kinethics in synchronized group-style dance, drawing on descriptions of Northern California Bay Area dancers to describe collective practices of touch and breath. Robotic dance styles connect all-girls dance group the Lady Mechanical Robots from the East Bay Area city of Richmond with San Francisco-originated group Medea Sirkas, the latter of whom continue to perform, working in and outside of professional industry dance. Their common aesthetic of synchronized dancing in close physical touch builds an intimate sense of belonging through a collective practice of feeling-knowing-moving as one.

Renée Lesley details the Lady Mechanical Robots' practice sessions in small spaces of home, revealing her local style of Richmond Robotting as a kinship practice that relies on touch—the dancers falling apart and coming back together in closely joined formations without losing their common sense of rhythm or solo sense of style. Medea Sirkas adds another dimension to kinship practice through their use of nonverbal percussive vocals as they move, showing the ways breath and touch work in concert with movement to support the group's performance of high-speed, tightly executed group choreographies.

Breath is the unseen partner of touch that trains dancers to feel familiarity in rhythm, which as I elaborated in chapter 1 is a common sense capacity fundamental to black social dance. Rhythm is multisensory and synesthetic, not simply seen-heard in music and dance but also felt in breath-touch as kinship practice. Following Ashon Crawley's assertion of the liberatory possibilities of "enfleshment as distinct from embodiment" that animate collective practices of black breath, I end the section putting dancers' nonverbal language of breath-touch in conversation with the studio-derived language of eight-counting, a standard practice in studio, competition, and entertainment industry dance.[102] While eight-counting can assist dancers in teaching and learning choreography as they negotiate social power dynamics and a fast-paced dance industry, the practice can also facilitate operations of racial capital that attempt to extract and commodify black movement. Felt slowly over time, through hours, days, and years of dancing together, breath-touch as kinship practice enfleshes relations of interconnectedness, training dancers to move in ways that disrupt the account of an individual body delineated as a unit of relation separate from the collective.

Robot is sometimes mimicked half-heartedly as a party trick loosely associated with old-school hip hop dance. Yet robot is special because of its linkages with local dance communities who have made and remade it into "over a thousand varieties," Boogaloo Dana expresses.[103] From the mid-1960s, dancers were interpreting hard-hitting beats of emergent funk sound, innovating robotic styles in the Northern California Bay Area. They were also drawing on special effects in popular postwar sci-fi fantasy films, kung fu movies, and cartoons. By the 1970s, robot was both a popular social party dance circulating to a national audience via *Soul Train* dancers and a solo street performance style.[104] A major influence on robot dance aesthetics was popular mime Robert Shields, a Los Angeles native who began showing up on San Francisco's Union Square in 1970 and later cocreated a series of televised skits with his wife, Lorene Yarnell, depicting the strange everyday life of a robot couple called the Clinkers.[105] Robotic dancers diverged from Shields and Yarnell's performances by incorporating rhythms of R & B, soul, and funk music—Temptations, Isley Brothers, James Brown, Sly & the Family Stone, Graham Central Station, Ohio Players, Parliament. Pop Tart asserts, "For us a robot would be something creating off of our background. My robot wouldn't be your normal robot. I would robot because of my conditions. All of what I'm doing is robotting."[106]

Future had been made present with the first launchings of humans into space in the 1960s and the first lunar landing in 1969, bringing televised images of space travel directly into people's homes. By the late 1970s, the advent of the personal computer meant an irreversible leap from industrial to information technology. On January 21, 1977, George Clinton's Mothership, accompanied by the Parliament-Funkadelic band, landed at the Oakland Coliseum. The mythic event took the concept of return to an idealized African past, prevalent in black nationalist and Pan-Africanist rhetoric, and projected it into a future space of possibility made present. P-Funk staged fantasies of moving far beyond social systems to access an otherworldly space of the unknown. Funk artists performed Afrofuturist acts to estrange reality, figuratively expanding and contracting space-time to imagine disorienting travels through uncharted territories of sound and movement.

The Black Panther Party (BPP) was founded in Oakland in 1966, and through the 1970s, members were creating material social infrastructures within black communities. By 1971, the party opened its Oakland school for black youth, directed by core party member Ericka Huggins. Dancers recall being beneficiaries of one of the BPP's most revolutionary services, the Free Breakfast for School Children Program. Young dancers lived in the same houses as BPP members, and the Black Resurgents were among youth dance groups who performed for BPP rallies.

Dancers' performances recycled sci-fi imagery but added layers of complexity to the formation of otherworldly identities as they mixed discourses of black power, pride, and upward mobility, drawing on black popular culture and local style. Black youth fashioned themselves as robots, space travelers, Frankensteins, and alien beings. Artistic performances of myriad groups such as the Black Messengers, Black Resurgents, Gentlemen of Production, Granny & Robotroid, Demons of the Mind, and Close Encounters of the Funkiest Kind were a pastiche of mass media, local culture, and the polished presentational style of contemporaneous black entertainers.

Dancers did not passively consume or imitate televisual representations; they made use of mass media materials for their own play. Observing, mimicking, improvising, and performing mechanized movement, they took machines out of the role of physical labor and into the discourse of outer space, futurism, and funk, conceptually transporting their bodies out of a system of capitalist profit and into a nonproductive, process-oriented space of symbolic, sensory-kinesthetic play. Science fiction and fantasy enabled dancers to flesh out mechanical, technological, and futuristic beings and at the same time shape an experimental representational space.

As he recalls studying the movements of robots, animated skeletons, an octopus, Bruce Lee, James Brown, and Looney Tunes characters, Fayzo accents his recollections with rapid staccato whispers, "*pow pow pow, tshyoo tshyoo tshyoo* . . . around the house it was music all the time and I'm just doing what I see on TV . . . that was my first interaction with the dance."[107] At grade-school age, dancers were shaping the new robotic styles in their home environments by improvising popular media materials to resonate with black vernacular rhythms, building new dance vocabularies in the process of watching, listening, and moving.

Growing from solo robotic dancing and bringing in local variations of rhythm and style, dancers began to twine arms and legs, melding movement of a collective body that kept them coming back in touch—the members disassembling and reassembling, changing smoothly between formations while sustaining one rhythm and flow. Touching shoulders, linking elbows and waists, overlapping legs, the dancers would move at sharp angles and shape accordion-like waves of motion. Their tightly choreographed performances included unison and "domino" chain reaction sequences, designing gestures of a collective body that could morph, taking humanoid, insectlike, and machinic form.[108] Groups also designed their original costumes, attaching battery-operated lights along seams of pants, pairing beauty store shoulder-length silver ladies' wigs with white face paint, accessorizing with white gentlemen's gloves, black top hats, and tuxedo ties. Dressing in matching costumes often with hats, light-colored accent gloves, and sometimes full face masks, synchronized dancers performed the sense of moving as a cohesive whole.

Preparations often took place in intimate home spaces—bedrooms and living rooms where dancers began to play creatively with time, manipulating the familiar technologies their home habitats afforded. Richmond Robotter Renée Lesley describes how, in a major innovation of the style, dancers began to switch the pitch control of home record players, nudging rotation speeds from 33 rpm to 45 rpm to 78 rpm:

> We used to take the Ohio Players. Back then we had 45s and LPs. We would put them on, double the speed. Miraculously fast. We felt that it was too slow. Speeding it up made the moves more crisp, sharper. It made you be able to be more technical. It made you go fast, do things, jump over people, and it was an effect. The effects looked better faster. We listened to it on such fast speed that I couldn't sing the original version 'cause I don't have a clue. All I know is in fast speed.[109]

While the dancers were moving at faster speeds, fitting more moves into shorter time frames, their practice sessions took time. Renée explains the technical precision involved in crafting a Lady Mechanical Robots group performance:

> We were in Cookie's small apartment or Bootsie's small apartment or our apartment in Crescent Park in the living room all night . . . it was just—*she slaps the back of her hand into her palm*—"Do it again! Do (*slap*) it over! Do (*slap*) it over! Do it over! Not right! Stop! Do it over!" And it went on for hours. And hours. Sometimes we would go all day and all night. Into the night, into the morning. If we knew the talent show was next week we'd practice. The minute I'd come home from school? Wherever we would meet. I would take my homework. I would ride my bike across Richmond. I lived close to Bootsie, and she lived in Deliverance Temple . . . across from Eastshore Park.[110]

Dancing in living rooms of small apartments into the night and morning, the Lady Mechanical Robots' rehearsal process is homework that extends into everyday life in excess of formal time schedules and spaces reserved for institutionally recognized learning. Their home assemblies touch on the idea of "homework" that Sara Ahmed invokes by way of Audre Lorde—a feminist self-assignment that collectively "aims to transform the house, to rebuild the master's residence."[111] Their laborious process of creation and rigorous technical practice describe a different ethic of schooling at home that the Lady Mechanical Robots undertake in the active sense highlighted by dancer Buddha Stretch to distinguish "the ones who take it seriously and school themselves." Referring to a dancer's effort to actively participate in dance study beyond the dance studio, Stretch suggests that getting schooled requires a deepening of intimacy with the dance: "don't just do the steps, learn the energy, the feeling behind the steps."[112] Immersed in their self-study and experimenting with new, high-speed choreographies, the Lady Mechanical Robots made a serious commitment to practice that creatively remade their homes as dancing places.

bell hooks locates black women's sites of healing and recovery beyond white supremacy, in places where "we had the opportunity to grow and develop, to nurture our spirits" and with an "idea of 'home' that black women consciously exercised in practice."[113] For hooks, "homeplace, as fragile and as transitional as it may be, a makeshift shed, a small bit of earth where one rests, is always subject to violation and destruction."[114] Deborah Granny Robotroid Johnson connects practice in homeplaces to the aesthetic of touch, nurtured by synchronized group dance: "It was small back in the day. When you did group routines you was close together, didn't have no space."[115]

At the same time, Renée embeds the Lady Mechanical Robots' close movement in homeplaces within a recollection of her solo travel across Richmond, tightly interwoven locations that inscribe her intimate memories of moving with Cookie and Bootsie, her dance family. She takes time to map her habitual bicycle path, reciting familiar place names of the subsidized housing developments where she and Bootsie live and the neighborhood park around the way. Renée highlights an everyday commitment to gather, which brings me and her in touch with a very material sense of Richmond Robotting's habitat. As the Lady Mechanical Robots cultivate feeling-knowing-moving overtime in their familiar homeplaces, they form dancing kinships that place Richmond in polycentric histories of Bay Area dance.

Yet if you ask many people who move to the San Francisco Bay Area what they know about the upper East Bay city, the last thing they're likely to say is "cultural center."[116] Richmond does hold the questionable distinction of being the 120-year-plus home to the Chevron oil refinery, once one of the largest in the world. When Richmond makes its bleep on the radar it's often been framed as the site of corporate scandal, pollution, violence, and, despite locals who dub it "the Rich," poverty. Nonetheless, by the late 1970s Richmond had birthed a land of robots. Richmond Robots, Androids, Audionauts, Criminons, Lady Mechanical Robots, and Green Machine, among many others, competed regularly in local talent shows, helping forge synchronized group dance style that grew robot's aesthetic discourse.

Like in San Francisco, Richmond's African American population before the 1940s had stayed relatively small, intermixing with Chinese, Japanese, Mexican, and Filipino residents. The promise of jobs and a socially integrated "California lifestyle" brought African American migrants from the South as wartime industry boomed. Detailing work life of World War II migrants in Richmond, Richard Rothstein evidences the US government's extensive acts of de jure segregation that typified urban/suburban development and expansion in the San Francisco Bay Area, despite its liberal, inclusive reputation. Regarding housing displacement, Rothstein writes, "black war workers in North Richmond . . . remained in cardboard shacks, barns, tents, or even open fields."[117] When the war ended and Richmond's Kaiser shipyards closed, unemployment and housing scarcity exacerbated intraracial tensions. The 1949 Housing Act escalated conditions of displacement.

Through the 1960s, working-class black Richmondites grew in number and were deeply involved in political leadership, social activism, and organizing. Shirley Ann Wilson Moore's native oral history documents the proliferation of mutual aid networks and cultural spaces as a mechanism of racial solidarity among black Richmondites, showing the accelerated growth of new cultural traditions during the war and postwar periods.[118] Moore argues that prior to the civil rights era, communities were organizing across class differences "to present a solid front in their challenges to the system that tried to shut them out, choosing to partially accept as a strategy for liberation the white stereotype that viewed blacks as an indistinguishable mass."[119] This strategy of congregation aerated the city's cultural terrain, creating fertile conditions for Richmond's local form of Robotting to seed.

Growing their local style through the 1970s and '80s, Richmond

Robotters enfleshed an aesthetic of congregation in young people's cultural innovation of vernacular dance techniques that chart "unofficial and oppositional geographies" of place. Katherine McKittrick argues that such geographies show how state-sanctioned "rules are alterable and there exists a terrain through which geographic stories can be and are told."[120] Renée maps an unofficial geography of Richmond's black cultural terrain that includes late-night rehearsals in small home spaces and a bustling talent show circuit. Mobile DJ vans, much like the Chicago caravan that inspired Don Cornelius's naming of *Soul Train*, were moving from school to school, helping generate robotting's locamotive practice. The cultural movement of Richmond Robotting was shaped in young people's collective artistry. Robotters were reimagining the landscape of displacement, contributing to unsettled, unfinished placings of home and habitat among black Richmondites.

Robottin' departed from formal dance training and in this respect brought young people into communication through informal forms of social mixing and dance practice, where they shaped study in terms that made their worldviews relevant. Renée recalls her interaction with an early childhood ballet teacher:

> She was like—*enunciates each word in a proper tone*—'Your. Butt. Is too big. For ballet. You are too. . . .' *She interrupts herself loudly.* 'I am a black girl.' And so for me [ballet class] was a terrible experience. I was maybe eight years old, and Robottin' fit right in because it allowed me to express my heritage, what I was feelin, how I got down. It fit my body."[121]

Robottin' shapes and grounds Renée's fleshly sense of cultural belonging in contrast with the ballet teacher's enforcement of normative standards that seek to limit her abilities and mobilities. She tells me how incessantly, insistently mobile were dancers' practices, moving them not only through and across their neighborhoods to fertilize one another's growth but also, importantly, creating sites of belonging, however incomplete, that imaginatively alter unjust hierarchies of static assessment and placement.

Formulating "home-spaces" differently from hooks's homeplaces, Judith Hamera's deftly crafted ethnography of a suburban Southern California ballet studio shows how elite and vernacular cultures converge as ballet's home-spaces diverge from "technical protocols of classical ballet [which] are deeply and heteronormatively gendered."[122] It's worth considering the ways ballet training is not wholly exclusionary but conditional—

based on intricate methods of assessment and calculation of bodily value. Nonetheless, racial dimensions of gender and sexuality are intimated in Hamera's close attention to ballet's discourse of beauty: "A rear-end sticking out beyond the heels, or a chest leaning forward beyond the toes, is an object of reprimand and ridicule, parodically labeled 'squaté'; the ugliness of the phoneme and its scatological connotations marks the violence of symmetry involved in improper corporeal 'placement.'"[123] Raquel Monroe's nuanced ethnography of student and teacher perspectives on contemporary university dance curricula highlights the persistent proprietary positioning of ballet technique in a Western dance canon that maintains a "cultural imaginary fram[ing] black dancing bodies, and the dances they dance as vulgar, excessive, hypersexual, and low class."[124] Echoing the squaté, the ballet teacher's reprimand and ridicule are evidence of ballet's symmetry-centered "position-orientation" that target Renée's removal from the ballet studio.[125]

Aimee Cox uses the concept of *shape-shifting* to highlight how Black girls collectively make "their own politics of the body" in urban spaces where they navigate institutional systems of control and containment.[126] Bringing their choreographies (of dance and social identity) to bear on black feminist theory, she asserts "the potential held in our capacity to embrace, rather than fight against, our displacement . . . to use our displacement as a starting point for regeneration and the creation of new lifeworlds and spaces that affirm our collective humanity . . . committed not to inclusion but to creation."[127] If the ballet teacher's assessment enacts an overseeing of the black body, Renée's story revises that violent negation in her fleshy articulation of robottin'—a radically different consciousness that "fits" her formulation of power: "Our body movements and styles express[ed] our feeling. [Robot] was cool, a form of strength. The moves were just smooth, they were electrifying. It signified toughness. A robot was well-oiled. Robottin' was a machine, and back then we were machines. [Robot] was a survivor."[128] The Lady Mechanical Robots do the homework of transformative world building as they shape-shift into fleshly machine. Renée articulates this electric, well-oiled, tough-textured way of otherwise world being.[129] As she dances to "miraculously fast" rhythms of Ohio Players records, sped up to adapt to robotting technique, Renée reinvents vocabularies of gesture to describe funk otherworlds she is imagining into being, when and where she, Cookie, and Bootsie gather.

Reflecting Granny Robotroid's recollection of moving in small spaces where group robotting's ethics-aesthetic grew, the Lady Mechanical Robots' transformative choreographies nurtured Renée's sense of shared embodiment by incorporating touch, carefully growing a technique of falling apart and coming back together:

> Doing that type of Robot you had to be uniform . . . every time you touch but you had to go to the ground and do something offbeat, when you came back up you had to make sure that you were touching . . . you were all one. You had to move like you were moving together. We had to walk each step. We had to walk together, arms together, legs, everything had to be together. And when you separated you had to pop back together. It was unbelievable. The practice was intense.[130]

As I imagine the Lady Mechanical Robots linking arms and crisscrossing legs, what surfaces for me is the shared sense of touch that keeps their focus on becoming "all one." Touch in group-style robotting is a practice of feeling-knowing-moving the rhythms of the dance in the whole body, simultaneously as soloist and collective. Even when a solo dancer moves away from the group to improvise—in the moment Renée explains "you had to go to the ground and do something offbeat"—the dancers keep time by keeping in touch. Learning to step together, walk together, move in and out of position together, is a collective practice of being in touch that bonds the dancers in rhythm.

Intrinsic to rhythm-sensing, touch never really lets the dancers be completely cut off from one another—they continue feeling-knowing-moving as one in rhythm, appearing to separate and "pop back together," yet not losing connection to the beat. Like with a jazz ensemble, the soloist is held by the collective. Solo moments function not to individuate so much as to show the soloist's continuity with the rhythmic sensibility of the whole, through the gift of interpretation. Separating is premised on coming back together, deepening a mutual obligation to make sure "you were all one." The tight place allows the conundrum of being at once excluded and included in dancing spaces, citing the material conditions that continue to determine how bodies are seen and the stakes involved in moving under such conditions.[131]

Robotting is both social dance and carefully crafted aesthetic. While rehearsing set choreographies, the Lady Mechanical Robots were "making do" with tight spaces—improvising an aesthetic of linked limbs, sped-up beats, flesh touched. Renée makes speakable the altering of geographic and physical terrain that would mark the black body's exclusion, creating otherwise worlds of the Lady Mechanical Robots' robotting style.[132] These improvisations of group robotting highlight training in terms that are repeated, ritualized, and enculturated. Not simply a response to structural exclusion, robot aesthetics are groove oriented, changing static place into a collective movement of displacement. Cox's careful insight into such practices that relate body, space, and home is helpful to cite at length:

> In the body as well as in home spaces, the ways of establishing inclusion are inherently unpredictable for young Black women. They are aware that if they rely on socially determined assessments to define their self-worth, they would be exiled from their own bodies and any home spaces they might establish for themselves—a state of eternal homelessness. Young Black women propose the possibility that *the body may be the space to which we may finally come home, or where we make a new one.* Staying in the body, therefore, may very well mean moving in and, most importantly, beyond it to locate new ways of imagining oneself and of remaking one's surroundings.[133]

Outside the ballet studio and after school, the Lady Mechanical Robots make home by organizing, directing, and shaping robotting's collective social body in ways that decidedly do not conform to the gender-sexual prerogatives of white patriarchal order.

Teaching within an innovative Chicago college dance program, Monroe argues for structural change in institutions that consistently place ballet at the foundation of all dance technique, calling instead for a shift to "dancing spaces" that articulate the hybridity of US American dancing techniques.[134] Teaching as a grad student at the University of California, Berkeley, I noticed this structural positioning firsthand when a guest teacher from the Alvin Ailey company matter-of-factly explained to students that "ballet is the base" with which they should be prepared even as they explore whatever other (African Diaspora) techniques they encounter. It's less that ballet needs to make space for robottin', and more that robotting's reinventive capacity allows dancers to articulate their creative kinship practices and forms of collectivity on their own terms.

Renée's experience outside the ballet studio can't be seen simply in terms of exclusion or as a plea for inclusion. Moving from the location of displacement, the Lady Mechanical Robots practice kinship as common touch that re-creates social bonds in tight spaces they make into homeplace. hooks's assertion applies to black girls' choreographies as resistive sites of healing and recovery: "calling attention to the skills and resources of black women . . . who have practical experience that is the breeding ground for all useful theory, we may begin to bond with one another in ways that renew our solidarity."[135] Robotting is a movement of isolation, but they don't move in isolation: they walk each step together, falling apart and coming back together as a practice of relation that takes time and goes slow. Richmond Robotting kinethics reorient the Lady Mechanical Robots to the intimate funk of shared embodiment, assembling their collective social body in motion.

Woom woom. Bam bam. Wop. Pow! As Medea Sirkas move, they whisper the dances' rhythms under their breath—*brrrrrrrrrrrdah*. Their synchronized dancing showcases San Francisco Strutting. The group's members, ranging from four to six dancers, sustain close contact in tight synchronicity while they ride funk, hip hop, and electro tracks, hitting at 170 bpm.[136]

Breath shapes their percussive vocals, emphatic undertones tracing a collective swooping of arms they deftly fold over and under one another. *Inhale. Silence. A tiny pause.* Masked figures hunch together, the surfaces of their metallic space suits mesh in a low-down freeze, heads bowed.

HAH! Breath returns with insistence, italicizing the sharp angles of their slicing salutes. They step boldly out and back in line in classic San Francisco Strutting style. Breath imbues the strong lines of their dance with polished confidence. Isolating neck, shoulder, elbow, wrist, hip, knee joints in various sequences, they design gestures of a collective body, feeling-knowing-moving as one.

In Medea Sirkas's nonverbal soundings, breath acts not as appendage to but in concert with gesture—of one movement. In *Blackpentecostal Breath*, Ashon Crawley asserts that varied black performance genres emerge and connect through breath, an aesthetic of the collective social body that is itself a form of intellectual practice.[137] As Medea Sirkas tell me, "Robots have to think together."[138] Breath practice makes feeling-knowing-moving as one possible.

Watching a video we filmed together without music, I become aware of their breathing and percussive vocalizations, suddenly magnified.[139] Guiding their rhythmic sense of touch in maintaining group form, breath registers so subtly as quiet—indiscernible in the rapid visual spectacle of a Medea Sirkas performance but, nonetheless, materially constitutive of their dance practice. Beneath chugging beats and hypnotic synths of

Kraftwerk's "Trans-Europe Express" or one of their self-produced electronic tracks, the dancers craft quiet performances of breath-touch. I ask Fayzo how the rhythmic vocals fit into Medea Sirkas's training process:

> "We've been doing it a long time. For us it's second nature. One of the things we don't do is count. I know a lot of professional industry dancers, and we've done stuff in the industry as well. We still have our way of doing what we do. Some dancers [go] "1-and-2-and-3-and-4," right. For us, it's about feel. An individual dancer he just feel the space around him and the music. That's it."[140]

Notice that Fayzo expresses a distinction between count and feel; the former he associates with professional industry dance. He makes an implicit connection between feel and the way Medea Sirkas use nonverbal vocal percussion as impetus and guide—dancing to a blasting 170 bpm electronic music track while rapidly isolating head-ribs-hips, flexing elbows-knees-wrists, performing domino effects, switching steps, directions, levels, formations, all without losing touch-timing as a group.

The counting language to which Fayzo refers is a common way of marking time for dance, widely used in street, studio, and stage settings alike, in which movement is measured in blocks of eight that repeat, starting again at "one" after each "eight." The conventional "five-six-seven-eight" directive cues a group of dancers to start a unison choreography coordinated on the next "one." Eight-counting is standard practice in competition and industry dance, and can simplify and speed up the rehearsal process, which is helpful for music video choreographers, who often have limited time to work on set. Trained dancers can "get" and reproduce the moves of a choreography quickly by matching it to eight-counts. Getting the moves is not the same, however, as feeling-knowing-moving the dance.

The practice of "five-six-seven-eight-ing" can quicken acquisition of movement for those not acculturated to nuances of vernacular rhythm and style, a situation that may arise when dancers of different cultural backgrounds and training are put together in a performance choreography. Eight-counting fixes movement into static units, numbering and spacing them evenly onto a linear timeline that repeats but stays the same. Numbering facilitates memorizing steps but also puts dance in the dancer's "head," as if the dance can be known separate from a whole-body movement.[141] Counting distances the dancer from rhythmic nuance, such as feeling a movement's layered polyrhythmic or syncopated capacities. Rhythm-sensing in black social dance, as I argued in chapter 1, transmits ways of feeling-knowing-moving embedded in the dance's ethics-aesthetic. The counting process makes dances structurally vulnerable to extraction and commodification, cutting movement off from ethics-aesthetic tradition and reinterpreting it as non-culturally specific.[142]

In chapter 1, locker Arnetta Johnson emphasized her ability to "keep up" and surpass as a girl in a male-dominated locking scene: unlike many of the guys, she explained, she had studio training and had learned to count. She asserted that she could "get" the guys' locking routines (though they wouldn't invite her into their groups) just by watching and ordering their moves to eight counts. Yet Arnetta also could dance in the vernacular. She and her dance partner, Skeet, reenacted for me the practice of vocal percussion as they recalled impromptu group dancing at house parties. Everyone in the party would improvise a groove together, calling out known steps like the Skeeter Rabbit: *Tchooka tchooka tchook ba boom boom! Skeeter Rabbit two times, FREEZE!* While eight-counting allowed Arnetta to shift gendered power dynamics in locking, she had the capacity to code-switch, translating between languages of counting and improvised feel—the common rhythm-sensing she practices in the party that vitalizes black social dance.[143]

Code-switching becomes audible evidence in a behind-the-scenes video, briefly posted on YouTube, of Medea Sirkas rehearsing on set for the filming of Justin Bieber's 2010 music video for the song "Somebody to Love."[144] They're running their choreography without music as they prepare their feature segment. They start off with eight-count phrasing yet, as they begin to physically connect, slip seamlessly into a whispered nonverbal language of breath and vocal percussion, now audible in the absence of recorded music. *One-two-three-four-woom woom. Bam bam. Wop. Pow! brrrrrrrrrrrrdah. HAH!*

"Somebody to Love" was the third single from Bieber's *My World 2.0* album, released as a remix with additional vocals by R & B pop celebrity Usher, who's also known for his love of dance. Along with Medea Sirkas, "Somebody to Love" featured an all-star array of dance crews, including winners of MTV's reality show *America's Best Dance Crew*. Director Dave Meyers expressed the video's aim to "brin[g] Justin into the world of dance . . . to integrate to different styles . . . no big story lines, no crowds of people, just real clean."[145] Embracing this idea, Bieber wanted to join Medea Sirkas in their routine, and the group was instructed to bring only three of their four members, who were Fayzo, Zulu Gremlin, and Mr. Getdown. Arriving on set, they showed their routine to the choreographer, at first doing their usual vocal rhythms. Fayzo recalls they were specifically asked to change to eight-counts: "The choreographer doesn't know it like that. You're going to have to 5-6-7-8." Here, the process of translation is revealed. Medea Sirkas translated their routine to eight counts, which a lead choreographer then memorized in order to teach Justin separately. However, Justin was not able to get their choreography in time for the shoot, and because the group was reduced to three members, Fayzo recalls staying up all night to redo the routine: "I hate dancing with three. To get the full potential of what we do, you need four or more."[146]

In the video's final cut, dance crews perform choreographed routines in quick, highly edited, and spliced-together segments. Justin is consistently positioned center frame, sometimes singing in front of the crews, sometimes joining their choreographies to perform a few moves or short phrases. In Medea Sirkas's segments, he distinctly appears inserted in front of the dancing crew and never physically joins them. Fayzo clarifies that they were shot separately and Justin's image was overlaid in the final cut. Cinematography and editing work together to manipulate the image, a magic that inserts Justin into, yet over, their dance.

Recalling this chapter's earlier discussion on animation dance style, the video editing process of masking reproduces Claymation's stop-motion technique of blacking out and overlaying multiple images so that animated characters and human protagonist can appear to exist in one taleworld.[147] Yet Medea Sirkas don't actually exist in Justin Bieber's world. In the final version of "Somebody to Love," Medea Sirkas have become doubly masked: white painter suits and black mesh face masks cover their bodies completely, anticipating a masking technique for creating areas of transparency and opacity in a clip that, ultimately, obscures "the full potential" of San Francisco Strutting and Richmond Robotting styles. While animation dance technique is transformative—as dancers reinvent Claymation technique "otherwise" from cinema's aim to produce racialized spectacles of otherworldly beings—an entertainment industry operation that centers whiteness stays static, reducing the dance's collectivity to separate and center the proprietary individual subject.[148]

I stay with this story for what surfaces in these moments of translation, when lines between street and studio blur, casting in relief the kinds of negotiations dancers make as they navigate the codes of black vernacular expression and the codes of industry dance. Hip hop dancer Nadine Hi-Hat Ruffin articulates the translation process in a video interview reflecting on her work as an industry choreographer:

> "I'm from New York. We danced with beat. Rhythm. *uhm DTAH! d' duhm duhm dtah!* We come to LA, it's a different style. They're all about counts. 1 and a 2 and a 3. *She laughs.* My style is different. I've always been creative. You have to have a passion for dance first before you move into choreography."[149]

As Hi-Hat cites her New York upbringing in rhythm, notice how she momentarily slips out of words. At this point in the video she begins to isolate her shoulders and chest, hitting the beats she enunciates in vocal rhythms akin to Fayzo's memory of watching Looney Tunes at home while funk music plays in the background: *pow pow pow, tshyoo tshyoo tshyoo*![150] Here, the "LA" to which Hi-Hat refers is specifically Hollywood industry dance—not the same Los Angeles located in the black social life of styles like locking and robot that share ethics-aesthetic practices of nonverbal rhythm-making.[151] Dancing "with beat . . . rhythm" points to the difference between industry dance choreography that's "all about counts" and the not easily captured sense of style, creativity, and passion Hi-Hat practices as the "we" of the place where *she* is from.[152]

Hi-Hat and Fayzo interanimate polycentric dance histories of New York hip hop, San Francisco Strutting, and Los Angeles streetdance as they root in a familiar language of rhythm-sensing, sharing the capacity to switch codes between vernacular rhythms of place and the language of eight-counts they learned to use working with industry dance.[153] Laughing, Hi-Hat explains, "My style is different." She understands the practice of counting at the same time she disavows it.

But why all this talk of counting? What does counting matter if the end result is the same—to learn the dance and get everyone moving together?

Eight-count translation bypasses the slow, intimate work of connecting with the dance's ethics-aesthetic sociality. A learning that does not take but gives away. Learning not to replicate steps but to attune to the dance's ineffable energy—seeing ways to relate to the steps by seeing "inside," as Wiggles's lesson teaches, giving up one's vulnerability and opening up to the dance's common feel.[154] The ones who interpret the dance in dialogue with black vernacular communities give away their gifts of interpretation in humble acknowledgment of a mutual incalculable debt that "cannot be repaid."[155] This is also kinship practice, an ethic that bonds dancer and dance, which asks for authenticity in relating to the dance.

The studio can be used to navigate the street, as Arnetta shows, using eight-counting to take her place as a black girl in locking. Dancers may use eight-counting to translate vernacular rhythms in cultural contexts unfamiliar with nuances of polyrhythm, syncopation, groove, bounce, funk, soul. This is not to say that eight-counting is inherently unethical, but that its language cannot capture the funk that's felt in parties at Netta's house or the exhaustive persistence of the Lady Mechanical Robots' homework or the intimacy of Medea Sirkas's breath-touch practice.

It bears mention here that of the dance crews contracted for the video, Medea Sirkas were the oldest in age as well as experience—all have been practicing their dances since the 1970s. Zulu Gremlin is a member of two foundational hip hop groups from the Bronx, The Rock Steady Crew and Universal Zulu Nation, and has been working in the entertainment industry since the early 1980s as a dancer well versed across different hip hop/street styles. Cultural conceptions of time and training are critical. What I've been describing as locamotive practice includes informal and everyday modes of dance training that do not conform to linear time schedules and regulated spaces more typical of dance studios, making it difficult to clearly assess when a dancer's training in any one style begins.

And, despite the fast-paced timing of a Medea Sirkas routine, the duration of their practice is slow—decades of dancing together that puts them in close touch. In 2022, I tried to access the link for the behind-the-scenes video, but the link had been switched to private, only underscoring the sense that Medea Sirkas's dance is a dis/appearing act that can't be fully captured. What the translation process removes to replace with counts, breath-touch generates as the ethics-aesthetic sociality of Medea Sirkas's collective movement practice.

When I shared this section with a friend, they told me their story of guest teaching hip hop in a prestigious university dance department. During class, a student asked pointedly, "Don't you count?" My friend took note and continued to teach the movement using vocal rhythm-sensing without counting, challenging the class to learn this different mode of relating to the dance through feel. Subsequently, the student, who identified as an extensively trained hip hop dancer, joined with several others to report my friend to department faculty and, ultimately, refused to return to the class. Aside from the offense the student apparently took when my friend undid their way of knowing hip hop dance as counts, there is a further suggestion, raised by this example, that counting is socially constructed as intellectual activity proper to higher learning, while rhythm-sensing lacks intelligence.

In a world that's wrapped up in antiblackness, black movement is something to be owned and policed. Racial capital is bound up with individuation—reproducing the body as a separable unit that is made to be counted. Kinethics are key here, as collective movement practices that "demand for nothing less than . . . return of the total value" of black social dancing that can't be captured or counted as separable form.[156] Black social dancing neither emerges from nor exists in the studio on its own. Breath-touch evidences a collective undoing, a different way that Medea Sirkas practice being and belonging in movement that is, as I listen, akin to the way Wiggles brings poppers to see "in-side" and feel on the "inner side" of the beat. It's the kind of shared embodiment shaped by Boogaloo Dana's practice of being-becoming Shiva-Kali and generated in animation dance technique. Kinethics escape racial capitalist modes of extraction to recover the careful kinship practice of common rhythm-sensing that generates dance lineages.

The ethics-aesthetic techniques I have described here figure wider social and political movement patterns. Reorienting their sense of place as they dance The Fillmore, dancers navigate a power dynamic that structures the removal of black life in San Francisco's Fillmore district. Dancing "where we're from," as Pop Tart expresses, becomes an ethics-aesthetic practice of fashioning expansive intimacies of place and belonging in motion and in flux that extend multiple kin relations acknowledged in the dance's cultural history. These dancing kinships are acts of "lateral care" by dancers who practice an obligation to become embedded in the places where they are.[157] They reinvent ways of belonging together in movement that reimagine experiences of being displaced.

Popping and other dis/appearing acts train principles like the zero, breath-touch, and becoming, preparing dancers to engage ways of seeing-feeling-knowing-moving in the world that do not sustain the separation of the individual over other bodies in a hierarchy of relation. While there has been a tendency to elevate single artist geniuses, usually male, in history, I bring attention to the ways dancers felt inspired to watch one another move, to study by inhabiting one another's movements. In doing so, they engaged collective artistic processes of circulating shared knowledges and innovating traditions—whether moving in group or in solo styles. Their dances emerge as fractal techniques, practiced by the dancer moving together with the collective social body.

Collective acts of naming dance (The Fillmore, The Fresno) and dancing place (Richmond Robotting, Oakland Boogaloo, San Francisco Strutting) shape stylistic lineages that don't align with a single center or follow a unidirectional line of origin but instead activate multiple dance histories located in dynamic polycentric relation. To reproduce the notion of a singular history or origin point of creation would be to devalue the ethics-aesthetic that dancers adhere to in practice. I am saying that ethics-aesthetic principles, embedded in technique and trained by the dancer, are repeated in the patterning of dance histories that figure multiple centers from which dances emerge as dancers form their relations in rhythm.

Kinship practice also brings California and New York dances in touch. To acknowledge the kinship bonds reinvented in the emergence of popping and other dis/appearing acts in hip hop/streetdance history is to acknowledge the ethos of black social dancing that emerges from their common "rhythm consciousness."[158] Dancing kinships, reinventing dance lineages, and activating polycentric dance histories, dancers assemble creative resources for practicing continuity and community as collective acts of being and belonging, in and as displacement.

Illustration:
Angel of Collective Discretion by d. sabela grimes

three
The Rebirth of Waacking/Punking

LIBATION

Arthur, Andrew, Tinker
Michael Angelo
Lonny
Billy
Danny
Gary
Lamont
Lil Tommy
Blinky
Micky
David
Chyna Doll
Fay Ray
Johnny
Jojo
Juan
Claude
Lizard Woman
Dallace
Shabba Doo
Tyrone

TYRONE (AUGUST 29, 1953–JUNE 6, 2020)

When I dance waacking . . . I reach back into my past . . . I feel that all of my mentors have to have a place in dance. I try my best to resurge them.

—TYRONE PROCTOR

There are ancestors to whom we become descendants . . . ultimately this decision to be ancestors requires descendance, it requires what transcends us.

—LEWIS GORDON

When Tyrone danced he stood still—chest puffed, eyes set on a distant horizon.[1] Only his arms would move—butterflying about his head almost distractedly, taut tracing reaching longing . . . until the moment he silenced their flutter, fingers curling into fists clutching air. His hips translated their pain in a frustration of arms twirling, striking down demons. He'd catch their mercurial movements, commanding them all to stop: "Be prepared. Pull up. *Touch.* Your head. To the ceiling. This dance is all about power. Power, attitude, control. They're everything."[2] He would temper stillness with extended drama pouring from fingers outstretched, beckoning an invisible lover. Yet their distraught striking movements, inevitably, would return.

What seemed a loss of mobility in Tyrone's hips and legs had transformed the dance called waacking in the early 2000s into a sweeping thrill of arms, a melodrama honed in many styles of his students—Princess Lockerooo, Aus Ninja, Kumari Suraj, Melanie Aguirre, Blak Kat, Nubian Nénè, Weon G, Waackeisha, Ebony, Cherry, Micky, Yasco, Sandrine Sainte Croix . . . and over the next two decades countless more. Tyrone's pain took flight in their hummingbird gestures, embraced in longing reaches and slowtender caresses.[3] Tyrone's influence on the dance was unmistakable, though he'd tell me dismissively, "Naomi, I'm just an imitator."

Then he'd invoke the stars I had come to know as waacking's legendary dancestors—a celestial ensemble of gay black men he often called down in triumvirate. With the spirited whip of an arm, he'd proclaim, "That's Tinker." His lips would push in a pout, and he'd narrow his eyes, steeling their gaze as his hand moved slowly upward, long fingers softly, firmly caressing their scalp from front to back, flirting with an imaginary lock of their hair: "That's Arthur. I'm channeling Arthur." Or he'd recall a dancer running across the floor on the tips of their toes: "That was Andrew." Those tiptoe flights Tyrone never showed. The somatic transformation of his pain re-created the dance waacking as a dialogue between stillness and motion. I understood his twirling arms, his slow touch to be more than imitation. I began to see Tyrone's dance as a collective practice of celebration in mourning them.[4]

Tyrone never described the pain in his hips and legs as a condition of disability. When I invited him to the Northern California Bay Area in 2012 to judge "Soul Train Ball & Battle," a memorial to Don Cornelius I was organizing with Oakland community activists Mario Benton and Traci Bartlow, Tyrone stubbornly refused my help getting his six-foot-plus frame into and out of my toy-size red convertible.[5] When we met again in New York, he insisted under the most unreasonable terms that he would take the subway late at night to meet me last minute in Brooklyn—miles from his Harlem apartment. He again insisted on driving me to visit my family in the Maryland suburbs—a five-hour ride in his beloved Mercedes-Benz sedan, transformed into a mobile dance studio to convene an extended history class on waacking. As he drove, Tyrone told stories and we danced—we were moving, and I felt their fluid presence moving with us in what writer M. Jacqui Alexander calls "a spiritual coming out."[6] With Tyrone, I felt an intimacy of the practice I was seeking to name.

In the twirling, flirting, reaching gestures, I felt a collective movement of dancestors who were becoming ensconced in the global contemporary style of waacking (and a lesser-known expression of the dance called punking). Punking was not a technical style, many 1970s generation dancers maintained, describing a fluid expression and feeling of longing that took form expansively in queer movement experiments they found themselves living out on the dance floor. Tyrone would say to me on more than one occasion, "Naomi, this dance was never meant for choreo . . . you can do that, but it wasn't made for that," and, "This was never meant to be a battle dance . . . they danced freely . . . they danced off of each other." I did not take his statements as an outright rejection of battles or routine choreography, which had become emphasized in elite dance competitions, community cultural events, social media, and studio classes in the 2000s. Tyrone articulated tensions between the dance's queer history and contemporary practice, expressing an obligation to search for waacking/punking's passed and lossed—an emergent ensemble of dancestors and collective condition of grief that moved him: "I reach back into my past . . . I try my best to resurge them."

The prominence of striking arms continued to mark Tyrone's signature on the dance, even when, after receiving two hip surgeries, he began moving his legs in short bursts on the dance floor, a few years before he became a dancestor. As I was researching hidden histories of the dance, emergent in queer nightlife of Los Angeles during the funk and disco era of the 1970s, I came to understand the pain Tyrone battled in his body as a condition of loss that is collective. Transformed in the millennium, waacking/punking continues to express a simultaneity of stillness and motion, a practice of celebration and mourning infusing the dance's global rebirth. The rebirth of waacking/punking is a story about finding queer kinship in movement—the ways dancers seek home and belonging as they return over and over to the dance floor to get lost, go in, let it out, and be touched by the dance.

STREETDANSCENDANCES

Loss gives rise to longing, and in these circumstances, it would not be far-fetched to consider stories as a form of compensation or even as reparations, perhaps the only kind we will ever receive.

—SAIDIYA HARTMAN

Queer people rarely exist in official history. We've always had to decode the past to find it.

—WU TSANG

How do we mourn and survive the violence of being known?

—ALEXIS PAULINE GUMBS

This chapter explores corporeal, kinetic, and spiritual dimensions of collective loss through danscendances that express yearning toward the past and accept the call to become dancestors.[7] Dancers of waacking/punking reinterpret movement styles of their progenitors, a wave of whom passed over the course of HIV/AIDS and the drug wars of the 1980s. Though I don't know how they may have chosen to identify, I offer the signifiers queer and trans* to call forth their fluid and open-ended movement experiments on dance floors of Los Angeles's disco underground, practicing possibilities of being that Marquis Bey elaborates as "the primordial force of unfixing openness . . . stars floating without laws set in motion."[8] Becoming kin to waacking/punking's floating stars, dancers call forth a collective commitment to be in mourning and celebration of them, reimagining expansively the ways they moved. To celebrate does not mean getting past their grieving, which is constantly present in danscendance's collective practice.

I tend to waacking/punking as a dance of mourning, following the dance's transition from queer nightlife of 1970s Los Angeles into global hip hop/streetdance culture in the 2000s. Waacking/punking moved through Los Angeles's first gay clubs like the Catch One and Gino's, traveled onto luxury entertainment stages like Caesars Palace in Las Vegas, and was screened on the Hollywood set of nationally syndicated TV show *Soul Train*, where glimpses of the dance appear in the context of freeform social dancing to soul, funk, and early disco music.[9] Unlike the dance style voguing, which has always belonged to black LGBTQ+ Ball culture, waacking/punking did not develop within an organized system of houses and families. As dancers traveled, reflecting the locamotive principle of black social dance practice that I define in chapter 1, they carried their style knowledges and common rhythm consciousness with them, helping set foundations for contemporary global hip hop/streetdance to emerge.

Leaving *Soul Train*, Tyrone moved from Los Angeles to New York, where he met dancers in the underground clubs who collectively formed the performance group Breed of Motion in 1982. One member was voguer Willi Ninja, who went on to form House of Ninja. Archie Burnett, also a core member, had already been exposed to waacking, he explained, through watching *Soul Train* on Saturday afternoons. By 1992, Archie was teaching clubbing internationally, including vogue and waacking styles.[10] Kumari Suraj asserts, "Breed of Motion is the main reason waacking and vogue began to resemble each other."[11]

Waacking/punking was reborn into hip hop/streetdance culture in the 2000s, with the expansion of transnational dance battles and competitions, studio classes, mass entertainment dance reality shows, and battle-themed dance films. In 2007, Brian Green organized the first waacking battle as a principal coordinator of New York City's House Dance Conference, an event dedicated to connecting dance and cultural education. In 2010, Kumari Suraj launched her International Waack/Punk/Pose Festival (Waackfest) in Los Angeles. Waacking resurged as a category in the battle scene.

New York-based waacker and protégé of Tyrone, Princess Lockerooo reflects on the dance's trajectory from the 1970s to 2000s: "Back then, nobody was looking at one person to know how to do [the dance]. Everybody would look at each other and then create. Now there's different [approaches] based on the styles of people who experienced the dance in the '70s and started teaching." Lockerooo highlights communal aspects of improvisation as key to the dance's early formation and cultural practice, describing an informal process of dancers watching each other and becoming inspired from the freeform dancing that was happening around them. Organizing waacking events in clubs and public spaces alongside her studio classes, she reflects:

> "As a teacher it's not about trying to get students to do it "right" or copy me. I believe it's most authentic to see students for who they are and help bring out their personality, talents and style, using waacking as a guide. This is how Tyrone taught me. What I can give [students] is freedom to be and create themselves. The freestyle aspect of street and club dance is not highlighted properly in mainstream media. It's not easy. Choreography is wonderful, but I wish freestyle was more celebrated in dance television shows. These are major art forms."[12]

Creating spaces for dancers to move beyond formal class settings is a key way dancers shape danscendances, as collective practices through which students apprentice themselves to the social life of the dance.

As the dance gained visibility in a global hip hop/streetdance scene, the term punking was less often used, while waacking became emphasized as a battle category and studio technique and, simultaneously, began to center women's performances within male-dominated and cishetero-oriented cultural spaces. Circulating online and in high-visibility contexts, waacking performances most often seemed to attach an emphasized femininity to assigned-female bodies. Gender-transgressive or gender-expansive performances of waacking/punking, while rare, became most recognizable among dancers who identified as male or gender fluid.

Women and girls in the 2000s were using waacking/punking in nuanced ways to challenge gender performance in streetdance. Young women to whom I listened would often express with deep emotion their indebtedness to the dance's progenitors, punctuating their expressions of gratitude with the statement, "waacking taught me how to be a woman." I was curious about deeper intimacies of queer embodiment, transmitted in waacking/punking practice yet obscured by the language and performance of binary gender. I started writing about waacking/punking as a technique of *corporeal drag*—a way in which dancers were inhabiting movement materials of the dance's gender-expansive progenitors.[13] In waacking/punking's resurgence, corporeal drag shaped dancers' practices of searching for their queer kin, who gave them access in arcing arms, yearning glances, self-loving caresses, seductive shimmies, and flits. Dancers were expanding their sense of "being woman" by reaching to waacking's dancestors, seeking to find themselves in the dance's queer and trans* history.

Performance scholar Marlon M. Bailey puts forth "kin labor" as the labor of care and recognition outside state systems that fail to protect queer black communities, practiced within black LGBTQ+ Ball culture and including the construction of alternative systems of kin relations that recognize gender-expansive being.[14] Though waacking/punking did not develop within an organized system of queer kin relations, dancers describe feelings of belonging and home in the dance. I find kin labor present in ephemeral and often understated moments of practice, as dancers interpret movement styles of waacking/punking's progenitors. These collective practices of danscendance reorient dancers to queer intimacies and shared embodiments, as they feel and find themselves in the presence of their dancestors.

Danscendances describe spiritual and emotional dimensions of kinethics, emerging from a common ethos of mourning as dancers find kinship with their dead. These practices reorient dancers of waacking/punking to their queer and trans* dancestors in ways that have shifted gender performance in contemporary streetdance and that offer forms of felt intimacy and shared embodiment vital to queer kinship and belonging. Not the same as repair or reconciliation, danscendances transform loss from a private to collective experience and, in the process, invite dancers to find and feel their wholeness. At the same time, danscendance carries an ethic of obligation to make queer histories known.

Danscendance extends feminist decolonizing practices of *rasanblaj*, a concept contoured by Haitian American artist-anthropologist Gina Ulysse in conversation with Afro-Caribbean writer M. Jacqui Alexander. Alexander says, "this work of reassembly, 're-memory' as Toni Morrison calls it, is a spiritual coming out, making Spirit public and not consigning Them to the underground, the basement, or the non-existent."[15] In waacking/punking's rebirth, teachers and students remember, reassemble, reinterpret, and reinvent the erotic gestures of an emergent ensemble of dancestors who continue to transform and grow. Inhabiting their ways of moving, dancers re-create the dance in the present, where they find themselves simultaneously within the presence of their dancestors.

This process of becoming is not frivolous, asking what the work of danscendances will be. These practices are less about a dancer's mastery of technique than about their commitment to the experimental gift of being/becoming dancestors: "The spirits have never left. It is just our consciousness in relationship to their presence and our interpretations of that presence that shift. That's why one of our collective petitions is to be endowed with the gift of interpretation, with the practice and grace of interpretation, so that when dreams come, we are able to *know* what they are telling us. . . . They do not come all at once. And they do not come once and for all."[16] Because the practice of rasanblaj is not outside systems of socialization with which the dancer-artist is inevitably enmeshed, the gift of interpretation holds weight. Interpretation is a lifelong process of bringing consciousness into alignment with spiritual presence—the "collective petition" of becoming kin that Alexander highlights as she assures us the spirits are not lost to us. As practices of belonging with and to waacking/punking's emergent ensemble, danscendances reorient dancers to possibilities of experimenting openly and expansively with form.

I study waacking/punking practices through participant ethnographic research of classes, battles, and cultural events, taking place primarily in Los Angeles, the San Francisco Bay Area, and New York, from 2011 to 2014. I include my recollection of first seeing the dance in a punking technique class taught by Brian Green during the summer of 2003.[17] I draw on personal interviews with contemporary and early generation dancers, the latter who told me stories of crossing gay/straight borders shaping the political geography of social dancing in 1970s Los Angeles.

In the 2000s, dancers bring waacking/punking into new global contexts, collectively reinventing hip hop/streetdance to reflect the culture's queer lineages. This is also a process of genre mixing that reveals the dance's entanglements with gender, sexuality, and race. In light of the historical connection between funk and disco music, discussed briefly in the book's introduction, mixing genres (at times considered taboo) also bears on hidden histories of gender-fluid innovators of hip hop/streetdance cultures. I bring queer and trans* theory to bear on politics of crossing, colliding, unsettling, blurring, and refusing strict categories of gender and style, as dancers find belonging within waacking/punking practices that both destabilize and reinscribe genre boundaries and gender norms.

Waacking/punking poses questions: How do we re-member our dancestors whose gender-transgressive and gender-expansive presence has been hidden within dominant historical narratives? What are we searching for in reinterpreting their dances and dance histories? How do we collectively mourn our lossed? As dancers shift their consciousness they prepare to receive the spiritual gift of dancestors, who find ways of being, becoming, and belonging to waacking/punking danscendances.

WHAT'S WAACKING/PUNKING?

Less-expected cultural moments at which punk has been figured . . . have more than a nominal relation to the canonical ones, and understanding something more of the connections between them—and the discourses of race and sex that simultaneously make and mask such connections—is an important part of the project of "punking" theory.

—TAVIA NYONG'O

It had been just over a month since Tyrone and I first found each other under the disco ball gracing the dance floor of Maverick's Flat.[18] The occasion for our meeting, "Celebration: The Life of Don Cornelius," was a Los Angeles reunion of *Soul Train* dancers gathering in memory of the TV show's celebrity host-entrepreneur, who had passed on February 1, 2012.[19] I had just embarked on my research into the contemporary streetdance style called waacking. I was curious to bridge the dance's emergence in queer-of-color nightlife of 1970s Los Angeles and resurgence in a global arena of streetdance battles, hip hop dance competitions, dance festivals, and studio classes in the first decade of the 2000s.

The 2000s also marked the global expansion of hip hop/streetdance in battle and competition culture. Now an international festival, Battle of the Year started in 1990, not as a competition but as a b-boy show at a local youth cultural center in Hanover, Germany. Japan Dance Delight in 1994 and San Diego, California-originated Freestyle Session in 1997 preceded the inaugural Juste Debout in the suburbs of Paris and World Hip Hop Dance Championship in South Beach, Florida (both in 2002). Importantly, Juste Debout, meaning "just standing," was created by dancer Bruce Ykanji Soné to give exposure to styles of popping, locking, hip hop and house. The Red Bull BC One breaking competition followed in 2004. Battle-themed dance films proliferated within the same period, alongside dance reality shows (Hollywood's new obsession), heightening the stakes for a multinational hip hop/streetdance industry: *You Got Served* (2004); *Rize* (2005); the *Step Up* film franchise (2006-19); *Feel the Noise, Stomp the Yard,* and *How She Move* (2007); the *So You Think You Can Dance* franchise (2005-present); *Dancing with the Stars* (2004-present); and *America's Best Dance Crew* (2008-15).

In 2012, waacking/punking's rise within global hip hop/streetdance was unprecedented. Dancers from New York to Mongolia were posting their solo freestyles and group choreographies to social media, starting group pages and promoting festivals and cultural events. Los Angeles-area dancers of the 1970s generation, including Tyrone Proctor, Viktor Manoel, Ana Lollipop Sanchez, Dallace Ziegler, Shabba Doo, and Toni Basil, were contributing their living histories of the dance, talking on panels, teaching master classes, and judging battles.[20] Brian Green and Archie Burnett, both well-established dancers of the New York underground, were disseminating their knowledge of the style as well.[21] Millennial waackers Kumari Suraj, Princess Lockerooo, and Johnny Waacks were each featured on FOX TV's *So You Think You Can Dance*, using the name *waacking* to refer to the dance.[22]

Off the mass media screen and elite competition stages, streetdancers were talking about waacking and punking as separate techniques, using the divided term *waacking/punking* to reference what appeared to be a relationship between two distinct styles often performed in combination. Some dancers were opting to use the spelling *whacking*, citing the English dictionary as an authoritative reference for the dance's characteristic arm movement—to strike with force. In 2003, Brian Green was teaching punking, offering smaller classes off the commercial grid at Fazil's—a New York City cultural institution where "even penniless artists could afford to rent."[23] Brian had initiated contact with Tyrone, who was living in Harlem, bringing him into the global hip hop/streetdance community as a first-generation dancer and caretaker of waacking/punking's repertoire. Still, the dance eluded easy definition.

Waacking/punking's resurgence felt like something between rebirth and reinvention. The rhythmic, striking arm movements seen in online footage of 1970s dancers had become an emphasized feature of global waacking style. In battle, waackers of the 2000s were re-creating a dazzling spectrum of isolated arm movements—training precise high-speed rotations of wrist, elbow, and shoulder joints—that, Nelson George writes, "move through space like summer fans in church ladies' hands."[24] Their whipping, whirling motions were accented by dramatic stops—a clenched fist, longing gaze, haughty pose. The restless yet commanding energy of the elongated arm gestures, timed precisely to hard-hitting beats of early disco tracks, echoed Tyrone's approach to waacking.[25] I was reminded each time Tyrone would enter or exit his beloved Mercedes sedan that the painful loss of mobility in his hips, which often kept him standing in place as he danced, had already become a kinesthetic element of waacking's rebirth.

While the superhero flights of arms served battle and television spectacle well, waacking/punking's resurgent story was also, less obviously, about a striking loss of movement. Between the dance's 1970s emergence and 2000s resurgence, there is a tangible sense of absence. It's not that the dance completely disappears. In 1984, Billy Goodson blends the dance in his choreography for *Breakin' 2: Electric Boogaloo*, working with Lonny Carbajal, Ana Sanchez, and Shabba Doo.[26] In 1985, Tyrone cameos in Jody Watley's "Still a Thrill," filmed at the Paris Opera House.[27] Viktor Manoel integrates the dance into television choreographies and performances with Danny Lugo as dancers for Grace Jones.[28] Ana Sanchez teaches punking in Orange County. Studios in Japan continue to teach the dance. Yet cultural knowledge of the dance and dancers is submerged, until the 2000s, when recognition of waacking/punking style ignites on a global scale.

During the two decades between, a wave of waacking/punking innovators vanished. I asked whether anyone knew where Arthur, Andrew, and Tinker, the dance's commonly celebrated ensemble of progenitors, had gone, but few dancers to whom I spoke could give details. Memory blurred with rumor and question, offered in softened voices, staggered pauses, and sentences that trailed off. Searching, dancers would sometimes recall a dancer who had fallen sick or another's transition surgery or another's murder or another's incarceration. Failures of words increased the sense of anonymity marking 1970s gay nightlife and those who moved through it.

The unfathomable loss and collective mourning of LGBTQ+ communities in 1980s and '90s Los Angeles, wrought by epidemics of incarceration, crack cocaine, and AIDS, amplified the dancers' disappearances and waacking/punking's cultural submergence. Waacking/punking's story is intimately shaped by this historical gap—a loss of time and memory that echoes in the ongoing enforcement of structural violence.[29] While beyond the scope of this chapter, a prolonged history of Los Angeles as a global capital of incarceration, elimination, and deportation entangles the dance.[30] Silence around the stigma of AIDS is challenged by the work of such artist-activists as Joseph Hemphill Beam, Essex Hemphill, Marlon Riggs, and Kenyon Farrow, who articulate intersections of HIV/AIDS with incarceration, militarism, and antiblackness.[31] Likewise I came to find that the slash at the heart of waacking/punking pointed to historical gaps and silences, presenting a challenge to bridge the divide between the dance's queer history and contemporary practice.[32]

I had become obsessed with the name *waacking/punking*. Why the forward slash? What was the relationship between waacking and punking? Were they one or two? I listened closely to explanations of the nomenclature, especially coming from 1970s dancers who had moved in the disco underground.

"Back then people would actually distinguish between them? No. Never. No! Never!" Margarita Disco Maggie Reyna breaks into peeling laughter as she responds emphatically to my questions. "Not like today. They never called it anything. They just did what they did."[33]

Tyrone echoed her, "They were living it . . . they didn't care about giving it a name. The only ones who started naming it was straight people."[34] Like other streetdances that populate this book, waacking/punking emerged from the social life of the dancers, and in the 2000s, the slash evoked an ethos in which dancers consistently sought to distinguish between labeling and living a dance.

Ana Sanchez added that the term *waacking* came about to protect dancers from the insult implied by *punking* in the straight world. The term *punk* in African American slang carries associations "from at least the late 1950s to the early 2000s . . . with extreme forms of imprisonment, slavery, and rape."[35] Punking called up the sexual politics of race at the intersections of homophobia and antiblackness. Among the dancers, Ana concluded, punking reclaimed their dance as "a collective movement . . . punkin' was how they lived, how they expressed who they were."[36] In the 1970s disco underground, dancers moved *punk* from noun to verb—"I'm punking"—switching the term from a static identity to a whole sense of self in motion.[37]

Viktor Manoel offered further clarification, "Waacking did not come first, it was punking." He described a Los Angeles nightlife of multiple crossings as gay dancers, refusing to stay within social lines, began entering contests at the straight clubs: "It was good money. Once they started competing outside the [gay] club, [straight dancers] started coming in to find out what the hell is going on and why are we getting beat. I think the division started happening when outsiders started coming in to learn the dance."[38] For many dancers who were jobless, the straight clubs presented opportunity; in the informal economy of the dance contest circuit, the money was better. Waacking/punking's slash directed me to the ways they negotiated both sexuality and class divides.

Tyrone recalled moments on the *Soul Train* film set and at Maverick's when he would show movement he was watching dancers do inside the discos:

> You know where the parking lot is at Maverick's? I was showing people how to waack. I said, "You have to *whack* your *arm* . . . literally throw it." Jeffrey [Daniel] was right there and said, "That's a good name for it. Let's make it two *a*'s." What he meant was the word *wack* had a negative connotation. Jeffrey wanted to think specifically for the dance. W-A-A-C-K. [Before] they were using only the word *punking*. Didn't nobody know what waacking was.[39]

Tyrone's story confirms Ana's and Victor's explanations of the etymology, exemplifying the ways dancers navigated racial-sexual politics as gay dances circulated beyond the discos. *Soul Train* dancer Jeffrey Daniel's reinventive spelling with two *a*'s plays with exaggerated style while sidestepping slippery connotations of both *wack* and *punk* in the black vernacular. I use the term *waacking/punking* to highlight an entangling of community histories and subsequent tensions made visible by the divided name, as well as to emphasize the reinventive spelling created by Jeffrey and Tyrone.

The emergent movement of waacking/punking's ensemble—the experimental life material of the dance—was becoming a collective style. Bringing these various explanations together, I draw the conclusion that naming the dance was not a deliberate aim by any clearly delineated social group to label a style but was part of dancers' ongoing process of collective identity formation as they moved through fluid social spaces.

The register of 1970s Los Angeles queer nightlife spaces is copious: Jewel's Catch One, Paradise Ballroom, After Dark, Sugar Shack, Circus, Ice House, Outer Limits, the Other Side, Gino's. Located in a North Hollywood strip mall at the intersection of Santa Monica and Vine, kitty-corner from a surplus store, Gino's did not have the economic resources of discos like Paradise Ballroom yet was uniquely renowned among dancers.[40]

To get to Gino's it was not uncommon to go by bus.[41] Walking up the long, narrow staircase, they'd queue at the entryway. Queer kids and runaways as young as eleven—no ID required—immigrants, refugees and children of refugees, hard-core cholas, pachucas, punk and disco kids, Cubanos, Chicanos, Filipinos. They wore angel wings and devil horns, painted their bodies entirely in gold.

"Everybody looked like they just came out of the dry cleaners. Pressed." Dancer Billy Goodson laughs, reminiscing about the time he sneaked in celebrity singer Diana Ross. "Then you went into this dump . . . dark, smoky, mysterious, small. Like you were walking into someone's apartment. Gino's in the best sense of the word . . . was a poppin' dive."[42]

Contests and theatrical performances were part of the entertainment bill, with specialty nights for African American and Latinx communities throughout the week. DJ Michael Angelo Harris was their renowned conductor, "the heartbeat" of Gino's and a dancer himself who knew how to bring the crowd to the floor. Producers traveled from across town to listen, watch, and break in new records, which Michael Angelo disguised with labels he painted over or switched, elevating his mystique among the disco elite.[43] On the tiny floor, open-ended movement mixed with popular social dances—the Bump, the Robot, and especially hustle, the ubiquitous partner dance of the day.[44] Dancing at Gino's could be best described as antigeneric in José Esteban Muñoz's sense of the "wildness of punk and its commons . . . refusal of cohesion and insistence on scatteredness"—a movement of belonging that invited unpredictable approaches.[45]

Extending punking's genre of refusal beyond the dance floor, Gino's bathrooms didn't follow gender binaries and inevitably became side stages for everyday dramas starring "a punk rock commons that certainly includes conflicted and passionate lovers, but also the scene itself, the social scene they dwell within, a commons of people who do not have the most predictable things in common."[46] Experimentation was plentiful, as were drugs and Cherry Coke. No alcohol was served at the bar, which nonetheless kept a counter lined with amyl nitrate for dancers to get high before they fell out, spinning, twirling, and sliding on the linoleum floor.[47]

Billy's recollection of dancing at Gino's dovetails with Ana's description of the "collective movement" of punking:

> One of our favorite songs to come on was "When Papa Was a Rolling Stone." The drama in the club you could cut it with a knife. I would want to sit it out. To just watch. Because it was too grand. Everyone in the club would pose that song down to the ground. A certain section, the whole club would hit the floor. That was the beauty of our club. Andrew . . . he'd pull out a mink from someplace and throw it on the floor. And it was over.[48]

In her punking classes, Ana further elaborated on the collective movement of the dance's ensemble. She recalled her first experiences going with Toni Basil to Paradise Ballroom in 1974, watching the dancers make the disco their playground. They moved around in a way she called "scatting" as she taught punking to her students, recalling their quick flights across the dance floor, winding in, out, and around the crowd, finding one another in the center, then suddenly disappearing out of sight.[49] Posing was a way of punctuating their movement with quick rhythmic freezes, timed with beats of the music. Dancers would pose and switch between dramatic gestures and facial expressions that drew inspiration from moving images of early Hollywood silent film stars, prompting self-references to their dancing as "Marlene" and "Garbo." These performances were less about expressing a normative desire to be female and white than about transforming the meaning of such identifications themselves.[50]

Shabba Doo explained punking's mode of reenactment: "If the doorbell rang it would say 'doorbell rings' in the bottom. They would bat their eyes all big and *over* and melodramatic. They became story based. They do *not* do routines. They do characters. You embodied that person, their spirit, their style."[51] Punking focused not on steps but on intensities of emotion and feeling, accessed through the movie characters yet more than imitation. Dancers consistently defined punking as a deeper revealing of self, which Billy Goodson articulated, "The dance is who we really are . . . everything that you were was happening in the club."[52] Inhabiting the movement materials of Hollywood film stars, dancers explored their intimately felt reality, reinventing the character's story in their terms of punking.

In the 2000s, 1970s dancers would often take time in classes to recall waacking/punking's emergent ensemble of dancestors and to show how they moved—performances that took on the resonance of ritual. Streetdancers were also going online, studying videos circulating on YouTube, including recordings of 1970s *Soul Train* episodes and, especially, one clip of Diana Ross performing "Love Hangover" at Caesars Palace in 1979. Drawing in part from the videos, as well as dancing together in classes, jams, and battles, dancers were reassembling waacking/punking's signature movements. Waacking/punking had become a mode of inhabiting the improvisatory materials of the emergent ensemble—a gathering of spirits forming and still growing. Stories and dances tethered them to their dancestors, offering ways of listening to the dead who speak through the dance. I was constantly reminded this is a dance of the passed, the lossed, and a continuous grieving of spirits. Returning punking to waacking is just as much a critical refusal to sustain silence over the dancers' irreparable loss.

SHABBA DOO (MAY 11, 1955–DECEMBER 29, 2020)

He's about six-foot-one. Wearing [his hairstyle] like Spock. Most women wore it, and it was famous in the late '60s '70s. The sideburns would come to a point, a widow's peak in the front. He also had red lipstick on. It looked to me like he was wearing mascara. And earrings. A long duster coat similar to what Lucille Ball wears. He wore pencil-tight pants. High platforms that were bedazzled . . . glitter or rhinestones around them. He was smoking a cigarette, with a cigarette holder. It was very long. He began to flit across the stage, running on the tip of his toes as though the floor was made of hot coals. He was running like that, with his hands in the air, with the cigarette holder. Flamboyantly feminine. He goes over to part of the stage, lays out all dramatic and blows his cigarette. Everyone sits stunned in the room. No sound. That's how it was in that room. The world stopped. He's doing this, and he's not doing it for any applause. He's just doing his thing.

—SHABBA DOO

Shabba Doo recounts losing a dance contest to Andrew Frank the first time they meet, at the Carolina Lanes, a bowling alley in back of the Los Angeles airport that he says drew a regular cast of Super Fly-type street characters.[53] The contest's presumptive winner, he feels awash in astonishment as he watches Andrew take his prize. Stressing that the "theater in which all this was playing out" is a social microcosm of hyper-heteromasculinity, he frames the story as a test of his ego and awe at Andrew's commitment to be completely who they are. The word *feminine* may reduce Andrew's gender-expansive dance to binary gender terms. Yet I also reimagine Shabba Doo's story through the spiritual practice of danscendance, listening for how Andrew reaches beyond performance of gender identity to a deeper sense of being-becoming in touch with self, akin to the "radical collective self-possession" that Alexander and Ulysse find in rasanblaj and that Shabba Doo moves on to elucidate through his observations of encountering punking in the disco underground.[54]

Critical to his storytelling style, Shabba Doo uses queer language to explain the deeper significance of Andrew's dance, resonating with 1970s dancers' consistent distinction between doing a technical style and living a lifestyle: "They were living out, as they called it, 'going in.' That meant I was really doing my thing. I was so far in my own imagination that nothing else mattered. I was in it. Fully. Committed to it. It's not a separate dance. They were not doing punking. Society has a tendency to label what they don't understand." Shabba Doo explains "going in" as the dancer's complete commitment to being in their imagination—not doing but "living out" the dance. Andrew's dance is a practice of going in that equates to nonperformance in the sense transfeminine artist Alok Vaid-Menon articulates: "I do not have the luxury of being. I am only seen as doing. As if my gender is . . . not something that belongs to me."[55] They trouble the repeated enforcement of gender performance on their gender-nonconforming embodiment, citing public interactions with people who call their clothing a "costume." The language of performance becomes a weapon of social policing, used to point out their failure to perform the gender binary. They describe an ontology of performance in which gender-fluid people are always already acting a role, their existence negated. Emphasizing that Arthur's dance is "not for any applause," Shabba Doo articulates a distinction between performing and going in. "Going in" is how Andrew commits to being-belonging-becoming in their dance, their imagination encompassing collective experiments with form. Punking poses expansive vocabularies of queer and trans* existence they are living out by going in on the dance floor.

Vaid-Menon goes on to vividly recollect their feeling of wearing a dress in public: "a reunification of my mind, my body, and my spirit—for the first time in a long time, I was able to be completely present with myself and the world."[56] That dancers may experience reunification in the club rather than public space does not make their practices of going in less consequential. Kareem Khubchandani asserts that queer nightlife does not escape political economies of affect and aesthetics, making these quotidian sites potent with "small opportunities for radical inclusion, pleasure making, and self-fashioning that dancers in the club 'fight for' in the face of the systemic exclusions that nightlife colludes with."[57] Exclusionary tactics were ordinary facets structuring straight/gay spaces at Carolina Lanes and Gino's alike. The dancers' practices were enmeshed with the contradictions of queer nightlife, not an escape from so much as a creative working out, with, and through nightlife's complexity and complicity.

Waacking/punking's queer and trans* dancestors who challenged rigid social borders practiced precarity, an impulse toward risk, and the possibility of expansive intimacies that tested the regulation of their gender-nonconforming embodiment and desire. Whether as sexual practice or dance style, dancers were following a common desire to move beyond bounds of normative expression. Shabba Doo's story is worth recounting at length as a rare firsthand description of dancers encountering one another in their shared desires to traverse social borders.

> I say, "Hey what's your name?"
> "I'm Andrew."
> "What is that dancing you were doing?"
> "Puuh! Oh chile, that's the Garbo."
> "Where do you do it?"
> "That's how we do where we hang out, where we go."
> "Could you teach me that? How to do the Garbo?"
>
> He looked at me, up and down. Like he was deciding whether I was OK to do it. Like I don't know if you got what it takes. He didn't say those words, but it was that sort of attitude there. And it was understood. So he says, "You have to come down to where we go. You're gonna need to come to Gino's."

Coming to Gino's and eventually to the Catch One with dancers Arthur, Andrew, and Billy Starr, Shabba Doo emphasizes how his socialization within organized religion and gang identity tangle with mixed feelings he experiences of fear, wonder, admiration, and longing: "We heard all these things . . . but I just wanted to know how this dance goes." He accepts the dancers' invitation, and they take him into their homes. At Arthur's, they make food, play music, sew clothes, do one another's hair and makeup, get high. They dress him, pluck his eyebrows, slick his hair, and rouge his cheeks. He details his transformation through a process of queer play that is queer care and queer love, the dancers refashioning him in their materials, helping him discover himself differently.

Shabba Doo goes on to express to me a feeling of consternation that arises in his experience of being transformed: "I'm stuck in between these two worlds now, cuz I'm not gay. And I can't go back the other way cuz now they think I'm gay anyways. So now, what am I! You know, what am I?" On one hand, his words would reduce sexual orientation to a straight/gay binary while suggesting an essential bind between dance style and sexual practice. Yet his twice-asked question—"What am I! . . . What am I?"—invokes a deeper trouble of feeling stuck at the limits of binary language, dividing a world of expansive experience into the requirement to choose. *What am I?* longs for an opening to the possibility of existing beyond the binary, a fluid sense of being-belonging-becoming given as a question rather than a foregone conclusion.

Moving to the crossroads of a gay/straight binary, Shabba Doo experiences a disorientation from cisheteronormative masculinity, suspended in a question. Shabba Doo's question expands with possibility to explore intimate vocabularies of feeling and spirit, found not in maintaining the forward slash but instead in unifying waackingpunking—found in ways I am suggesting are the dance's undoing of gender-normative imperatives of embodiment through ethics-aesthetic practice.

* * *

We are resting between classes at the Performing Arts Center Annex in Van Nuys, a twenty-minute drive on crisscrossing Los Angeles highways from Gino's 1970s North Hollywood location. Studio D is not atypical of a private dance studio: smooth, off-white walls match the light grain of the sprung floor and double ballet bars; a stretch of polished mirrors runs along one wall from the stereo cart at the entrance door to the grand piano in the opposite corner. This summer Shabba Doo is teaching beginner-level Saturday classes in locking and his brand of punking technique, which he's dubbed *shway*. There's never more than five students in class, though we all stay for the full three hours plus.

Shabb has finally called a water break, and some students have left the studio, while another stands facing the mirror, slowly moving through the waacking/punking gestures we've just learned. I linger at the ballet bars, taking sips from my water bottle and typing notes into my phone. Suddenly Shabb moves to the dance floor. He nonchalantly announces, "This is Andrew."

He shifts into slow-slow motion. His eyes close. Ecstasy mists his face, touching his skin with a soft glow. Gently, he traces a single toe across the dance floor, the invisible arc semicircling him. I catch my breath, silently watching. A release of energy into the fold of a knee, a coquettish bending inward, a protrusion of the opposing hip, a loosening at the shoulder girdle. His arms float slowly upward. They appear as birds wings gently suspended in flight. Now he's being lifted, hovering, arm-wings flapping slowly, softly. A pause. One index finger snakes slowly upward. Stillness.

Nothing Shabba Doo did in the handful of seconds during which he finally introduced me to Andrew looked anything remotely like what I had come to know as waacking/punking. Not like anything anyone had taught me in class or that I'd see again. The movement did not look like the precise steps and bold strikes of shway choreography he would proceed to teach us when he called class back to order for the last hour of the day. In the moment Shabba Doo danced Andrew I felt studio time falling away in the sense Billy Goodson confided "has always been part of my battle about teaching [the dance] . . . I couldn't possibly whittle it down to an hour."[58]

Shabba Doo showed us Andrew's felt presence as a gift of their collective imagination. Not a gift that could in any way be taught or apprehended as a formula of style. Their gift was all the more felt in the moment of the water break—given over in the free time before the "call to order" during which, Fred Moten explains, differently organized forms of collective study and knowledge transmission can happen in excess of institutionally recognized learning.[59] Inhabiting Andrew's movement materials through danscendance, Shabba Doo activates queer kinship, a practice that does not demand mastery of form or professional skill, but is not the same as saying form has no value. Rather than the aesthetic transferred as a static object, the aesthetic becomes intimately known through shared embodiment and feeling, touching me.

As he commits to going in, finding self-connection in their dance through queer kinship, he shows what Omise'eke Natasha Tinsley writes, drawing on gender-illusioning performance artist MilDred's invocation: "all people have the possibility to be simultaneously man and woman because they're always surrounded by multiple, multiply gendered spirits and may temporarily become any of these spirits at any time."[60] I experience Andrew through Shabba Doo's practice of shared presence—their way of going in. We commune with Andrew.

GOING TO GINO'S

What happened was, a lot of kids were runaways, kay I was one of um. I met Raul . . . he was a Cuban guy who had a lot of money. He says, "I have to take you to Gino's." We walked in and he paid. He was hot, he had money. His parents loved me. They bought me clothes, they owned their own factory. I went on the dance floor with him, and I have to be completely honest with my feelings. (softening voice) *I said what the heck am I doing with you? I don't wanna dance like this. I wanna dance like* them. (raising voice to a shout) *I wanna be* me *now! And so I thought, let's leave. I thought, I'm going back tomorrow but I'm not* ever *going back there with him. So I broke up with him. To go to Gino's. I went to Gino's time after time. I had something in me, and I had to* (growls) *LET IT OUT! When I went there by myself, and I let it out, I felt like I was* (whispers) *at home. And I felt complete.*

—DISCO MAGGIE

Margarita Disco Maggie Reyna calls herself by turns a 1970s dancer, a salsera and hustle champion, and an underground dancer.[61] As her story of punking at Gino's unfolds, she vocalizes with intermittent shrieks, breathy and guttural sounds, an untamed longing "to go to Gino's . . . to LET IT OUT!" Going to Gino's is a journey to finding herself, one that she feels she has to take by herself, alone, apart from anybody else. To go to Gino's she decides to break up with her boyfriend. Longing to "dance like them," Margarita calls up the *I* of her experience, telling herself "let's leave" in order to return, taking herself there—alone but not separate from dancing with them on the dance floor.

Going to Gino's is a practice of belonging to self in queer kinship with waacking/punking's emergent ensemble who move Margarita to renounce all that's signified in hetero-coupling, an ideal that she constructs through markers of gender and class, accented by a hierarchical Latinidad. She is very clear that her Cuban boyfriend's moneyed status offers a dream of upward mobility she otherwise lacks as a teen Chicana runaway: "We walked in and he paid. He was *hot*, he had *money*. His parents *loved me*. They bought me *clothes*, they owned their own factory." She underscores the benefits she would be receiving as his girlfriend—parental love, material gifts of money and clothes, a potential share in the family-owned business. Yet in Margarita's story, the potential of normative family success works in contrast to a different capacity for home and belonging, the one she finds on Gino's dance floor.

> What punking was back then was not dancing today. Kay? They were posing, or moving their body while scratching their head. Whippin their hair around, having a seizure on the floor, doing all kinds of freekin things. Today all of that's considered weird. Kay? To some people! Especially studio people. But in that time, these people felt completely that place was a sanctuary for them. It really brought out being gay, owning who you are. Just believing in yourself, you know?

Margarita's description of punking on Gino's dance floor is not about attaching "craziness" to black and queer cultures, but it is helpfully elaborated in Anna Martine Whitehead's love for queens who fall with "freak technique," which she describes as movement teetering on the edge of "a devastating lack of hegemonic protection and a legacy of sensuous and spirited cultural inventiveness."[62] Freak technique animates more dancers' descriptions of punking dancestors: Tinker, whom Ana Sanchez remembers teetering in platform heels, almost losing balance, then incorporating that motion of constant falling into a complicated footwork style that can be seen "to embellish an expectation of failure and collapse . . . always already presumed in the case of both Black and/or queer bodies is a queer Black."[63] Freak technique is found in punking's taste for dances that revolt against the palatability of pretty aesthetics—dancers whipping, scratching, seizing, shrieking. Punking at Gino's played with abjection and transgressive capacities of the dance.

I was curious what Margarita meant by "studio people" who would think punking was too freeky and weird, so I asked her.

"You couldn't teach punking. Punking was not a professional dance. It's whatever came up. Punking came out of your spirit and your heart. Whatever you felt like doing at that moment—was punking." Tyrone's words came back to me, "They were living it, they didn't care about giving it a name." Questioning me back, Margarita was curious what I knew of waacking/punking's contemporary studio practice:

MARGARITA: Some teachers have labeled their dance moves. But I'm not sure about the syllabus of waacking and punking. I'm not sure if they have created a syllabus. You know? They have?

NAOMI: What do you mean, like different kinds of moves that go under that style?

MARGARITA: Yes.

NAOMI: People have their own . . .

MARGARITA: *Interrupting.* No I don't think so. Yeah. Uh huh. No. It's not a syllabus. *Never!* Today people are trying to own what happened yesterday, and that's such a big mistake. I think. I think that's what you call political. What's going on today is people wanna hijack. These dances. And market them. I totally respect business. I respect all that. But the truth is, since you are writing a story. I mean, nobody owned *ANY*thing.

Margarita's choice of *syllabus* is compelling as a term less common in the dance studio than in the university. The syllabus is the prescheduled order of an academic course, including rules, policies, and required texts, which Margarita associates with the studio and professional dance that would reduce punking from the fullness of experience queer people are living to a technical genre to be acquired as a preset lexicon of steps and moves. The syllabus points to the process of institutionalization that Margarita associates with marketing dance. She points me to tensions surfacing in waacking/punking's rebirth at the intersection of underground spirit and studio technique.

At this point in the interview she also shifts our power dynamic, turning to question me about what I know. Her comments throw light on my self-identifications and commitments, both as dancer and as academic who is implicated in a need to identify and put labels on the dance.

Reborn into the 2000s, waacking/punking was navigating a new context of the studio-trained dance industry professional who learns street-dances as part of the standard offerings among a roster of techniques. Susan Leigh Foster historicizes the studio, explaining, "Where the dance studio formerly institutionalized a community's process of transmitting the knowledge of dance, it now functions as the training ground for entry into the labor force of dance, replacing a community function with a market function."[64] A neoliberal discourse of the professional, she further argues, shapes a narrative of the individual dancer who must acquire mastery over techniques in a search for self-improvement or self-advancement. Professionalization arranges and presents techniques on a diverse menu of options, from which the contemporary dancer exercises freedom to choose. As Foster emphasizes, professionalization demands that the dancer demonstrate their ability to incorporate a "diversity" of genres without disrupting the hierarchical standard of ballet, ultimately reinscribing the Eurocentrism of the contemporary dance industry.

Waacking/punking was contending with being reduced to a label, queer dance included in a dancer's diverse repertoire yet detached—by Western aesthetic standards linked to operations of racial capital—from the less consumable, palatable, or governable experience of queer and trans* life. Rejecting the idea that punking might be apprehended under the terms of a syllabus, Margarita challenges claims of ownership and marketing that she associates with the studio.

Punking reorients her to a spirited sense of self-with-others, away from propertied relations of cisheterocoupling signified by the couple dancing she quickly rejects after her first time on Gino's dance floor—"*I* don't want to dance like this." She explains that studio dancers began coming into Gino's to find freedom in their dance, pointing to passed dancer Dallace Ziegler: "she opened up her spirit to punking . . . and what she was doing when she walked in wasn't as exciting as what she was doing towards the end of the night." In a 2013 interview, Dallace reflects on her experience of early waacking/punking culture, rejecting the idiom of family to describe the forms of relationality that developed among dancers: "We were all a cohesive unit, yes . . . but it was *not* a family dynamic like a House of Ninja, like Vogue is."[65] Her reflections dovetail with my description of waacking/punking kinethics as collectivities that opened dancers to experiment with moving together.

On the dance floor Margarita also experiences coming home to herself.

MARGARITA: Sometimes when I'm dancing I feel better than just having sex. Because I did it all myself.

NAOMI: *Laughing*. That's a quotable phrase.

MARGARITA: Without needing *anybody* to satisfy, anybody else. Without having to worry about how anybody else feels. Just doing something for myself that makes *me* feel good, and me satisfied. After a night of dancing and I'm driving home, I think about that and I think, I just *love* the feeling.

Punking gives Margarita complete access to herself, an intimacy her boyfriend cannot provide—an objectless love. Going to Gino's, Margarita practices self-loving, asserting her power to move beyond cisheteronormative constructs of beauty or coupled gender relations. As I listen to her story, dominant meanings of love, kinship, mental health, sexuality, and morality, secured through heteropatriarchy, are refused.

So I also want to talk about queer kinship and belonging as a way of being with self that is a radical self-possession—a practice of dancing alone that is not separate from belonging with and to others on the dance floor of Gino's punk rock commons. Kinethics reveal Margarita's pointed critique of a kind of "self that is in mastery over the world"—a self positioned in relation to waacking/punking as a technical challenge to be overcome.[66] This professionalized self can be made in the studio and marketed on the studio's terms, but rather than disrupting a Eurocentric aesthetic regime it is bound to be evaluated by the standards of that regime. Listening to Margarita's story of going to Gino's, I also feel familiarity, as an underground dancer, connecting to my experience of growing up in Los Angeles's queer nightlife. We both seek home and long for a sense of belonging that keeps returning us to the dance floor. What Margarita practices at Gino's is a way of finding herself that is also about finding home in queer kinship and the open invitation to experiment with form.

AT FAZIL'S (INNERLUDE)

What is Punking? It's a sweaty summer day sometime in the early 2000s. That morning I had been perusing a paper schedule for Fazil's dance studios. Those days I often visited New York during the summer to train, explore the dance clubs and the city, staying at a friend's house bordering Prospect Park in Flatbush and not far from the house where my father was raised when the neighborhood was home to largely middle-class communities of Italian and East European Jewish immigrants. Now West Indian immigrants are the predominant ethnic group. The area's diverse and changing composition continues to pose questions not only of race and ethnic but also of class divides, as the gentrification of New York City neighborhoods runs parallel with the commodification of black culture.

My eyes study the unfamiliar word printed in miniature on the paper schedule of classes. Punking—Instructor: Brian Green. Brian is well established in the global streetdance scene, an Ailey-trained dancer who has taught in all the major dance studios. A widely trained dancer who can as quickly break down a fast footwork flow as pull up into an arabesque. I finish breakfast and head to Fazil's in Midtown Manhattan.

I'm launching myself determinedly up four possibly five flights of steep wooden stairs—a rickety journey of devotion that's been intimately undertaken by so many dancers before me. I catch myself from doing a double take when Savion Glover brushes past me with a group of young guys. They jaunt casually down to the lower-level street entrance. Fazil's was just like that. Dance seeps out floorboard cracks blunted and creaky from the infinite fall of foot rhythms. Planked wood grimy with sweat and splinters. I wouldn't dare walk without shoes. Tap shoes, toe shoes, Pumas, Adidas. Hot city summers are prime time for young streetdancers traveling to New York to take classes, many from Japan.

What's Punking? My curiosity percolates as I step inside the small windowless room. A mirror lines one low wall. I am one of maybe five to seven students—the majority of us are Asian. We are all cis-presenting young women, ranging from early to late twenties, dressed in the obligatory training gear of streetdancers: loose-fitting cargo pants or sweats, oversize t-shirts, and floor-worn sneakers. Brian guides us through a choreographed sequence, and we group loosely around him, facing the mirror. He dances effortlessly, his limbs loosening their muscularity into sensuous arcs of motion that fall and softly enfold themselves within the music's gentle one-two beat. My shoes rub the ground-in grit tracing other dancers' work.

A piercing stare in my direction. Are you keeping up? Where's the rhythm? Our sweat lingers and congeals in New York City humidity. My eyes follow his weighted fall, with each one-two catch step turning and turning as I try to mimic the rhythm-loving curve of hips, a flirtatious wrist, a delicate head whip. My lips play with a smile. The dance flirts with me. I let go and feel a release. Punking tells me to soften.

After class I grab my water bottle and bag and make the trip down rickety wooden steps. I step out from studio heat into the hotter New York City summer. Leaving Fazil's, I have a sense of Punking that's more than the steps I repeat . . . a flirtation, a glance, a release into hip sway sensuality. I flirt with the dance's longing for me. I have yet to know Punking as a felt sense of place that dancers made for themselves collectively—a home within a dance. I have yet to go in, to feel myself within their dance.

* * *

WAACKING AND HIP HOP DANCE

Hip hop was built on this thing that happened called disco. . . . Black and Latino mobile DJs in New York that went around with they sound systems . . . inspired what became known as hip hop. In the beginning every other group was disco this, disco that . . . but another form of disco, not the commercialized Saturday Night Fever *kind of thing.*

—FAB 5 FREDDY

In August 1978, *Soul Train* dancers Cleveland Moses, Kirt Washington, Jeffrey Daniel, Jody Watley, and Tyrone Proctor were featured in a full-page color spread for an *Ebony* magazine special issue, highlighting the inventive fashions and twirling, dipping dance moves of Los Angeles's "New Generation" of black youth.[67] Shot at Maverick's Flat, the spread titles their story in bold: "The Outrageous Waack Dancers." Famed jazz, soul, and R & B musicians mixed with Hollywood celebrities and amateur artists at Maverick's Flat, located on Leimert Park's iconic Crenshaw Boulevard. Five minutes' walk down the 'Shaw was Total Experience, another club popular among dancers and rising funk, soul, and disco artists. The rare presence in print of the word *waack* ("an outrageous name we thought up," Jeffrey Daniel explains) marks the emergent style's circulation through early gay disco and high-profile black cultural spaces alike.

In this section, I show how waacking's queer/punk past blurs music and dance genre divisions that become attached to social constructs of race, gender, and sexuality. Dancers in the 1970s were crossing straight/gay social lines, blending stylistic gestures as they moved to music that blended stylistic genres. A long-standing relationship between disco and funk is less widely discussed, in no small part shrouded in the social stigma attached to disco music and gay identity and exacerbated in the wake of the AIDS epidemic, entrenched antiblackness, and homophobia. While funk has long been acknowledged as hip hop's precursor, a return to the promiscuity of music genres from which waacking/punking emerged ultimately shows the dance's early links to hip hop via gay dancers and disco culture. As waacking/punking and hustle gained visibility in 2000s hip hop/streetdance culture, dancers circulated their living knowledge of disco's cultural relationship to hip hop.

Ebony's document of youth dance cultures is likely what prompted dance historian Katrina Hazzard-Donald to make a decisive link between California and New York hip hop dance. In her cornerstone 1996 essay "Dance in Hip-Hop Culture," she writes, "Hip hop dance can be characterized in three stages: waack, breakdancing, and rap dance. Waack dancing appears in 1972. Dance moves such as locking . . . the robot, and the spank . . . were part of waack's outrageous style."[68] She classifies locking and robot as "dance moves" within waack style, a slip that likely arises from the televised mixing of black vernacular and social dances on *Soul Train*. While the Robot was a social party dance that often did combine with locking in everyday practice, both locking and robotting were also growing as separate lexicons, innovated by dancers building local movement vocabularies, cultural histories and rhythms of their own, as I noted in chapters 1 and 2.

More provocatively, however, Hazzard-Donald names waack as hip hop's progenitor—placing the dance genealogically prior to New York breakdance. Breaking's creation in the Bronx in the early 1970s is well established, controverting the essay's timeline. Still, the geographic connection she makes between East and West Coast cities is fundamental. Though the *Ebony* article and essay overlook waacking's association with gay disco culture, Hazzard-Donald's genealogy reveals a cultural crossover between locking and waacking that is key to reckoning with hip hop culture's queer lineages.

Hazzard-Donald inadvertently spotlights a conundrum of classification presented by waacking/punking, indirectly linked to racial-sexual politics of boundary keeping that underlie a funk/disco divide. Street-dancers generally associate dances with music genre: waacking emerges from disco; locking and robot emerge from funk. Funk has largely been considered hip hop's musical progenitor, meaning that locking and robot are likewise considered the funk progenitors of hip hop dance. Yet these distinctions have not been consistently maintained in the dances' cultural histories.

While DJ Michael Angelo crafted a disco soundscape for waacking/punking at Gino's, it was the *Soul Train* camera that first captured waacking/punking on syndicated television, where the music was often funk and soul. As stories of 1970s generation dancers attest, gay dancers were competing and performing in straight venues, prompting straight dancers to travel to gay discos, mixing dance styles in practice. Dancers were bringing waacking/punking from the discos onto the *Soul Train* Line—showing the dance alongside locking, robot, and the spank, in support of Hazzard-Donald's genealogy. Keeping with Muñoz's punk rock commons, waacking/punking can be seen to proliferate wild kinships of style. And regardless of what viewers may have thought they were watching, *Soul Train* was bringing gay black club cultures to international exposure at a time when black and gay were largely imagined antithetical.[69] While gay identity was not openly celebrated and Don Cornelius exercised control over the dancers' more flamboyant dress and makeup play, the show did support a fluid environment for dancers to display their outrageous style. The medium of dance as a form of identity experimentation, specifically, supported waacking/punking's wild gift in this early period of growth, as dancers inhabited one another's movements, trying out and trying on an unpredictable mix of movement styles.[70]

As disco music accelerated in mainstream popularity through the 1970s, and became more complex in terms of production processes, recording techniques, effects and engineering, abusive attacks on the genre were entangled with social policing that aimed to enforce an always already racialized gay/straight binary.[71] Disco music was critiqued on aesthetic lines across a range of contemporaneous communities, including white rockers, feminists, and funk, soul, and R & B musicians, who attached the absence of the live band to the death of the natural body. Disco was described as an artificial, manufactured, highly managed synthetic sound. Lightening the heavy tone and often overtly confrontational lyrics of funk, disco lyrics were sparse evocations of a ritualistic dance floor culture in which themes of sex, slavery, and demonic fire mixed with affective heat, fever, and ecstasy. Funk was often seen as the politicized black popular music of the period and positioned against "apolitical" disco.

Tavia Nyong'o complicates social implications of the gay/straight divide, arguing that the perceived threat presented by disco is its "disorganized modulation" of normative oppositional categories—a fear of same-sex desire but also the discomfort of disorganized heterosexual desire.[72] More than an essentially antigay stance, antidisco sentiment in the 1970s had to do with flipping the role of heterosexual masculinity from active to passive. The disco movement presented the idea that male bodies could be sexy and objectified, consolidating "a male demand for a return to the position of gazer rather than gazed upon."[73] Transferred in aural-kinesthetic-affective club space, disco's "oceanic feeling-tone" could open normative desires, whether in acts of singing, dancing, or both.

Normative conceptions of sexuality enmeshed with black power discourse, as well, staging queerness (figured as depoliticized and antithetical to blackness) as a crisis to authentic black masculinity (figured as always already heterosexual and politicized). Hip hop masculinity would become aligned with black power masculinity, upholding the racialized sexual binary that infused the language of genre: "disco killed the funk."[74] Discomfort with black queer politics played out less visibly as disco and the dances associated with it continued to take form, bringing dancers across social divides to experiment with identity and embodiment.

Hip hop came of age in 1980s New York. In the decade prior, hip hop culture's seeds were planted by breakers and party rockers dancing to early disco music that DJs manipulated through their innovation of cutting and scratching techniques.[75] Although waacking is performed in *Breakin'* and *Breakin' 2*, now considered classic 1980s hip hop films, the dance was not directly affiliated with hip hop, unlike the California "funk-style" dances of locking and popping, which both appear alongside waacking in the films. What appeared to be fixed genre classifications and straightforward lineages were more unruly in the context of people's everyday lives—where, why, and how people were actually moving to music. Waacking/punking's transit across social borders regulating gay/straight club life played a key though not consistently acknowledged role in the affiliation of 1970s California dances with New York hip hop.

Waacking/punking's embodied practice by dancers seeking to bring wider cultural recognition to the style has opened the door to more nuanced telling of hip hop dance histories. With the last two decades of waacking/punking's resurgence, these lineages have become more publicly recognized and discussed by hip hop culture practitioners. The everyday practiced kinship of dances has also set foundations for the emergence of streetdance as a contemporary global culture. Kinethics invite consideration of the nonlinear ways hip hop/streetdance lineages have formed in practice.

I am not arguing that waacking/punking is hip hop dance. I am saying that waacking/punking's kinship with hip hop dance via early disco music and gay culture is key. Though binary power hierarchies can be upheld by the language of genre, regulation and enforcement of social divides are not consistently maintained by the behaviors of dancers who move in and through cultural space. Despite a desire for neat origin narratives, people's lived experiences show the messy and wild kinships that re-create dancestries.

Borders can be used to protect identities as well as make them static and resistant to change. Drawing on border theory, put forth by Édouard Glissant as a poetics of relation, I am also suggesting that a border is not simply a wall that separates but a way to regulate difference in relation to an imposed standard—specifically, for waacking/punking, the double imposition of heteronormativity and antiblackness. The sonic-kinetic kinship of styles shows the *practiced* ambiguity of genre divisions, as such divisions reveal the historical entanglements of sexuality, gender, and race in how people actually *do* culture.[76]

The fluidity of waacking/punking histories continues to invite dancers to feel familiarity with others through the entanglements of movement practice. Dancers' desire to cross geographic, social, and aesthetic borders shows they were/are thinking relationally and, in practice, expanding their imaginations of who they could/can be.

RESOURCING FEMME-ININITY IN WAACKING

. . . queer as being about the self that is at odds with everything around it and it has to invent and create and find a place to speak and to thrive and to live.

—BELL HOOKS

Femininity does not belong to one body.

—ALOK VAID-MENON

By the 2000s a new generation of dancers was shaping waacking/punking style, reborn from 1970s gay discos and underground clubs into queer nightlife's afterlife.[77] As I noted earlier in the chapter, a global culture of competition and studio dance was increasingly centering technical styles, alongside a Hollywood entertainment industry enamored with dance reality shows and dance films. Transnational dance battles, competition choreography, and festivals promoted style categories like breaking, popping, locking, hip hop, house, and, increasingly, waacking—in a scene that was visibly male dominated. It wasn't until 2010 that Niki Tsappos and Martha Nabwire became the first women to be named hip hop dance world champions, winning Paris transnational battle event Juste Debout after "battl[ing] it out in numerous hip hop dance-offs against dudes . . . after dudes . . . after dudes."[78] Women in hip hop dance were also refashioning waacking/punking—trying on, trying out, and reinterpreting the movement materials of the style's 1970s queer and trans* progenitors—opening new possibilities to explore gender identity through dance.

This section spotlights waacking/punking's reinvention as a style category within global hip hop/streetdance culture of the early 2000s, looking to ways dancers continue to navigate the social reality of gender in shifting contexts. I put kinethics in conversation with black feminist, trans* feminist, and queer theory to focus on waacking/punking as queer kinship practice, resourced by dancers who shape and shift their experiences of gender in tension with social expectations.

Women and girls in hip hop shape their identity and belonging, which includes navigating choices of dress and ways of moving. In the 1990s and into the 2000s, b-girls typically dressed in less revealing clothing: tracksuits, baggy sweats, oversize T-shirts, sneakers.[79] With waacking/punking entering into a largely straight-cisgender oriented hip hop/streetdance culture, young women were entering battles twirling skirts that showed skin, posing in pantsuits that contoured hips and breasts, lips popping with color. They were dancing in heels, sequin bras, lace, and pearls, rustling across stages in floor-length feathers and fur. The spectacular clothing changes made a gender binary more visible, suturing an emphasized femininity onto women dancers' bodies.

Undoubtedly waacking/punking was putting a focus on women and girls—from grade-school-age through adulthood—allowing dancers to challenge the idea they must "cover up" or perform "like dudes" in order to show power. Yet gender-normative spaces could also reinscribe ideas of binary gender, invoked in dancers' language and effecting how they experience the dance. The style's passage into global hip hop/streetdance posed a challenge to new generations of dancers who confronted the systematic operation of the gender binary, with the potential to both secure and move beyond it.

Waacking/punking's 1970s innovators certainly challenged binary modes of self-presentation. They experimented expansively with possibilities of "femininity," moving beyond limited constructs of gender. Their cultural codes, abstracted in the style, transfer through time, such that even in their absent presence the social values of their lived experience "remain encoded in the dance" and continue to be activated through waacking/punking technique.[80] Not defined as spectacular mastery over form but felt in intimate experiences of longing to free the body, waacking/punking's ethics-aesthetic becomes a resource for expanding all dancers' potential sense of self.

Like clothing, a dancer's physicality and affect which she shapes in performances of technical skill need not attach to gender descriptors. Breaking trains rounded shoulders, curled-in chest, straight hips, a squared jaw, the signature crotch grab. In battle, hip hop draws out a hard stare, a weighted bounce on bent knees preparing to thrust forward, arms thrown in taunting curves through the air or wrapping the chest in a defiant pose. Critiquing cliché characterizations of breaking as "masculine," Imani Kai-Johnson studies "badass femininity" in gender performances of women breakers, acknowledging, "most of the b-girls that I have met claim femininity, even when they operate outside of social expectations of what femininity is supposed to be."[81] For Kai-Johnson, b-girls refashion movement materials presumed masculine, to perform a "strong, fierce, powerful" femininity.[82] The words *strong*, *fierce*, and *powerful* echo in the ways I've heard waackers describe the style, showing that women in hip hop can draw on multiple styles, including queer dance, to continue performing badass femininity. In this way, *queer* has the potential to move beyond gender identity and sexual practice, into political critique that unsettles gender and genre categories.

Attaching gender to fashion (and dance) is fraught, both revealing and obscuring dancers' experiences of self. While gender is not the only way dancers understood their artistic choices, they were certainly aware of the gendered aspects of identity in relation to being and belonging that a shift to waacking/punking presented. Dancers in the scene with whom I spoke often used gendered terms to highlight a transformation they were experiencing in relation to waacking. The move to abandon a pair of Adidas shell toes for platform stilettos provokes the question: how *does* waacking/punking work with and potentially unsettle gender norms?

When I asked what they valued most about waacking, I often heard some form of the response, "Waacking taught me how to be a woman." Their words were often heavy with emotion and expressions of gratitude for the dance. The prevalence of this sentiment suggests a shared understanding that "womanness" could be trained by apprenticing to waacking style—here personified as the dancer's teacher. It also suggests dancers' recognition of the ways gender is trained and culturally and socially constructed, rather than existing as a biological fact.

Leah Waackeisha McKesey attributes a change in her battling approach to her transition to waacking/punking style. "I felt I was missing something in my dance. I had too much popping, growing up battling guys so much. Showing them an aggressive tone like, 'yeah I'm a girl, but I have skills and I'll kick your ass.' I did that everywhere I went. [Waacking] helped me get into that femininity."[83] Waackeisha's badass femininity which she accesses through popping—an aggressive tone and physically confrontational moves—is transformed in waacking as the dance guides her into other dimensions of the feminine: "Waacking made me use my legs. Let people know, these are my curves. Curves I've never shared with people cuz I used to wear baggy pants. All the time. Big T-shirts. Waacking was a very, very special moment in my dance career for exercising my sexiness. To feel sexy? I was not used to sharing that with people. The Waackeisha you see now? Me dancing in underwear? Never did I dream that would be me."[84] Waackeisha associates her change in clothing and movement style with an intimate loving of her physicality, reflected in a shift in her language from showing aggression to sharing her curves and feeling sexy. In battle, Waackeisha's shivers and trembles tell of her exposure. She suggests a growing openness and vulnerability in connecting with people that I find compelling as a softening of a defensive investment in hip hop's philosophy of show and prove.

She also describes sexiness as a feeling she exercises and shares creatively—statements that work in dialogue with the black feminism of Audre Lorde, who articulates "uses of the erotic" that relate personal and social transformation:

> There are many kinds of power, used and unused, acknowledged or otherwise. The erotic is a resource within each of us that lies in a deeply female and spiritual plane, firmly rooted in the power of our unexpressed or unrecognized feeling . . . the power which comes from sharing deeply any pursuit

> with another person . . . forms a bridge between the sharers which can be the basis for understanding much of what is not shared between them, and lessens the threat of their difference.[85]

Waackeisha resources sexiness as a feeling and sharing of self-connection—a self she reinvents through waacking/punking practice. Black women dancers with whom I spoke also associated experiences of being misgendered from childhood with their desire to find themselves as a woman in waacking. In reflection of them, Waackeisha's gift of sharing a feeling of sexiness is also an intimate practice of self-care and self-love that goes beyond "a matter of personal self-expression," as Omise'eke Natasha Tinsley writes: insisting on "the importance of expressing a black femmeness, curviness, bejeweled-ness, open-thighed-ness that never has to be erased," including when dancing in underwear.[86]

Waacking finds Waackeisha in her practice of a reinvented dance that resources feelings of femininity. Growing in a womanness that needs not desire normative femininity, Waackeisha flexes codes of a historically male-dominated cultural scene as a girl and woman in hip hop, shifting identities between b-girl Leah McFly and waacker Waackeisha. Yet, her dance styles go beyond always-already assumptions of the categories of girl and woman, for Waackeisha dreams up the same pleasure to name who she is that brings Tinsley to ask with regard to Ezili ("the lwa of the black femme function")—"isn't it best just to call her Manbo Metres Ezili Freda Daome, and to try to understand all the complexities that entails?"[87]

These feelings do not require a binary gender to exist. As collective practices, waacking/punking kinethics call on all dancers to feel queer kinship with the style's dancestors, while also finding self-connection in relation to femme-ininity not attached to binary gender. Marcia Ochoa offers a framework they call "the accomplishment of femininity" to study the discourses, techniques and technologies that cisgender and transgender women share: "not because any of these people were miming the other but rather because all were using similar symbolic resources to produce and perform femininity." [88] Black feminist work, Kai M. Green writes, has "challenged us to consider the limitations of the gender binary and made us think about how Black cisgender women in particular have always already functioned as excess of that category, making it necessary to trouble the usefulness of the category 'woman' in the first place."[89] Following Sojourner Truth, Green presents the meeting of black feminism and trans* feminism as a gift that provides us with resources to explore the question of being-woman. Their critique is generative for finding waacking's significance not in gender-normative performances of "woman" but instead in the less easily seen or identified feelings that dancers learn from the style.

Still, cishetero relations set conditions of possibility for a cultural scene in which outright transgressions of the gender binary are rare and cisgender self-presentation is the norm. In a cultural context where performances are literally taught and judged, the language of gender could also be used as a rubric of social control—taking away its potential for political critique by reinscribing the category of "woman" onto an assigned-female body. Stakes rise in the battle arena, where community approval is mired in decisions of respected judges (who are also community members), whose opinions carry weight, affecting competition, training, and teaching practices. Attending battles in the 2010s, I would at times hear judges instruct the few guys entering the waacking round to dance "like a man" or "be more masculine"—then adding that the "women" should dance like "women." The presence of cismale bodies doing waacking suddenly threw into relief the operating assumption that "femininity" belonged to cisfemales. In the face of a judge/dancer hierarchy—a relation that centers visual power in the role of judge as observer versus dancer as performing body—a dancer's order to perform binary gender roles for an audience of observers effectively identifies and controls gender variance and delegitimizes queerness, regardless of the participant's gender orientation. Likewise, for dancers seeing the possibility to learn "womanness" from waacking/punking, the reinforced binary gender understanding limits the expansive power of such practices by retraining the idea that "femininity" is an innate attribute of bodies assigned female at birth.

No matter a judge or teacher's gender or sexual orientation—because gender binary trauma can be reproduced by straight and gay dancers alike—such comments evoke anxiety over compulsory gender binary identification and cisgender heteronormativity in general. Marlon M. Bailey has similarly pointed to the judging operation in the Ballroom scene for voguing, which, despite its celebration of gender-fluid performance, can also reinscribe normativity: judges "apply and adhere to these criteria, often conflat[ing] notions of anatomic femaleness and maleness with performance and presentation," and then participants "[end] up reinscribing and relying upon these same norms to view and judge each other within the community."[90] Cisgendering of movement secures gender boundaries to counteract an embattled history of racialized sexualities, obscuring how a normative gender and sex binary bolsters (white) heteropatriarchal power.

A young black woman in her late twenties recalled her fraught entry into waacking from hip hop dance, explaining: "One of my teachers told me I was too masculine. You're a girl, you should look like a girl. . . . He told me you will never be able to dance like a girl. I always dressed like a guy. If I didn't have waacking, I would still be not knowing how to be a woman. . . . We have the power that we don't use. It taught me how to use my power and be confident that I'm a girl and it's okay."[91] Her reflection on practice reveals the ways gender works as a rubric of social control, limiting her possibility of being-woman under her teacher's patriarchal surveillance and disciplining of her dress and dance style. Yet, her words—"We have the power we don't use"—echo Lorde's naming of an inherent sense of power, previously unused. If reoriented to the collective call of waacking/punking's dancestors, such erotic power moves an experience of being girl/being woman beyond the terms of patriarchal power and the policing of a cisgender binary, embracing a spectrum of possibilities.

In our interview she went on to describe this different kind of power that has remained unused as "flow and a subtle feeling." Her felt consciousness of power echoes descriptions of watery flow that I find compelling as they diverge from the often-used phrase "striking with force" that describes more muscular performances of waacking. This power she resources in relation to waacking becomes a practice of "knowing how to be a woman." She exercises this power—while not experienced as un/gendering or maintained within fraying limits of binary gendered language—through her "practice and grace" of interpretation.[92]

Reggie Prince Lavince Seale reflects on his battle and club experiences, nuancing the ways dancers name and use power in waacking. As I noted in events of battle judging, the gender binary was often complicated more visibly for men dancing waacking/punking, and Reggie spoke to his struggle finding belonging in waacking/punking as a gay African American male. His experience is critical to put in dialogue with those of women and girls, as he expands gender categories in the same way that waacking/punking's dancestors carefully crafted "femininity" beyond binary gender socialization.

Battling in the early 2000s streetdance scene, Reggie found himself challenging battle judges' demands that he dance with more power: "Breakdancers do power moves . . . I'm not [that] kind of power person. I am powerful. I have strength. My power comes in my connection to the music. I can hear things people will not normally hear. That's how I beat people, in that power. I'm a very flowy kind of person. My hands are like water. I'm able to express the music more when I'm softer, rather than hitting everything like a pin needle. Light like a feather."[93] Reggie insists that power doesn't always require shows of muscular athleticism. His articulation of power surfaces sense knowledges—sound, movement, touch—that tend to be backgrounded to visual power and more striking spectacles of breaking (and waacking) performance. Likening his waacking style to the flow of water and a feather's airborne ease, he enhances these erotic sensibilities stylistically by connecting to music. His references to water and flow are especially potent, considering that water can appear as a gentle and completely permeable substance, yet its associated qualities of flow, slipperiness, and heaviness enable it to be an extraordinarily destructive mobile force.

Reggie connects power to the sense of freedom that he reaches for kinesthetically in his self-styled approach to waacking, which he places outside the normative masculinity he attributes to breakdance kinesthetics: "I feel more empowered doing waacking as a gay male . . . when I waack I have some type of power. It's like how when you breakdance it makes you feel like yeah, I'm a man . . . I feel free and like I have some type of power." His words echo a refiguring of power that scholar Darieck Scott approaches by describing black power as an abject status: "I want to talk about that which is not-power according to the ego-centric (and masculine and white) 'I' definitions we have of power, but which is some kind of power, if by power we mean only ability, the capacity for action and creation in one or several spheres, be they internal or external to the empowered."[94] Reggie's experience shows how within the dance community, normative assumptions of muscular "power" can become coded language for reinforcing masculinity on assigned-male bodies.

Reggie also disarticulates gender expectations from a definition of power in his waacking practice that challenges his childhood experiences of socialization: "Growing up I always felt weak being a gay man. I didn't play football. I'm not a man. I don't have any power. You're a sissy boy. [With waacking] I have control over the people watching me . . . it feels so good to walk inside the club and everybody's just staring at you with your awesomeness and the music. Keep looking at me I don't care." The control Reggie exercises does not manifest as guarded defensiveness but is a working with power, felt as a capacity to direct the gaze of the club crowd. He contrasts the power practice honed in waacking/punking with his childhood knowledge of power as something that divides "man" from "sissy boy" by enforcing a hegemonic masculinity—football as manly and gay identity as bound to effeminacy and a feeling of weakness.

Reggie's description of entering a straight club in 2013 dovetails with Shabba Doo's story, earlier in the chapter, of encountering Andrew's "flamboyantly feminine" presence during a straight dance contest in 1973: "Everyone sits *stunned* in the room. No sound. That's how it was in *that* room. The world stopped. He's doing this, and he's not doing it for any applause. He's just doing his thing."[95] Fiona Buckland offers a critique of currencies of the fabulous and fierce—a desire to look extraordinary and practice moving through space to command attention.[96] Andrew and Reggie both practice the erotic power to be looked at, which is also the erotic power to be fierce. Andrew's gender-expansive dancestry touches Reggie in the present, as they both refuse a world's refusal to care for them, feeling pleasure in opening fully to being gazed on. Practicing erotic power, Reggie finds waacking/punking kinethics that refuse to enact hegemonic gender and sexuality.

Not a direct challenge to gender policing or social constructions of binary gender and sex, waacking/punking practice nonetheless gives the potential of feeling a more expansive sense of woman and feminine. Dancers explore this capacity as a gift of reinterpreting the movements of waacking/punking's queer and trans* dancestors. They find and celebrate themselves in waacking/punking, highlighting a coded femininity that is queer—even while the codes are read through a binary lens.

Clothing is another layer of this practice that adds to the ambivalence of queer kinethics. Battle fashion crafts sensual identities to augment dancers' reinterpretations of movement style. Costuming often reinscribes a cisgender aesthetic of palatability, even if waacking/punking invites all dancers to access and perform the feminine as a somatic experience of power felt from within that doesn't rely on externally imposed markers. An aesthetic regime of beauty is reinscribed, not only on women's but on all bodies, in which visual markers (race, sexuality, gender, size, able-bodiedness) are constantly shifting to frame the degree to which a dancer's performance of "woman" appears appropriate and palatable to those watching them.

The rebirth and reinvention of waacking/punking style in the 2000s have shifted the dance from more gender fluid queer nightlife spaces to newly open space for women's gender performances in global hip hop/streetdance. Waacking/punking has created a platform for women and girls to gain visibility and expand a sense of their power and freedom to move and find self-connection within a male-dominant scene. Within these changing contexts, a cisgender binary has also been variously enforced, challenged, and kept intact.

Waacking does not escape the real-life impacts of gender policing and reinforcement of social division in club, battle, class, or other cultural spaces. Linked with a queer/punk past, the dance exposes the fragility of the social fabric with which dancers constantly contended and still contend. For black women who collectively refuse the prerogative of normative gender, waacking/punking emphasizes intimate encounters with the feminine beyond a normative construct of being-woman. Putting their practice into conversation with black feminism and trans* feminism is important to complicate the possibilities and limits of the dance.

It's vital to talk about the feminine beyond gender, in ways that do not limit understandings of sexuality and the body. There are also radical ways that terms like *woman, girl, feminine*, and *female* can be expanded and opened up as part of the necessary work of undoing. Part of the power of longing to free the body is transforming the categories that have been imposed, that we want to live beyond, and that we often can't live without. Kinethics as collective movement practices of queer kinship resource a power that is yet elusive. They give waacking/punking as a resource for imaginative world-building artistic practices of dancers who undo patriarchy and are yet undone.

LOSSED

I've never gotten lost in my dance like I remember getting lost in waacking.
—BILLY GOODSON

"This is what I did the moment I got back from Russia," Tyrone states.[97] I bounce on the passenger seat of his white 2001 Mercedes sedan, inhaling leather and varnished wood. I allow my eyes to glide the distance of the console, following the flourish of Tyrone's hand.

For Tyrone, getting into the driver's seat is a choreography that lasts several minutes. More when he is in severe pain. He bends his head down first, then launches his whole body forward. *Pause. Breathe.* Next, he rotates his torso and pelvis in slow motion, returning to vertical. There he tilts. Legs, pinned together, jut at an acute angle to the door. *Pause. Breathe.* A matter-of-fact look passes over his face. Then he moves. The third sequence begins with both hands grabbing and lifting his right leg. Without embellishment, he maneuvers the leg into place and proceeds to grab and lift his left leg in a parallel manner. *Pause. Breathe.* The task is finished. Tyrone pulls up in his seat, straightening his back. Again, the look. Unwavering, his hands release their grip. Finally, he rests.

A moment of silence.

Now we are ready to depart. Tyrone's controlling the music. "Do you want to ride in my Mercedes boy . . ." Singing gaily, we begin a five-hour car ride to the DC suburbs where my family lives. Despite my concern, Tyrone has insisted on driving and I've learned it's best to follow along.

We've come to the outskirts of town. The highway's gray expanse is gradually fading to dark in the still-chilly early springtime breeze. The road narrows, twisting with fields that roll and blur into clumps of trees. Occasional houses sprinkle their little warm glows outward to the road.

"What's next?" Tyrone's tone is antsy, my reverie interrupted.

I'm trying to find our location, and my Wi-Fi's not working.

"I'm not really sure," I answer Tyrone hesitantly.

Silence.

I quickly reenter my home address and press "search." The pinwheel spins hypnotically, and my mind wanders. *Does anyone really know what happened . . . where they've gone?* I recall the layers of urgency in Tyrone's voice. He'd recited the list of names again at my request, after I'd grasped for my pocket notebook and pen—a well-rehearsed move. This time I'd been determined to commit their names to written memory.

"They *say* they're going to do this. That *I* have to find them." The voice registers indignation, as if talking to a very bothersome person. "Well why don't *you* go find them!"

No results found.

"I forgot my family lives so far out." I steal a glance sideways at Tyrone. He looks straight ahead.

"It was just me, Archie, and Willi in the hospital room with the nurse." He breathes in deep and lets it out, reviving Willi Ninja's last breath.[98]

"You know who I can hustle with better than anyone in the world? You'll never guess." *A long pause.* "Archie . . ." The lilt of his tone and careful pacing of words allow me in. Darkness. Sweat. A pulsing dance floor across which flicker flash of spirit moves. The music's no longer coming to you. It's washing over you. I'm suddenly imagining Tyrone and Archie *twirling* the dance floor, their height, build, and skin tone meshing—balancing the weight of their body, moving tightly, arms interlocked then separating and leaning away. How beautiful to move with the whole weight of loving embrace, revolving moons magnetized to a common center, pressing into each other's soft places, intimating a flesh movement that's all but a blur for those who sneer.

"They raped them." The voice flattens. Tyrone's moved on to another story. This time *Paris Is Burning*. "You know those young boys died with nuh. Thing. Nuh. Thing." He tells me they'd wanted to film Breed of Motion, but he refused. "What would I want to have to do with that fucking film." The words slice, and I find myself falling silent, words kited across a hollow terrain of feeling, lost in the corridors of spirit. I let go of my questions. Their testimony washes me over. The voice has to get out whatever it is, so I wait, listening.

A soft sigh.

"I'm really crazy, I can get very crazy at times . . ." the voice mists up the gathering darkness. A nervous giggle escapes out the side of my mouth.

"It's *not* funny." The voice sharpens.

My throat closes around a ballooning giggle.

"Maybe we took a wrong turn," I concede.

"Okay, well you just figure that out."

Tyrone releases his foot slightly from the accelerator. His hand briefly clutches his left thigh. I take peripheral note of the fleeting movement—a secreted gesture that's become familiar to me.

"You know," the voice suddenly interrupts my thoughts again. "You know this is really just wonderful. I just love this. Don't you just love this? I'm just having so much fun! Oooo! *Honey!*"

Sometimes Tyrone's manner switches from annoyed to ecstatic, commanding to generous, provocative, loaded with innuendo. "Put it in there *honey*. No! I said *shove* it in there. No. You've got to shove it *in*!" He has everyone laughing at his antics. "That's Arthur. I'm channeling Arthur."

Sometimes, many times, I'd felt them there with us. Especially when he'd go on a rant. Maybe that's why at times I sensed melancholy, like he was possessed by restless spirits. Most often I would hear dancers call them down in triumvirate—Arthur, Andrew, Tinker. The legendary first-generation stars of waacking/punking. Other times the list would bloom, and I'd find myself searching for my pen again, scribbling the scroll of names in an attempt to keep pace with the dancer's reminiscence. I keep writing until the repetition of their names assumes a rhythm of its own.

"My world is empty without you, babe . . ." Tyrone sings out, explaining that there was no specialty music for gay people in the '60s. Except for Diana Ross.[99] "The reason they connected to her was because when you hear her voice sing these songs it was a bit over the top. Straight people liked her, but they didn't really, really, really like her. It was her tone. She had a gay persona. She knew how to use it . . ."

The sounds from the car stereo blare and insist. They feel luxurious as Tyrone's leather seats. Underground disco is completely different, more akin to deep house, with its scatty nasal vocals, twinkling melodies, and thick horn loops. This is music for lovers and dancers. Bass lines syncopate against a steady kick drum or shaker's rapid fire. The music pillows me, and I feel that dry ice smoke lights clamp teeth feeling. Each songstress warms and wraps me close with clear-toned chords cascading through electronic melodies. They generate sequin glitter like sunlit oceans. The light froths up, forming droplets on wave crests coming back over and over to shore.

"What year is this?"

"Hmmm. Maybe '76? '77? Michael Angelo would play a plethora of songs. Top 10. Scorpio. Disco Connection. They would say things like, 'baby, the beats in Voyage! Oh my god! Those beats are the way!' He would go back years before and reintroduce songs that were flops, like 'Sweet Lucy.' That's what made him the greatest DJ on the West Coast at that time. He was trying to figure out what kind of songs will get these bitches on the floor."

"Has anyone ever tried to find them?" My eyes search the passing trees. It's just occurred to me—*what if this whole time they've been right here . . . with us?*

I pause my spinning thoughts, straining my eyes at blurry trees clutching darkness. "I'm not sure . . . I think this place is sort of starting to feel familiar?"

"I said I didn't want any part of it. Leave. Me. *ALONE*!" Sometimes I'm not sure if it's Tyrone speaking or someone else. I'm not sure who I'm hearing. And I definitely wasn't sure if he was talking about someone else who pissed him off or about me. In fact it felt pretty much ambiguous on purpose.

"They take everything from me. All they want to do is take. All *anyone* wants to do is take." I breathe in and feel the reprimand resounding in my ears.

Are you really, really serious?! They might not even be . . . ? But I can't write about this without even knowing? I mean . . . I can't say they're gone and . . . what if they're not?

I edge the pointer back and forth over my map. "I think we should just keep going in this direction," I conclude.

Tyrone's words whip air between us, jolting me from my task at hand.

"Did you ever think maybe they don't *want* to be found?"

TOUCHED

Lightning is a reaching toward, an arcing dis/juncture, a striking response to charged yearnings.

—KAREN BARAD

When you infuse your life experience into dance, dance becomes more beautiful than just the outside form. Get in touch with that thing.

—ARCHIE BURNETT

"Did you ever think maybe they don't *want* to be found?"[100] Tyrone's pointed question brings me back, momentarily, from my search for direction. "I'm very, what's the word . . . I'm trying to find the feeling . . ."

"Sad?"

"No."

"Melancholy."

"No. Different from that."

"Angry."

"No. It's bitter. I'm just very bitter."

Swallowing the sharp edges of his words, I began to think of the way he gulped soda like it's going out of style. Coke was the only liquid I had ever seen Tyrone drink. I'd point to dietary studies connecting overconsumption of sugar to joint stiffness, and still he'd refuse water. Now we'd lost our way on a five-hour car ride that was turning out to be less about getting me home safe to my bio-family and more about finding my queer dancestors in waacking/punking history. I was beginning to sense the ways Tyrone contended with their loss as a psychosomatic condition that is collective.

Tyrone pointed me to a fraught articulation of feeling, entangled in his struggle with loss and with being found in waacking/punking's rebirth. He had shared with me his ambivalence about returning to the dance world as a teacher and oral historian of this dance. The stillness in Tyrone's hips, highlighted in my telling—my rasanblaj of waacking/punking's queer history—signifies loss and longing in complex ways, no less of mourning dancestors than of articulating a practiced, sometimes painful, effort to celebrate them.

Tyrone reoriented me to the emotional labor of queer kinship, of feeling constantly moved by the spiritual weight of dancestors to whom he expressed an obligation of danscendance: "When I dance waacking . . . I reach back into my past. . . . I feel that all of my mentors have to have a place in dance. I try my best to resurge them."[101] His story also mirrors Scoo B Doo's backward dance that concluded chapter 1; as first-generation dancers and carriers of legacy, they both had experienced a kind of rebirth into global streetdance in the 2000s. To borrow Julian B. Carter's phrasing, "re-memory is hard," meaning that the intergenerational work of danscendance is experienced differently for dancers who carry living memories of the dance in its historical contexts.[102] The collective practice of mourning dancestors is entangled with sustaining queer kinship with our dance elders who are still here.

Transitioning from 1970s queer nightlife into 2000s global streetdance culture, waacking/punking's afterlife materializes in danscendance as practices of intergenerational healing. AB Brown finds such work to be concerned with "belonging to a genealogy of resistance, community, and support," meaning that the afterlife of queer nightlife sustains relations "not only to people of different ages, different ways of moving, bodily abilities, desiring, and coming together, but to time and history themselves."[103] Connecting black queer history to waacking/punking dancestries is intergenerational work.

Finding ourselves in queer history extends the unfinished intergenerational work of helping our dance elders live, knowing that transforming their loss from private to public comes also with distress, unease, discomfort, envy, bitterness. For dance elders, moving, traveling, remembering, retelling is often physically difficult work. Tyrone revealed his kin labor in touch during fleeting moments when he'd move a hand to his legs, the grip traveling silently from thigh to jaw to eyes, looking into the distance. His question posed to me—*Did you ever think maybe they don't want to be found?*—resounds an "ethics of relation emergent in queer nightlife" and its afterlife.[104] Adding punking to waacking protects the dance's black queer past and the dancestors who have passed, so we don't lose them.

Kinethics refuse the ongoing disappearance of black queer and trans* people from dance histories and contemporary practices of waacking/punking. Dancers describe feelings of going in and getting lost, acts of reaching, touching, and being touched, that are part of waacking/punking's expansive experimental practice. These ethics-aesthetics are also transferred in dancers' practices of shared presence, of dancing queer and trans* dancestors, given in the dancers' gift of interpreting them.

Gestures of self-touch are common in waacking/punking—the back of a hand gently caressing cheekbones, fingers feeling up fleshly contours of thighs, hips, belly, slipping across the chest to end in a tight embrace.

Archie describes his approach when teaching punking elements of the dance: "The hips . . . then if they're that daring. After the hips, I start with caressing of the face. For men it would be like a fist on the head here . . . maybe a whole hand on the head here. Maybe against the face. Maybe a hand on the shoulder. Maybe come across the chest. Then maybe I can make them start to use the hands differently."[105] Billy Goodson connects Archie's studio pedagogy to the stage and the club, recalling the moment he touches Andrew as they pass each other in solo sequences onstage at Caesars Palace, during Diana Ross's 1979 performance of "Love Hangover": "I remember running down the stairs. Andrew had the next solo. I always knew, don't throw your energy all over him. Because I played football. I'm big. *Don't invade.* Just caress the back of his jacket and let him take off into his stratosphere. It reminded me of just that kind of sharing we had for each other in the club."[106] Ablaze in circles of light and a glittering backdrop of streamers, the sequence is one of the only visual archives circulating of the stars of waacking/punking, and it's spectacular. Barely visible in their explosion of movement, yet returning in Billy's memory, the fleeting caress connects the high-profile entertainment stage of Caesars Palace to the dark of Gino's dance floor—an expansive intimacy that Billy gives as he tempers his football player physicality with the sharing of soft touch.

Billy deeply knows to express touch in ways that undo invasive acts of gender socialization, which both recall Reggie's trouble with football and become thrown into relief in dancers' critiques of studio industry dance. David Johnson is an Oakland-born dancer who came up through 1990s hip hop and trained in Hollywood. He describes a liberating shift into finding black nonbinary identity in waacking movement that rebels against predictable form:

> Gender was forced onto me in Hollywood. Waacking said fuck you. This is what dance is. Free and liberated. I identified and gravitated towards it. Industry dancing wants you to make them money and be marketable. Tyrone uses [dance] as a tool to expand your expression. He uses choreographed phrases as exercises, for the dance to register in your body—not to say "look like me when you stand in the mirror," which is the format and formula that's expressed in every dance studio today. Emotionally it put me in a fucked-up state. Going into a jazz class and being told, "guys, you need to dance like men." Waacking was rebellious. I felt free . . . touching my face feels flirty and it feels like "come join me."[107]

David allows me to consider touch as a longing to free the body, inviting intimate connection in ways that refuse the violent management of nonbinary embodiment and queer relationality. Hapticality, or love, Stefano Harney and Fred Moten write, is "the capacity to feel through others, for others to feel through you, for you to feel them feeling you."[108] Hapticality is a fleshly feeling expressed in the ways dancers feel queer kinship as they become touched by their queer and trans* dancestors.

What I came to see is how waacking/punking's dancestors live through the dance. It's not only the geographic locations but also our body that stores memories of waacking/punking. The dance for Tyrone was a queer black history he lived as felt intensities of loss, joy, bitterness, and love. He called up and moved with these intensities constantly, allowing the dancers to be intimately a part of him, to be touched by his dancestors. As Tyrone shows me Andrew, Arthur, Tinker, he invites me to join their dance and their dance touches me. These fleshly flirtations surface a longing to feel through others living on in waacking/punking danscendances.

This process of danscendance is not frivolous. Doing this work is less about a dancer's mastery of technique, than about their commitment to the expansive experiment of being/becoming dancestors. The gift of interpretation is incomplete and undone, allowing the dance to change our recognition of who we are in unfolding relation with them.

To be touched is to move with a freak technique that allows Margarita to growl and *let it out!* on the dance floor, knowing her power to satisfy no one but herself is her way of finding belonging alone in queer kinship. Margarita emphasizes: "I don't think we were crazy. We took it serious. Our craziness was seriously crazy."[109] To be touched is also how we find our divinity.

This capacity to be touched emerges when dancers open their dance to the genre of refusal found in the punk rock commons and "the enduring habit of transforming oneself through significant loss into something desirable, vulnerable, and fierce" that is freak technique.[110] It is possible that dancers become most devoted to queer kinship when they invite a promiscuous mix of genres that allow a spiritual coming-out of dancestors as a gift of interpretation. In mourning their loss, danscendance means unfixing categories that have been used to deny their existence, where they move in ways more than *woman* or *feminine* could describe, where they find beauty in the infinite play of the universe, where they answer Tyrone's question by refusing to be found.

It's just as true that waacking/punking's most compelling nonperformances of danscendance are about deeply getting lost, "almost never recognized . . . not much noticed."[111] Billy recalls such a moment at the dance festival StreetStar in Sweden, when he suddenly came across a dancer alone in a room waacking: "It was just him getting lost in him. It wasn't about a dance class. It wasn't about anything you learned. It wasn't that aspect of the dance. It was something else. I don't know how you resolve that or how you fill that void."[112] Getting lost in punking also describes an ethic of unknowing the dance that can't be about learning anything. The refusal to be found allows infinitesimal possibilities of moving, which escape definition and codification.

In getting lost, dancers forge this bond between the living and the dead—a bond that is core to danscendance. Getting lost finds different forms of belonging and familiar intimacy, of being touched by spirits. The dance's passed progenitors reach into their future, longing to touch those who reach into their past. Their unfound movement may also get lost in longing to feel whatever you feel and release whatever you have to let go of on the dance floor.

Bedtime Story

I've been listening to artists speak of gardens. It was the beginning of a new year when I signed in to my pandemic grief group, a regular online gathering that bloomed in the beginning of 2020 from a pledge of love given in concert by a community of activists, artists, and thought leaders, who through counsel, prayer, testimony, song, and collective witness materialized the powerful antidote of locating ourselves (personally-politically-socially-historically) in the unpredictable balance of ongoing death and movement toward life. With lyrics woven from Malkia Devich-Cyril's opening sermon, Abigail Bengson led us in song: *The future is the garden of the past. First imagined in the dark. Planted in the dark. I'll meet you in the garden.* We sang, and I remembered a few weeks earlier stepping into *Cosmic Garden*, an immersive installation in green set inside a mobile shipping container designed by Holly Bass and Maps Glover. The *Cosmic Garden* was part of their ongoing collaboration *Double Rainbow: Future Archives*, in which the artists stage, perform, document, and therein create their place in a previously undocumented lineage of DC black performance artists.[1]

In this pandemic context of collective loss and distended mourning, acts of planting—turning over soil, seeding, plotting, growing life underground, in the dark—make fertile metaphors for building liberated lifeworlds. Contemporary artists are reaching into the archive to find themselves in histories they reimagine and reinvent to grow their legacy, which future artists can pick up and pass on. They describe archiving projects they're planting now in soil persistently turned over, seeds chosen with care.

Planting is a process by which we reach into our pasts to know ourselves in the movement, which is to say the breath, of our dancestors—"to resurge them," Tyrone tells us. To resurge is neither to replicate nor to master their movement. Resurging simply means we practice our past and with our passed. To feel comfort in knowing we're not unprecedented. That's what it means to be in the shared presence of dancestors.

To find ourselves in history is also slow and careful practice, beginning to reimagine the archive that has functioned to extract, reduce, objectify, classify, itemize, order, measure, count, erase. To be able to tell stories, to critically fabulate, borrowing from Saidiya Hartman's body of work, is also what it means to prepare the "undoing of the plot."[2] The poethical undoing of ethical indifference, to borrow Denise Ferreira da Silva's words.[3]

Ethical principles, Sylvia Wynter says, are the seeds of domination.[4] Kinethics extend poethics, embedding aesthetic principles that subvert domination's ethics. They foster dancing kinships that return dancers to legacies they keep growing. Returning to the garden of the past, turning over the soil of the plot, replanting the garden are metaphors for the work of preparing a radical imagination to sustain life.

Once there were dancers who imagined themselves in movement. They felt rhythms growing in the darkness within them. They were children at the time they began to imagine their dances. They reached for their community's traditions, and their rhythms grew. They got involved in one another's movements, and their dances wandered, flowing in the currents of black social life that moved them. They listened with the sounds around, watched over one another in schoolhouses, backyards, and house parties. They moved themselves in their rhythms, entangling in the darkness of the clubs. They tuned in to struts, leans, rolls, poses, strikes, that told them secrets of how to be. They danced, and the secrets they breathed freely became embedded within the body of their dance.

They were not crusaders. They didn't have a grandiose statement to make, yet they made statements. They most longed to impress one another. Their dances were pledges of love to one another. They belonged to themselves yet found themselves in one another. Their artistry was not seen as significant, yet they were seen by one another. They unearthed their movement, found hiding in the open secret of their everyday surroundings. They grew in style, keeping watch over one another, breathing their dances in darkness growing lifeworlds.

Their future archive will begin with weeds with root systems stringent, resilient, pushing underground, hiding in dark soil. They will always grow out of place, scattered among the cultivated plants yet following a system of their own. The gardens they will plant will be seen as overgrown. Wild, their dances persistently keep growing. They will creep around corners. They will lean back to recognize monstrous beauty and flesh movements of lower creatures. Their dances will steal away from what's been deemed too beautiful to ever be reimagined. They will be too beautiful to never be reimagined.

The dancers whose movement stories shape the body of this book were youth at the time they began planting—children as young as grade-school age who imagined worlds by taking the form of silent stars, skeletons, and goddesses. They fell on the One, twirled their bodies to four-on-the-floor. They attended neighborhood talent shows, stayed up late nights in living rooms. They showed out on film sets and kept watching over one another. The dances they tend are their legacy, careful plantings of future archives, passed on in dancestries and danscendances.

This book remembers a small part of their collective project, reaching back into their hidden histories to reimagine future archives. This project traces the ethics-aesthetic in dance practices that will have seeded-imagined a world otherwise.

Their dances shape ways of knowing how to be. They teach us to open, to soften, to empty. They teach us to give away and give up. They teach us how to break. They teach us how to resist. They teach us how to fall. They teach us how to be held and be whole. In dancing, we shape our body into gestures, postures, breath, that give us access to the ethics secreted within the dance.

In the last two years, many dancers passed. Some were dancers with whom I conversed over years, listening to their stories and tending to their words, writing and rewriting, revising, looking for the hidden meanings they were telling collectively. As I interpret their stories, a circle takes shape, into and out of which dancers fall. This circle is a ritual work simultaneously of celebration and of mourning.

The dances that seed this book are their common project. This book reimagines their art as the garden to which generations of dancers return to grow future archives. Going into the garden, turning over the soil, preparing the ground for life. The ways of knowing-being-becoming-belonging found in their dances are seeds for a world that's growing now. This book calls for more of their stories.

NOTES

Damita's Solo Flight

1. "HER-story 'Damita Jo Freeman' Soul Train Dancer Receives an Appreciation Award," YouTube video, posted by God Bless Hip Hop, September 11, 2013, 11:34, https://www.youtube.com/watch?v=EKObcjkon_A

2. *Soul Train* began broadcasting live in Chicago, Illinois, in 1970.

3. "The 'Outrageous' Waack Dancers," *Ebony*, August 1978, 64–68.

4. Joe Tex's performance career interanimated Brown's in curious, at times intensely combative, ways. For an insightful reading of Tex and Brown's relationship, see Hanif Abdurraqib, *A Little Devil in America: Notes in Praise of Black Performance* (New York: Random House, 2021), 223–37.

5. Music scholar Steven F. Pond follows the growth of jazz-funk in the reciprocal creative process between musicians and dancers, citing Damita's solo dancing in dialogue with the always highly anticipated performances of the *Soul Train* dancers that closed out each episode—dancing on the *Soul Train* Line. See Pond, "'Chameleon' Meets *Soul Train*: Herbie, James, Michael, Damita Jo, and Jazz-Funk," *American Studies* 52, no. 4 (2013): 125–40.

6. Abdurraqib and Blount Danois quoted in Sam Sanders et al., "There Was Nothing Like 'Soul Train' on TV. There's Never Been Anything Like It Since," *It's Been a Minute*, NPR, September 28, 2021, MP3 audio, 36:00, https://www.npr.org/2021/09/14/1037118049/

7. Sandra Sainte Rose Fanchine, interview by author, April 26, 2022. Black vernacular dancers have always been part of the global conversation on which this book draws. This sense of global modernity was an intimate aspect of how young Diasporic Africans saw themselves, then and now.

8. Christine Acham, *Revolution Televised: Prime Time and the Struggle for Black Power* (Minneapolis: University of Minnesota Press, 2004), 63.

9. In this narrative, I capitalize the dance styles that I introduce by name. For the remainder of the book, dance styles appear in lowercase unless prefaced by their city/location of emergence.

10. See James Higgins, "The Robot: The Dance or the Act?," Locker Legends, accessed June 15, 2023, https://2022.lockerlegends.net/the-robot/

11. Demons of the Mind are now known as Medea Sirkas. The final section of chapter 2 features Medea Sirkas and Richmond Robotting group Lady Mechanical Robots.

12. See "What Is the Campbellock a.k.a. Locking," Don Campbell (website), accessed June 15, 2023, https://campbellock.dance/about-locking/what-is-the-campbellock-aka-locking/. Don Campbell passed on March 30, 2020.

13. Steps and moves that have been named and are now considered part of Locking style include the Campbellock (Don Campbell), Scoo B Doo and Scoobot (Jimmy Scoo B Doo Foster), Skeeter Rabbit (James OG Skeeter Rabbit Higgins), Leo Walk (Leo Flukey Luke Williamson), Alpha (Alpha Omega Anderson), Stop-and-Go (or Quickies), and Which-a-Way. Women's absence in streetdance lexicons indexes gendered tensions of naming practices. Women lockers of the 1970s include Arnetta Johnson, Freddie Maxie, Fawn Quiñones, Toni Basil, and Ana Lollipop Sanchez.

14. See chapter 1, "*Soul Train* Locamotives."

15. Freddie Maxie, interview by author, Fontana, California, 2014. California State University, Fullerton, in Orange County, also held dance contests organized by the Black Student Union, helping bring locking culture east from its early growth in South Central Los Angeles.

16. The 1973 film *Wattstax* evidences the popularity of Locking as a social party dance centered in the Watts neighborhood of what was at the time considered South Central Los Angeles. By 1973, Locking is already set to go overseas, with *Soul Train* recordings (and later the dancers) carrying the dance to the Philippines, Japan, and Indonesia, among other international locales.

17. Natasha Jean Bart, Zoom conversation with author, November 4, 2022. Don was known not to teach choreography, and I remember only freestyling in his classes. As a founding member of the celebrity dance group The Lockers, he did performance choreography on *Soul Train* and entertainment stage shows. However, dancers also recall Don's particular dislike of learning choreography.

18. Jacqui Malone, *Steppin' on the Blues: The Visible Rhythms of African American Dance* (Chicago: University of Illinois Press, 1996), 34 (emphasis added).

19. Malone, 35. Also see Zora Neale Hurston, "Characteristics of Negro Expression," in *The Jazz Cadence of American Culture*, ed. Robert O'Meally (New York: Columbia University Press, 1998), 298–310.

20. Damita Jo Freeman, "Diary of an Ex-Soul Train Dancer Presents: The One and Only Damita Jo Freeman," interview by Stephen McMillian, *Soul Committed Productions* (blog), August 20, 2012, https://soulcommitted.wordpress.com/2012/09/01/diary

21. Damita Jo Freeman, speaking in "Talk: Nick Cave and Friends, with Linda Johnson Rice, Damita Jo Freeman, and Nona Hendryx," moderated by Naomi Beckwith, Facebook Live video, posted by Museum of Contemporary Art Chicago, November 17, 2020, 1:08:09, https://www.facebook.com/43871522761/videos/1225021567876301

22. Nick Cave, speaking in "Talk: Nick Cave and Friends."

23. Rickey Vincent, *Funk: The Music, The People, and the Rhythm of the One* (New York: St. Martin's Griffin, 1996).

24. Laura Harris, "What Happened to the Motley Crew? C.L.R. James, Hélio Oiticica, and the Aesthetic Sociality of Blackness," *Social Text* 30, no. 3 (2012): 49–75.

25. See chapter 3 for hidden histories of waacking/punking, whose 1970s innovators danced on *Soul Train*.

Introduction

1. Global hip hop/streetdance as a kind of US exceptionalism is certainly complicated by frictions within US borders as well as sea changes in the contemporary production, circulation, and transmission of African Diaspora vernacular dances, significantly, in relation to immigrant and refugee movement across nation-state borders, as well as the internet and viral social media. Critical study of hip hop, club, and streetdance across and beyond US national borders, though not within the scope of this project, follows shifting undercurrents of codification and exchange that drive processes of reinvention and making of dance lineages in sub-Saharan Africa such as contemporary Afrobeats, Nigerian street-hop, and South African Pantsula (alongside dances outside the region, such as *passinho* in Rio de Janeiro, Brazil) and continental African immigration to western Europe, among many other flows. Anna Scott's "It's All in the Timing: The Latest Moves, James Brown's Grooves, and the Seventies Race-Consciousness Movement in Salvador, Bahia-Brazil," in *Soul: Black Power, Politics, and Pleasure*, ed. Monique Guillory and Richard C. Green (New York: New York University Press, 1998), 9–22, draws on Sylvia Wynter's deciphering practices to critique western European hegemony in the reading of aesthetic codes and theorizes a counterpractice of "tenaxis" that opens up possibilities for liberated black enfleshment; see Wynter, "Rethinking 'Aesthetics': Notes towards a Deciphering Practice," in *Ex-iles: Essays on Caribbean Cinema*, ed. Mbye Cham (Trenton, NJ: Africa World Press, 1992), 237–79. April K. Henderson's "Dancing between Islands: Hip Hop and the Samoan Diaspora," in *The Vinyl Ain't Final: Hip Hop and the Globalization of Black Popular Culture*, ed. Dipannita Basu and Sidney J. Lemelle (London: Pluto Press, 2006), 180–99, uses the terms *street dance* and *hip hop* to trace poppin' as "diasporic currency" that circulates multidirectionally in/beyond the United States and between the Polynesian islands of Samoa, Aotearoa, and Hawai'i. Halifu Osumare's *The Africanist Aesthetic in Global Hip-Hop: Power Moves* (New York: Palgrave Macmillan, 2007) builds a theory of "connective marginalities" to study hip hop (1990–early 2000s) as a global culture of rebellion, taken up by youth who experience cultural and class marginalization. *The Hiplife in Ghana: West African Indigenization of Hip-Hop* (New York: Palgrave Macmillan, 2012) is Osumare's more recent study of global hip hop cultures. Imani Kai-Johnson's *Dark Matter in Breaking Cyphers: The Life of Africanist Aesthetics in Global Hip Hop* (Oxford: Oxford University Press, 2022) builds on Osumare's body of work to explore principles of ritual circle practices that animate dancers' social worlds, proposing a "global diaspora" frame for grounding hip hop in Africanist aesthetics.

2. "Traci Bartlow $ Oakland $ Mikeyice #50yearsofhip hop #oakland #tracibartlow," YouTube video, posted by Mikey Ice TV, August 28, 2023, 1:11:35, https://www.youtube.com/watch?v=Vbo8U37WRxk

3. Steffan Clemente, "What Are Hip Hop Dances," *Mr Wiggles* (blog), accessed June 15, 2023, https://wigzee.biz/blog/?post=what-are-hip-hop-dances

4. Jorge Pabon, "Physical Graffiti: The History of Hip-Hop Dance," in *Total*

Chaos: The Art and Aesthetics of Hip-Hop, ed. Jeff Chang (New York: Basic Civitas, 2006), 18.

5. Robert Farris Thompson, "Hip Hop 101," in Perkins, *Droppin' Science*, 213 (originally published in *Rolling Stone*, March 27, 1986). Also see See Katrina Hazzard-Donald's chapter "Dance in Hip Hop Culture," in *Droppin' Science: Critical Essays on Rap Music and Hip Hop Culture*, ed. William Eric Perkins (Philadelphia: Temple University Press, 1996), 220–35, and Henderson's chapter "Dancing between Islands." Carla Stalling Huntington's monograph *Hip Hop Dance: Meanings and Messages* (Jefferson, NC: McFarland, 2007) mentions "waack" dance in California. Thomas Guzman-Sanchez's study *Underground Dance Masters: Final History of a Forgotten Era* (Santa Barbara, CA: ABC-CLIO, 2012) is the first book-length study to systematically address the historical development of California dances including early forms of boogaloo and popping in Oakland (Worming, Creeping, Posing, Ditallion) and Don Campbell's creation of Campbellocking, alongside other Los Angeles styles like posing, punking, waacking, and krumping.

6. See "Boogaloo, Robottin' & Struttin': The Untold Story of the West," Hip Hop Congress (website), accessed June 15, 2023, https://www.hiphopcongress.com/boogaloo-robottin--struttin.html. Also see Spencer Wilkerson, dir., *If Cities Could Dance*, season 4, episode 2, "Boogaloo: The Dance That Defined Oakland's Culture," 8:33, aired January 15, 2021, on KQED. For a critical history of Oakland Boogaloo that incisively locates the dance in relation to the recent rise of far-right extremist group Boogaloo Bois and information age surveillance capitalism, see "Boogaloo: The Greatest Story Never Told (Official Trailer)," One Cypher (website), posted October 8, 2021, 3:15, http://www.onecypher.com/2021/10/08/boogaloo. Also see Alan D. Mar, "The Funk behind Bay Area Street Dance" (master's thesis, San Francisco State University, 2012). An important premise of these studies is dancers' ongoing research into previously untold histories that will shift the mapping and thereby the conversation about hip hop/streetdance culture.

7. Lonnie Pop Tart Green organizes an annual dance event called the Strutter's Room that draws dancers from out of state, bringing attention to Bay Area dance histories and style. See "San Francisco Strutter Lonnie 'Poptart' Green," Strutter's Room (website), accessed June 15, 2023, http://www.thestruttersroom.com/about/

8. Clemente, "What Are Hip Hop Dances." Important precursors to these films are *Breakin' 'n' Enterin'* (September 14, 1983, dir. Topper Carew) and *Wild Style* (November 23, 1983, dir. Charlie Ahearn). *Breakin'* (dir. Joel Silberg) came out on May 4, 1984, and *Beat Street* (dir. Stan Lathan) came out on June 6 of that year. *Breakin' 2: Electric Boogaloo* (dir. Sam Firstenberg) came out in December 1984. *Style Wars* (dir. Tony Silver) came out in 1983, and *Graffiti Rock* (presented by Michael Holman) came out in 1984.

9. Dancers Ana Lollipop Sanchez, Lonnie Carbajal, and Billy Goodson all appear in the films, blending waacking movements with popping, locking, and jazz dance styles.

10. Speaking on a 2022 panel, James Cricket Colter cited the music video

for Chaka Khan's "I Feel for You," released September 24, 1984, as a primary resource, showcasing the hybridity of street and club dance cultures, including popping, locking, waacking, and breaking. The video features four dancers from *Breakin'*: Adolfo Shabba Doo Quiñones, Ana Lollipop Sanchez, Bruno Pop N Taco Falcon, and Michael Boogaloo Shrimp Chambers. With respect to sonic hybridity, Prince originally wrote the disco song for his 1979 album *Prince*, and this version includes rapping by Grandmaster Melle Mel and harmonica by Stevie Wonder. Colter was speaking on the panel "Street Dance x Screen Dance: A Visual Call and Response," organized by Amanda Adams-Louis and Brian Polite (Black Portraiture[s] VII: Play and Performance, Rutgers University, Newark, NJ, February 17, 2022).

11. Tim Lawrence, *Love Saves the Day* (Durham, NC: Duke University Press, 2004), 113.

12. Rickey Vincent, *Funk: The Music, the People, and the Rhythm of the One* (New York: St. Martin's Griffin, 1996), 10.

13. Tony Bolden, *Groove Theory: The Blues Foundation of Funk* (Jackson: University Press of Mississippi, 2020), 5.

14. Bolden, 12 (original emphasis).

15. LaMonda Horton-Stallings, *Funk the Erotic: Transaesthetics and Black Sexual Cultures* (Chicago: University of Illinois Press, 2015), 3.

16. Tavia Nyong'o, "I Feel Love: Disco and Its Discontents," *Criticism* 50, no. 1 (2008): 101.

17. Lawrence, *Love Saves the Day*, 4. Lawrence opens *Love Saves the Day* with thick description of two key nightlife spaces for disco—the Loft and Studio 54.

18. Lawrence, 120–22.

19. Early disco artists and tracks include the O'Jays' "Love Train" (1972), MFSB's "Love Is the Message" (1973), Gloria Gaynor's "Never Can Say Goodbye" (1975), Donna Summer's "I Feel Love" (1976), and the Trammps' "Disco Inferno" (1976).

20. Nyong'o, "I Feel Love," 110.

21. Nyong'o, 111.

22. Zora Neale Hurston studied how black vernacular speech tends to use the active form of nouns, apparent in the naming of these styles. See Hurston, "Characteristics of Negro Expression," in *The Jazz Cadence of American Culture*, ed. Robert O'Meally (New York: Columbia University Press, 1998), 298–310.

23. Brenda Dixon Gottschild, *Digging the Africanist Presence in American Performance: Dance and Other Contexts* (Westport, CT: Greenwood Press, 1996), 11.

24. James Higgins, text message to author, May 4, 2018. Deputy, in conversation with author, Dallace Winkler-Zeigler Memorial, Star Dance Center, Newhall, California, February 15, 2014.

25. Jeff Kutash, a dancer-choreographer who recruited many dancers with whom I spoke, promoted the material he staged in entertainment shows and commercial film as "street dancing," without mentioning the black dancers whose artistic-cultural labor produced these styles. See Lewis Segal, "Jeff Kutash's Street-Style Dancing," *Los Angeles Times*, August 31, 1986. Sima Belmar notes that both Kutash and Deney Terrio were key players in the circulation of street/

club dance on TV and film screens. See Belmar, "Behind the Screens: Race, Space, and Place in *Saturday Night Fever*," in *The Oxford Handbook of Screendance Studies*, ed. Douglas Rosenberg (Oxford: Oxford University Press, 2016), 461–79.

26. Anthea Kraut, *Choreographing the Folk: The Dance Stagings of Zora Neale Hurston* (Minneapolis: University of Minnesota Press, 2008).

27. Marcel Mauss, *Techniques, Technology and Civilisation*, ed. Nathan Schlanger (New York: Durkheim Press, 2006), 20, 18.

28. Marya McQuirter, "Awkward Moves: Dance Lessons from the 1940s," in *Dancing Many Drums: Excavations in African American Dance*, ed. Thomas F. DeFrantz (Madison: University of Wisconsin Press, 2002), 91.

29. See Greg Tate, *Everything but the Burden: What White People Are Taking from Black Culture* (New York: Broadway Books, 2003).

30. Jonathan David Jackson, "Improvisation in African-American Vernacular Dancing," *Dance Research Journal* 33, no. 2 (2001): 49.

31. Susan Leigh Foster, "Dance and/as Competition in the Privately Owned US Studio," in *The Oxford Handbook of Dance and Politics*, ed. Rebekah J. Kowal, Gerald Siegmund, and Randy Martin (Oxford: Oxford University Press, 2017), 64-65.

32. Foster, 68.

33. Michele Byrd-McPhee, quoted in Steven Vargas, "Jacob's Pillow: How Competition and Performance Harmonize in Dance Battles," Redbull (website), August 25, 2022, https://www.redbull.com/us-en/competition-performance-harmonize-dance-battles

34. See J. Lorenzo Perillo's ethnographic study of the World Hip Hop Dance Championship during the years 2012–14 in his monograph *Choreographing in Color: Filipinos, Hip-Hop, and the Cultural Politics of Euphemism* (Oxford: Oxford University Press, 2020), 109–42.

35. Heather Wisner, "From Street to Studio: Hip Hop Comes Inside," *Dance Magazine* 80, no. 9 (2006): 74–76.

36. Denise Ferreira da Silva, "Toward a Black Feminist Poethics: The Quest(ion) of Blackness toward the End of the World," *Black Scholar* 44, no. 2 (2014): 81-97.

37. Édouard Glissant, *Poetics of Relation* (1997; Ann Arbor: University of Michigan Press, 2010).

38. Sylvia Wynter, "Black Metamorphosis: New Natives in a New World," Unpublished manuscript, n.d. and "Rethinking 'Aesthetics': Notes Towards a Deciphering Practice," in *Ex-iles: Essays on Caribbean Cinema*, edited by Mbye Cham (African World Press, 1992) 237–279).

39. Sylvia Wynter, "Sambos and Minstrels," *Social Text* 1, no. 1 (1979): 151.

40. Denise Ferreira da Silva, "1 (life) ÷ 0 (blackness) = ∞ − ∞ or ∞ / ∞: On Matter beyond the Equation of Value," *E-Flux* 79 (2017), https://www.e-flux.com/journal/79/94686/

41. Wynter, "Sambos and Minstrels," 156.

42. Anna Scott, "It's All in the Timing: The Latest Moves, James Brown's Grooves, and the Seventies Race-Consciousness Movement in Salvador, Bahia-Brazil," in *Soul: Black Power, Politics, and Pleasure*, ed. Monique Guillory and Richard C. Green (New York: New York University Press, 1998), 9.

43. Katherine McKittrick, "Rebellion/Invention/Groove," *Small Axe* 20, no. 49 (2016): 90–91, quoting Sylvia Wynter, "Black Metamorphosis: New Natives in a New World" (unpublished manuscript, c. 1970s), 900.

44. Examples of this work include Ana Rokafella Garcia and Gabriel Kwikstep Dionisio's Bronx-based non-profit Full Circle Productions; Ladies of Hip Hop, founded and directed by Michele Byrd-Mcphee; E. Moncell Durden's documentary film *Everything Remains Raw* (2018) and online course "Intangible Roots: Exploring the Heritage of Black Dance, Culture and People" (2020); jumatatu m. poe and Donte Beacham's J-Sette performance project *Let 'im Move You: This Is a Formation* (2019); Camille Brown's dance programs Every Body Move and Social Dance for Social Distance; Shamell Bell's Street Dance Activism; and the spectrum of streetdance pedagogies that emerge within and beyond studio, concert, and competition/arena stages.

45. Saidiya Hartman, *Scenes of Subjection: Terror, Slavery, and Self-Making in Nineteenth-Century America* (New York: Oxford University Press, 1997), 61.

46. Christina Sharpe, *In the Wake: On Blackness and Being* (Durham, NC: Duke University Press, 2016).

47. Silva, "Toward a Black Feminist Poethics," 85.

48. For the language of "dancestry," I am indebted to dancers Sekou Heru and Buddha Stretch, who began collaborating on an Instagram Q and A series about hip hop and club culture during the COVID-19 pandemic.

49. For the asterisk in trans*, see Marquis Bey, "The Trans*-ness of Blackness, the Blackness of Trans*-ness," *TSQ: Transgender Studies Quarterly* 4, no. 2 (2017): 284.

50. Elizabeth Freeman and Tyler Bradway, eds., *Queer Kinship: Race, Sex, Belonging, Form* (Durham, NC: Duke University Press, 2022), 4, 3.

51. Silva, "Toward a Black Feminist Poethics," 85.

52. "Blackness, Aesthetics, and Liquidity," *liquid blackness*, 2014, https://liquidblackness.com/blackness-aesthetics-and-liquidity

53. Alessandra Raengo and Lauren McLeod Cramer, "Editors' Notes," *liquid blackness* 5, no. 1 (2021): 2–3.

54. Nicholas Whittaker, "Case Sensitive: Why We Shouldn't Capitalize 'Black,'" *Drift*, no. 5 (September 17, 2021), https://www.thedriftmag.com/case-sensitive/

55. Sharpe, *In the Wake*.

56. Dixon Gottschild, *Digging the Africanist Presence in American Performance*, 14.

57. Ronald A. T. Judy, "On the Politics of Global Language, or Unfungible Local Value," *Boundary 2* 24, no. 2 (1997): 105–6.

Chapter 1

1. Rufus Thomas's Stax Records hit "The Breakdown" reached number two on the Billboard R & B chart in 1971, and in 1989 it set the base groove for rapper Eazy-E's track "Easy-er Said Than Dunn."

2. "Soul Train Show with Bobby Hutton, Eddy Kendricks, Gladys Knight &

the Pips, the Honey Cone," YouTube video, posted by Bee Music, July 24, 2017, 42:45, https://www.youtube.com/watch?v=sinT7B5Q_-E

3. Chicago natives including Jody Watley and siblings Fawn and Adolfo Shabba Doo Quiñones also joined *Soul Train* as dancers.

4. Ahmir Khalib Thompson, *Soul Train: The Music, Dance, and Style of a Generation* (New York: Harper Design, 2013), 97.

5. Blount Danois speaking on Sam Sanders, "The Legacy of 'Soul Train,'" *It's Been A Minute*, NPR, October 17, 2021, MP3 audio, 36:02, https://www.npr.org/2021/10/15/1046380826/

6. Laurence Ralph, "Love, Peace, and Soul," *Transition* 108 (2012): 24–25.

7. Tyrone Proctor, interview by author, February 26, 2012.

8. Adolfo Shabba Doo Quiñones played the influential lead role of Ozone, dancing alongside costar Michael Boogaloo Shrimp Chambers, in the 1983 top-grossing dance film *Breakin'*, followed by 1984's *Breakin' 2: Electric Boogaloo*, considered hip hop movie classics. Shabba Doo passed on December 29, 2020.

9. Jonathan David Jackson, "Improvisation in African-American Vernacular Dancing," *Dance Research Journal* 33, no. 2 (2001): 49.

10. Katherine McKittrick, "Rebellion/Invention/Groove," *Small Axe* 20, no. 49 (2016): 90.

11. The section epigraph is from Avery Kelley, dir., *Soul Train Soul Change*, short film posted to Vimeo by Lynne O'Hara, June 10, 2020, 9:59, https://vimeo.com/427723480

12. Chicago's importance as a major site of black cultural production through the Great Migration and after the civil rights movement demands a much greater body of scholarship. For a study of Chicago House music, see Micah E. Salkind, *Do You Remember House? Chicago's Queer of Color Undergrounds* (New York: Oxford University Press, 2019).

13. Nelson George, *The Hippest Trip in America: "Soul Train" and the Evolution of Culture and Style* (New York: HarperCollins, 2014), 9.

14. Dancing on TV gives the new *Soul Train* dancers local recognition and cachet, conferring a degree of freedom to travel through the city and even cross otherwise precarious city trails. Ericka Blount Danois writes about dancer Crescendo Ward, whose moves drew respect from Cabrini Green gang members during a street confrontation. Los Angeles dancers told me similar stories. Blount Danois, "The Story of the Soul Train Dancers," *Wax Poetics*, no. 57 (2013): 66–70.

15. Clinton Ghent, quoted in Ericka Blount Danois, *Love, Peace, and Soul: Behind the Scenes of America's Favorite Dance Show, Soul Train: Classic Moments* (Milwaukee, WI: Backbeat Books, 2013), 15–16.

16. Leela Ghandi uses the term *affective communities* to propose a postcolonial theory of transnational collaboration against imperialism that doesn't reify a binary construct of the West. While my use of *affective community* does resonate with Ghandi's project, especially when considering the anti-imperialist philosophy of the US black power movement, I focus on the somatics of community, specifically rhythm as a feeling that is synesthetic and that holds the capacity to form dance communities engaging in communal acts of listening and grooving.

Ghandi, *Affective Communities: Anticolonial Thought, Fin-de-Siècle Radicalism, and the Politics of Friendship* (Durham, NC: Duke University Press, 2006).

17. *Soul Train* moves from Metromedia Square to A&M Studios in 1981.

18. Haili You, "Defining Rhythm: Aspects of an Anthropology of Rhythm," *Culture, Medicine and Psychiatry* 18 (1994): 361–84; Marcel Mauss, *Techniques, Technology and Civilisation*, ed. Nathan Schlanger (New York: Durkheim Press, 2006), 77–96.

19. Imani Kai-Johnson, "Music Meant to Make You Move: Considering the Aural Kinesthetic," *Sounding Out!* (blog), June 18, 2012, http://soundstudiesblog.com/2012/06/18/music-meant-to-make-you-move-considering-the-aural-kinesthetic/

20. Horton-Stallings poses a revisionary critique of Jean Baudrillard's use of the term *transaesthetics*, in order to offer a description of the erotic that reorganizes human relations, especially normative sexualities and sexual relations. LaMonda Horton-Stallings, *Funk the Erotic: Transaesthetics and Black Sexual Cultures* (Chicago: University of Illinois Press, 2015).

21. Jacqui Malone, *Steppin' on the Blues: The Visible Rhythms of African American Dance* (Chicago: University of Illinois Press, 1996), 36. Malone further defines vernacular dancing as a way "black Americans *ritualize their lives*," allowing them to renew communally held values, even as forms change over time (27 [original emphasis]).

22. Saidiya Hartman, *Scenes of Subjection: Terror, Slavery, and Self-Making in Nineteenth-Century America* (New York: Oxford University Press, 1997), 61.

23. Sterling Stuckey, *Slave Culture: Nationalist Theory and the Foundations of Black America* (1987; Oxford: Oxford University Press, 2013), xvi, 104. Also see Katrina Dyonne Thompson, *Ring Shout, Wheel About: The Racial Politics of Music and Dance in North American Slavery* (Urbana: University of Illinois Press, 2014).

24. For a careful exploration of circle practices, see Imani Kai-Johnson's *Dark Matter in Breaking Cyphers: The Life of Africanist Aesthetics in Global Hip Hop* (Oxford: Oxford University Press, 2022).

25. "Camille Brown: A Visual History of Social Dance in 25 Moves," TED.com, June 2016, https://www.ted.com/talks/camille_a_brown_a_visual_history_of_social_dance_in_25_moves/transcript?language=en

26. Anna Scott, "It's All in the Timing: The Latest Moves, James Brown's Grooves, and the Seventies Race-Consciousness Movement in Salvador, Bahia-Brazil," in *Soul: Black Power, Politics, and Pleasure*, ed. Monique Guillory and Richard C. Green (New York: New York University Press, 1998), 21.

27. Thomas Guzman-Sanchez, *Underground Dance Masters: Final History of a Forgotten Era* (Santa Barbara, CA: ABC-CLIO, 2012).

28. See "Don Campbellock Signature Moves," Don Campbell (website), accessed June 15, 2023, https://campbellock.dance/about-locking/the-campbellock-aka-locking-moves/. Also see "Don Campbellock Explains the Origin of 'Locking,'" YouTube video, posted by John Carluccio, March 31, 2020, 2:00, https://www.youtube.com/watch?v=5KhsfDg30Nw

29. "I still harbored one secret humiliation: I could not dance." Malcolm X with Alex Haley, *The Autobiography of Malcolm X* (New York: Grove Press, 1966), 56.

30. "Don 'Campbellock' Campbell on the History of 'Locking' at HHI 2015," YouTube video, posted by PacificRimVideoPress, August 9, 2015, 3:34, https://www.youtube.com/watch?v=qROnQORvHHc

31. Don's dance was first called Campbellocking. He recorded the eponymous song "Campbell Lock" with Stanson Records in 1972. This song later sparked a legal dispute around the commercial use of "Campbellock," resulting in the name change to Locking. The Lockers dance group was originally called the Campbellockers.

32. Malone, *Steppin' on the Blues*, 28.

33. Arnetta Johnson and James Higgins, group interview by author, 2014.

34. See, for example, "Official Tyrone P Waacking & Soul Train Tribute by 'The Chapter' Mtl," YouTube video, posted by the Chapter Waacking, August 29, 2020, 11:12, https://www.youtube.com/watch?v=GaUHZGnTzhw

35. Two years after *Soul Train*'s premiere, Bay Area promoter Jay Payton launched a variety show called *Soul Is*, which became an important platform for local artists. For two 1976 episodes, donated to the African American Museum and Library at Oakland by Payton's family, see Sean Heyliger, "The Jay Payton Show: Oakland's Own Soul Train," *Oakland Public Library* (blog), December 1, 2017, https://oaklandlibrary.org/blogs/post/the-jay-payton-show-oaklands-own-soul-train/

36. This section weaves together content from recorded interviews and informal conversations with dance partners Arnetta Nettabug Johnson and James OG Skeeter Rabbit Higgins, which took place over an eight-year period from 2014 to 2022, by phone and Zoom and in person at Johnson's family home in Carson, California.

37. Netta went on the show once, after performing with other *Soul Train* dancers for James Brown's concert at the Inglewood Forum.

38. Watts Writers Workshop in Charcoal Alley is where Netta first comes to practice, by invitation of her uncle Spelman Ward, who is producing music groups there. She invites Lorna Dune (Lorna Cox) and Shelly Cepeda to join her. They soon become known as the Toota Woota Sisters. Netta invites Skeet, who brings Tony and Buddy GoGo from South Central. Greg Pope joins. And Scoo B Doo. Netta brings Freddie Maxie, too, who's just moved to Compton. All together they form the youth performance group of Watts Writers Workshop—Creative Generation. For more on Watts Writers Workshop, see Johnie Scott, "The NEA," *Artforum*, Summer 2017, https://www.artforum.com/print/201706/the-nea-68668

39. William McKinley Covan opened the Covan Dance Studio in 1936, teaching with his wife, Florence, until closing its doors in 1974.

40. Here, Netta uses her studio training to indirectly challenge and outshine a male-centered dance experience, quickly memorizing and recalling the dance by watching and assigning numbers to the young men's moves in eight-count sequences. Netta's observation differs from my argument at the end of chapter 2 that studio counting practices reduce rhythmic nuance in black vernacular dance to extract moves in uniform linear temporal-spatial units.

41. Eddie Cole, interview by author, April 23, 2014. *Soul Train* dancer Eddie Cole was on the cheer team of Fremont High School in Los Angeles, which lock-

ers and *Soul Train* dancers Scoo B Doo and Freddie Maxie both attended. Netta attributes much of her gymnastic skill in locking to competition performance training on her high school's drill team, practicing seven days a week.

42. Ron Gatsby, speaking in "When I Move / You Move: The Conversation #2 'Hip-Hop' Dance in Seattle Perspectives in Black," YouTube video, posted by Dani Tirrell, August 25, 2020, 1:58:17, https://www.youtube.com/watch?v=iQTmJyIa9no

43. Greg Campbellock Jr. Pope passed on January 28, 2010, and is a core contributor to locking's global circulation in hip hop/streetdance culture.

44. Section epigraph is from "What Is the Campbellock a.k.a. Locking," Don Campbell (website), accessed June 15, 2023, https://campbellock.dance/about-locking/what-is-the-campbellock-aka-locking/

45. "Master Locker Jimmy 'Scoo B Doo' Foster Interview (Guest Host Lil B)," YouTube video, posted by Funkd Uptv, August 15, 2011, 26:09, https://www.youtube.com/watch?v=YnG1gcNOsOM

46. James Foster, interview by author, 2022.

47. Jason King, "Which Way Is Down? Improvisations on Black Mobility," *Women & Performance* 14, no. 1 (2004): 25–45.

48. Rahsaan Mahadeo, "Funk the Clock: Transgressing Time while Young, Prescient and Black" (PhD diss., University of Minnesota, 2019).

49. James A. Snead, "On Repetition in Black Culture," *Black American Literature Forum* 15, no. 4 (1981): 146–54.

50. A related move is the Backslide, often referred to as the Moonwalk, which is a backward move that was popularized by dancer Jeffrey Daniel on *Soul Train* and performed most famously by Michael Jackson.

51. James Foster, interview by author, 2022.

52. Christina Sharpe, *In the Wake: On Blackness and Being* (Durham, NC: Duke University Press, 2016), 20.

53. Scoo B Doo's second two-room apartment was located on West Thirty-Ninth Street, about a block from Los Angeles Memorial Coliseum, where the Wattstax concert took place in 1972. Greg Pope, Fluky Luke, and Shabba Doo all lived there with Scoo B Doo.

54. This move, which was first called the Quickie by Greg Pope, was named the Stop-and-Go by Damita Jo. Both Greg Pope and Fluky Luke attended Wattstax and appear in the eponymous 1973 documentary film, dancing the Stop-and-Go together during Rufus Thomas's performance of "The Breakdown." See "Rufus Thomas - 'Breakdown' & 'Funky Chicken' Live @ Wattstax 1973," YouTube video, posted by ianwoodsman, November 25, 2011, 9:45, at 3:13, https://www.youtube.com/watch?v=KCFyKRtlLOI. For the connection between the Breakdown and Stop-and-Go, which demonstrates what I'm calling the locamotive power of black social dance, see this chapter's section "The Breakdown."

55. James Foster, interview by author, 2022.

56. Foster.

57. Sharpe, *In the Wake*, 21.

58. In chapter 2, I examine eight-counting in music video choreography as a language dancers use to code-switch between sensory-vocal rhythms of their vernaculars in contexts of professional industry dance.

59. Another resource that helped me do the research for this story of locking is the Korean website Lockorea (https://lockorea.com), which gives maps, lyrics, photos, clips of the Wattstax documentary, and an extensive history of locking culture in 1960s and 1970s California.

60. Michel-Rolph Trouillot writes, "If the account was indeed fully comprehensive of all facts it would be incomprehensible. Further, the selection of what matters, the dual creation of mentions and silences, is premised on the understanding of the rules of the game by broadcaster and audience alike." Trouillot, *Silencing the Past: Power and the Production of History* (Boston: Beacon Press, 2015), 50.

61. James Foster, "Diary of an Ex-Soul Train Dancer: Q&A with Former Soul Train Dancer Jimmy 'Scoo B Doo' Foster, the Master Locker," interview by Stephen McMillian, Soul Train (website), August 24, 2011, http://soultrain.com/2011/08/24/diary-of-an-ex-soul-train-dancer-qa-with-former-soul-train-dancer-jimmy-scoo-b-doo-foster-the-master-locker/ (site discontinued).

62. James Foster, interview by author, 2022.

63. Michel Foucault, *Security, Territory, Population: Lectures at the Collège de France, 1977–1978* (New York: Palgrave Macmillan, 2009).

64. King, "Which Way Is Down?," 42.

65. Alicia Garza, *The Purpose of Power: How We Come Together When We Fall Apart* (New York: One World, 2020). Also see adrienne maree brown, *Emergent Strategy: Shaping Change, Changing Worlds* (Chico, CA: AK Press, 2017).

66. Joshua Chambers-Letson, *After the Party: A Manifesto for Queer of Color Life* (New York: New York University Press, 2018).

67. By drawing a link between *Soul Train* and the BPP, I don't mean to essentialize black power in the historically specific phase of the BPP's formation. There is certainly a history of black power struggle prior to the 1960s and well before the twentieth century. Yet I find the potential for a conversation between traditions of black political organizing and black vernacular dancing to be essential to building a robust theory of black social dancing as ethics-aesthetic consciousness. See Fred Moten, *In the Break: The Aesthetics of the Black Radical Tradition* (Minneapolis: University of Minnesota Press, 2003), for a related approach via sound and philosophy. Also see Sterling Stuckey's *Slave Culture* and his article "Through the Prism of Folklore: The Black Ethos in Slavery," *Massachusetts Review* 9, no. 3 (1968): 417–37.

68. Foster, "Diary of an Ex-Soul Train Dancer."

69. Foster.

70. Sharpe, *In the Wake*, dedication.

Chapter 2

1. "Traci Bartlow $ Oakland $ Mikeyice #50yearsofhip hop #oakland #tracibartlow," YouTube video, posted by Mikey Ice TV, August 28, 2023, 1:11:35, https://www.youtube.com/watch?v=Vbo8U37WRxk. Boogaloo also became a prefix for dancers' names, for example, Boogaloo Dana, Boogaloo Vic, Boogaloo Bill, and Boogaloo Dan. For a short-form, award-winning study of Oak-

land Boogaloo and early innovators the Black Resurgents in the context of Bay Area Funk, black power, and Black Lives Matter movements, see Spencer Wilkerson, dir., *If Cities Could Dance*, season 4, episode 2, "Boogaloo: The Dance That Defined Oakland's Culture," 8:33, aired January 15, 2021,' on KQED. This episode won a Northern California Area Emmy. Also see "Watch 'Bay Area Street Dance' with Traci Bartlow, Lonnie 'PopTart' Green, Iron Lotus and More," KQED Live, February 2, 2023, https://www.kqed.org/arts/13925415/bay-area-street-dance-hip-hop-traci-bartlow-poptart-iron-lotus; Dave Cook, "Oakland's Boogaloo Reunion BBQ: A History Lesson in West Coast Street Dance," Davey D's Hip Hop Corner (website), September 22, 2015, https://hiphopandpolitics.com/2015/09/22/oakland

2. Will Randolph, interview by author, December 26, 2009.

3. Will Randolph named the second dancer as Donald Duck Matthews but could not recall (nor was I able to confirm) Lester's surname. In the mid-1960s, One Plus One and Pirate & the Easy Walkers were two key groups to get known through neighborhood dancing in schoolhouse and community center talent shows. In the 1970s, the Black Resurgents and Black Messengers brought the dances into nightclubs and mainstream entertainment venues, performing with noted R & B musicians. Dancers I spoke with have consistently named Jerry Rentie, Michael Enoch, Albert Ironman Milton, and Michael Sanders, as well as Patricia Scott and Doris Cooperwood, two women dancers of early boogaloo history. Will Randolph, in conversation with author, February 19, 2023.

4. See Brenda Dixon Gottschild, *Digging the Africanist Presence in American Performance: Dance and Other Contexts* (Westport, CT: Greenwood Press, 1996), 14. For an up-close view of polycentrism in styles of Richmond dancer Riley Moore, see "Scarecrow Riley Moore," YouTube video, posted by Robonati, November 12, 2009, 0:32, https://www.youtube.com/watch?v=mmsqYBsomyw

5. See "(BRS) Boogaloo Robot Strut (Bay Area Dance)," YouTube video, posted by dizzrockn, May 5, 2008, 7:46, https://www.youtube.com/watch?v=DuYqpWVAiz4

6. Dana Dorham, interview by author, Berkeley, California, 2015.

7. Tommy Washington, interview by author, Berkeley, California, 2015.

8. Dana Dorham, interview by author, Berkeley, California, 2015.

9. Dorham.

10. Naomi Macalalad Bragin, "On the Front Porch: Deborah McCoy and Fresno Streetdance," *Tropics of Meta: Historiography for the Masses* (blog), April 3, 2018, https://tropicsofmeta.com/2018/04/03/on-the-front-porch-deborah-mccoy-and-fresno-streetdance/

11. See the following sources, also quoted in the introduction: Steffan Clemente, "What Are Hip Hop Dances," *Mr Wiggles* (blog), accessed June 15, 2023, https://wigzee.biz/blog/?post=what-are-hip-hop-dances; Jorge Pabon, "Physical Graffiti: The History of Hip-Hop Dance," in *Total Chaos: The Art and Aesthetics of Hip-Hop*, ed. Jeff Chang (New York: Basic Civitas, 2006), 18–26; Robert Farris Thompson, "Hip Hop 101," in *Droppin' Science: Critical Essays on Rap Music and Hip Hop Culture*, ed. William Eric Perkins (Philadelphia: Temple University Press, 1996), 211–19; and Thomas Guzman-Sanchez, *Underground Dance Masters: Final History of a Forgotten Era* (Santa Barbara, CA: ABC-CLIO, 2012).

12. Steffan Clemente, "Mr. Wiggles Hip Hop Camp," Mr Wiggles (website), accessed June 15, 2023, https://wigzee.biz/contact/book%20hip%20hop%20camp/. While it's beyond the scope of my study to trace the historical timeline of these dances' emergence in detail, the proliferation of dance styles invites in-depth research into histories of the region, extending for example through the California cities of Sacramento and San Jose.

13. Slusser highlights the stakes of competing origin stories in hip hop and streetdance in "Defying Gravity, Breakin' Boundaries: The Rise of Fresno's Climax Crew," in *Dispatches from the Straight Outta Fresno Archives*, by Valley Public History Initiative: Preserving Our Stories (Oakland: California Humanities, 2018), n.p., https://calhum.org/wp-content/uploads/2018/04/FSU_SOF_booklet_low-res.pdf

14. Lonnie R. Green, interview by author, San Francisco, California, October 22, 2011. The Fillmore dance discussed in this chapter is part of the San Francisco Strutting movement. See also "San Francisco Strutter Lonnie 'Poptart' Green," Strutter's Room (website), accessed June 15, 2023, http://www.thestruttersroom.com/about/; "Poppers Picnic #7 2014 Pop Tart & Harry Berry aka Frisco," YouTube video, posted by Chineserobot, July 13, 2014, 2:47, https://www.youtube.com/watch?v=vPiGso6j_hc

15. See "Boogaloo, Robottin' & Struttin': The Untold Story of the West," Hip Hop Congress (website), accessed June 15, 2023, https://www.hiphopcongress.com/boogaloo-robottin--struttin.html

16. Deborah Johnson, interview by author, East Oakland, California, January 12, 2010. See Granny dancing center stage on the historic Gong Show, "Granny & Robotroid Inc - 1977," YouTube video, posted by SkillzOne, February 15, 2016, 2:00, https://www.youtube.com/watch?v=Ka2qHrizK6A. Deborah Delois Johnson (1949–2013) founded the group in 1975, taking on the role of choreographer, producer, chaperone, and, often, informal caretaker for the grade school-age boy dancers who danced alongside her. She explained to me that she didn't work with girls except in her early years of directing.

17. Christina Sharpe, *In the Wake: On Blackness and Being* (Durham, NC: Duke University Press, 2016), 81.

18. See Diamond D dancing solo and group Bay Area styles in Oakland's Fruitvale neighborhood, filmed by Beto Mooncricket Lopez: "Part 1: Homeless Man-Diamond D 'Red' Original Oakland Boogaloo Popper 52 Years Old," YouTube video, posted by Mooncricket, October 5, 2011, 4:55, https://www.youtube.com/watch?v=fsoAF5yo-aM

19. Katrina Hazzard-Gordon, *Jookin': The Rise of Social Dance Formations in African-American Culture* (Philadelphia: Temple University Press, 1990), 20.

20. Jason King, "Which Way Is Down? Improvisations on Black Mobility," *Women & Performance: A Journal of Feminist Theory* 14, no. 1 (2004): 32.

21. Fascinatingly, in the UK context, British poppers were initially disconnected from the funk foundations of poppin', since their early studies were often based on poppin' scenes from the New York movie *Beat Street* (1984), the soundtrack of which centers hip hop and electro beats. UK poppers weren't widely dancing to funk until the early 2000s. See Jo Read's research on poppin'

and animation styles in proscenium stage performance. Read notes that UK poppers have often favored classical music when choreographing for theater stage institutions. Read, "Cadences of Choreomusicality: Investigating the Relationship between Sound and Movement in Staged Performances of Popping and Animation in the United Kingdom" (PhD diss., De Montfort University, 2017), 30.

22. See Marie Pandora Medina improvising robot styles in "Pandora Marie Female Popper Popping Freestyle Robot Dancer x Mechanical Monday," YouTube video, posted by Pandora Marie, December 4, 2017, 3:16, https://www.youtube.com/watch?v=rDDAHc9848A

23. Danielle Goldman, *I Want to Be Ready: Improvised Dance as a Practice of Freedom* (Ann Arbor: University of Michigan Press, 2010).

24. Goldman, 46.

25. Renée Lesley, interview by author, Richmond, California, 2010. See Riley dancing in front of the Richmond Memorial Auditorium, where regular talent shows were held, in Ralph Plik Plok Montejo's *Robotter's Room* video docuseries: "Robotter's Room (Featurette #4) [HD] - The Solo Robotter's / Richmond Robottin History," YouTube video, posted by Ralph Montejo, August 26, 2013, 5:13, at 0:32, https://www.youtube.com/watch?v=cW2Dsew7XqQ. This clip gives an up close view of polycentrism in styles of first-generation dancers Riley and Willie Professor Shields Boyd.

26. Rizvana Bradley, "Black Cinematic Gesture and the Aesthetics of Contagion," *TDR: The Drama Review* 62, no. 1 (2018): 23.

27. Ashon Crawley, "Otherwise Movements," *New Inquiry*, January 19, 2015, https://thenewinquiry.com/otherwise-movements/

28. See dancer OG Harry Joseph Berry (a.k.a. the Legendary Frisco Popper, 1965–2020), filmed in the Bayview/Hunters Point neighborhood of San Francisco, in "The Fillmore Strut by OG Harry Berry of SF," YouTube video, posted by dizzrockn, April 16, 2008, 4:20, https://www.youtube.com/watch?v=myD4MWmewuI. That he dances seven miles southeast of The Fillmore's eponymous neighborhood shows ideas developed in this section of place in motion and the dance as an ethics-aesthetic practice of displacement.

29. Savannah Shange contextualizes the landscape of San Francisco's contemporary development within a history of native Ohlone people's enslavement, laws restricting housing for Chinese laborers, and Japanese American internment, this last of which cleared Japantown in the Fillmore district and opened housing to a large-scale influx of black migrants, recruited to work in the World War II shipyards. Shange, "'This Is Not a Protest': Managing Dissent in Racialized San Francisco," in *Black California Dreamin': The Crises of California's African-American Communities*, ed. Ingrid Banks et al. (Santa Barbara: University of California, Santa Barbara, Center for Black Studies Research, 2012), 97. Jasmine Johnson and Sean Ossei-Owusu note a relative absence of interethnic coalition addressing Japanese disappearance at the time, in light of the district's marked transformation into a thriving African American community. Johnson and Ossei-Owusu, "'From Fillmore to No More': Black-Owned Business in a Transforming San Francisco," in Banks et al., *Black California Dreamin'*, 87.

30. Jaimal Yogis, "What Happened to Black San Francisco?," *San Francisco*

Magazine, January 18, 2008, https://sanfran.com/what-happened-black-san-francisco (article removed from site).

31. Albert Broussard, *Black San Francisco: The Struggle for Racial Equality in the West, 1900–1954* (Lawrence, Kansas: University of Kansas Press, 1993).

32. "Harlem of the West: The San Francisco Fillmore Jazz Era," conversation with Elizabeth Pepin Silva and Lewis Watts, YouTube video, posted by California Historical Society, February 16, 2021, 1:55:07, https://www.youtube.com/watch?v=M2Ku1d78csU

33. Johnson and Ossei-Owusu, "From Fillmore to No More," 82.

34. Johnson and Ossei-Owusu, 82.

35. I'm describing how place functions within hip hop/streetdance as a movement of displacement with geographic, cultural, and ontological dimensions. My wording and thinking on acquisition and displacement are indebted to Fred Moten, who has said, "the objects of black study have been displacement and acquisition. . . . I do have hopes for displacement, more complicated and not simply disavowed. What if there's something about how we dance that bears a secret about how we should live and how we should not take up space but be embedded in the places where we are." Quoted from the online broadcast of the event, "Fred Moten, Theaster Gates & Adrienne Brown Live in Conversation," Center for the Study of Race, Politics and Culture, University of Chicago, May 20, 2020. For critical theories of displacement, see Katherine McKittrick, *Demonic Grounds: Black Women and the Cartographies of Struggle* (Minneapolis: University of Minnesota Press, 2006); David Bailey and Stuart Hall, "The Vertigo of Displacement: Shifts within Black Documentary Practices," *Ten.8* 2, no. 3 (1992): 14–31; Nahum Dimitri Chandler, *X—The Problem of the Negro as a Problem for Thought* (New York: Fordham University Press, 2013), 129–70.

36. Nathaniel Mackey, "Other: From Noun to Verb," *Representations* 39 (1992): 51–70.

37. McKittrick, *Demonic Grounds*, xxiii (original emphasis).

38. McKittrick, xxii; and see Édouard Glissant, *Poetics of Relation* (1997; Ann Arbor: University of Michigan Press, 2010).

39. Nikki Jones and Christina Jackson, "'You Just Don't Go Down There': Learning to Avoid the Ghetto in San Francisco," in *The Ghetto: Contemporary Global Issues and Controversies*, ed. Ray Hutchison and Bruce D. Haynes (Boulder, CO: Westview Press, 2012), 218.

40. Jasmine Johnson, "Dear Khary (An Autobiography of Gentrification)," *Gawker*, August 31, 2013, https://gawker.com/dear-khary-an-autobiography-of-gentrification-1227561902

41. Jasmine Johnson, "Sorrow's Swing," in *Race and Performance after Repetition*, ed. Soyica Diggs Colbert, Douglas A. Jones Jr., and Shane Vogel (Durham, NC: Duke University Press, 2020), 140.

42. Johnson, 140.

43. The birth of hip hop culture in the Bronx tells a connected history of disinvestment, displacement, and development. See Jeff Chang, *Can't Stop Won't Stop: A History of the Hip-Hop Generation* (New York: St. Martin's Press, 2005). Dancer and cultural historian Jay Jenkins echoes many streetdancers' reminders

to me that a quick attachment to dance labels overlooks attention to the dances' commonly lived experience: "It wasn't even called hip hop. It was life. You have to have a sense of that historical process. A lot of young folks from the Bronx don't even know the history of their own buildings." Jenkins, "Stretch Music and Movement," Zoom meeting, March 26, 2020.

44. Laura Harris, "What Happened to the Motley Crew? C.L.R. James, Hélio Oiticica, and the Aesthetic Sociality of Blackness," *Social Text* 30, no. 3 (2012): 49–75.

45. Mike Muse and Tommy Washington quoted from "Legendary Dance Crew Medea Sirkas Break Down the History of the Culture and Demonstrate Live," YouTube video, posted by Sway's Universe, November 11, 2018, 20:38, https://www.youtube.com/watch?v=z_4AVyqihmI

46. The section epigraph is from Dana Dorham, interview by author, Berkeley, California, 2015. See also "Boogaloo Dana from Medea Sirkas Demonstrating Robot/Animatronics," YouTube short, posted by medeasirkas-legacytv808, April 21, 2022, https://youtube.com/shorts/kRpdqJhXIfo

47. See "Animation Exhibition Battle // .stance // Highlight the Style," YouTube video, posted by stance, September 12, 2019, 28:25, https://www.youtube.com/watch?v=gXJ46GaSysU

48. I am drawing here on the hip hop pedagogy of d. Sabela grimes, who teaches a movement system he calls Funkamental MediKinetics. See "4 Ways d. Sabela grimes is Making the Case for Hip Hop in Higher Ed," *Dance Teacher*, August 9, 2018, https://dance-teacher.com/d-sabela-grimes. I am also thinking of these dances as "generating a critical praxis of being," along the lines of Zakiyyah Iman Jackson's theorization of *Becoming Human: Matter and Meaning in an Antiblack World* (New York: New York University Press, 2020), 2.

49. *The 7th Voyage of Sinbad* (dir. Nathan H. Juran) was released in 1958. It was later followed by two more films on the Sinbad story: *The Golden Voyage of Sinbad* (1973, dir. Gordon Hessler) and *Sinbad and the Eye of the Tiger* (1977, dir. Sam Wanamaker). *Jason and the Argonauts* (dir. Don Chaffey) came out in 1963.

50. Read, "Cadences of Choreomusicality," 60.

51. Melissa Blanco Borelli, introduction to *The Oxford Handbook of Dance and the Popular Screen*, ed. Melissa Blanco Borelli (Oxford: Oxford University Press, 2014), 1. For a critical collection of scholarship on the making and circulation of dances for screen, see Melissa Blanco Borelli and Raquel Monroe, eds., "Screening the Skin: Issues of Race and Nation in Screendance," special issue, *International Journal of Screendance* 9 (2018). Also see Douglas Rosenberg, ed., *The Oxford Handbook of Screendance Studies* (Oxford: Oxford University Press, 2016). Two foundational monographs for the study of dance and screen are Sherril Dodds, *Dance on Screen: Genres and Media from Hollywood to Experimental Art* (New York: Palgrave Macmillan, 2001); and Douglas Rosenberg, *Screendance: Inscribing the Ephemeral Image* (Oxford: Oxford University Press, 2012). Danielle Goldman's careful study of Bill T. Jones's *Ghostcatching* (1999) and *The Breathing Show* (1999) discusses the use of motion-capture technology in concert stage dance works of the late 1990s. Between private spaces of improvisation in the motion-capture studio and the blending of live and mediated dance in public presentation

of the pieces, Goldman asserts that sweat escapes the technology's attempts to capture and record Jones's performance, to the degree that the "material outpouring of Jones's work actually stopped the motion of production." Goldman, *I Want to Be Ready*, 125.

52. Childhood is an important context for the development of animation and related dance styles, where play and make-believe hold core functions. Dancers now well into their sixties continue to get together for annual reunions such as the Oakland Boogaloo Reunion at West Oakland's Middle Harbor Shoreline Park (whose tenth anniversary was in 2021) and OG Popper's Picnic in Los Angeles (which had eleven gatherings between 2007 and 2018).

53. Tony Bolden, "Groove Theory: A Vamp on the Epistemology of Funk," *American Studies* 52, no. 4 (2013): 29.

54. Bolden, 29.

55. Read, "Cadences of Choreomusicality," 65.

56. Gregory E. Rutledge, "Futurist Fiction & Fantasy: The *Racial* Establishment," *Callaloo* 24, no. 1 (2001): 237.

57. Sianne Ngai, *Ugly Feelings* (Cambridge, MA: Harvard University Press, 2005), 90–91.

58. Read, "Cadences of Choreomusicality," 75.

59. See, in chapter 1, "Locamotive Power" and "All the Ways We Dance Backward."

60. Jonathan David Jackson, "Improvisation in African-American Vernacular Dancing," *Dance Research Journal* 33, no. 2 (2001): 40–53.

61. André Lepecki, *Exhausting Dance: Performance and the Politics of Movement* (New York: Routledge, 2006), 1.

62. Lepecki, 3.

63. Goldman, *I Want to Be Ready*.

64. "Animation Dance Style Tutorial (JRock) Advanced and for Beginners," YouTube video, posted by Styles upon Styles, October 16, 2018, 7:53, https://www.youtube.com/watch?v=oV-soLRxMRU

65. Locating Shiva and Kali within indigenous belief systems, Braj Ranjan Mani builds a critique of casteism in contemporary Indo-Aryan Brahman Hinduism. Mani writes, "Shiva, as is well-known, has two divine consorts, the first one is Kali (of black colour), while the priests have to procure him a second one, Gauri (of white skin) to placate the God of Destruction." Mani, *Debrahmanising History: Dominance and Resistance in Indian Society* (New Delhi: Manohar, 2005), 59. Thanks to Meena Murugesan for this reference and her critical feedback on this section.

66. See the introduction; see also Sylvia Wynter, "Sambos and Minstrels," *Social Text* 1, no. 1 (1979): 149–56.

67. Shiva is also invoked as a gender-fluid god, in one form depicted as half man and half woman.

68. LaMonda Horton-Stallings, *Funk the Erotic: Transaesthetics and Black Sexual Cultures* (Chicago: University of Illinois Press, 2015), 181.

69. For a critique of the nature/technology binary, see Jasbir Puar, "'I Would Rather Be a Cyborg Than a Goddess': Becoming-Intersectional in Assemblage Theory," *Philosophia* 2, no. 1 (2012): 49–66.

70. Ashon Crawley, *Blackpentecostal Breath: The Aesthetics of Possibility* (New York: Fordham University Press, 2016), 2.

71. Rizvana Bradley, "Black Cinematic Gesture and the Aesthetics of Contagion," *TDR: The Drama Review* 62, no. 1 (2018): 28.

72. Bradley, 26.

73. Horton-Stallings, *Funk the Erotic*, 181.

74. Bradley, "Black Cinematic Gesture and the Aesthetics of Contagion," 24.

75. The section epigraph is from Calvin Warren, "The Catastrophe: Black Feminist Poethics, (Anti)Form, and Mathematical Nihilism," *Qui Parle* 28, no. 2 (2019): 359.

76. In the 1990s, Japan, Taiwan, and South Korea grew as centers for global streetdance. For a documentary on this dance scene, see Kozo Okumura, dir., *Far East Coast Is in da House: Street Dancers in Japan* (Michigan State University, 1998), 32 min.

77. Schloss highlights this function in b-boy culture, arguing for a shift from object-centered to discourse-centered analyses of hip hop. He asserts that unmediated participation is fundamental to serious engagement of hip hop forms as aesthetic developments of social dance, showing the systematic ways that breakers link aesthetics, philosophy, and history. Joseph Schloss, *Foundation: B-Boys, B-Girls, and Hip-Hop Culture in New York* (New York: Oxford University Press, 2009), 156.

78. See Wiggles dance in a more recent video, "All Judges Demo," YouTube video, posted by Boog Studio TV, January 27, 2019, 10:13, https://www.youtube.com/watch?v=kGhDpX8aQE. The Electric Boogaloos include Sam Solomon, Timothy Popin' Pete Solomon, Steffan Mr. Wiggles Clemente, Steve Suga Pop da Silva, and Stephen Skeeter Rabbit Nichols (1960–2006). Early members included Robot Dane, Puppet Boozer, Creeping Sidney, and Scarecrow Scalley.

79. For up-close examples of this appearing/disappearing act, see Taylor Pierce (@taylor_thatdancer) on Instagram.

80. Quoted from a video posted to the now-defunct website West Coast Poppin (http://www.westcoastpoppin.com) in 2009: Steffan Clemente, "Mr. Wiggles Gives Advice on Popping."

81. The focused use of muscle tension and relaxation to encourage deeper relaxation and efficiency of movement is also present in release techniques and therapeutic movement methods often incorporated into European-derived modern and postmodern dance traditions. I'm thinking for example of Alexander technique and the Feldenkrais method.

82. See Leigh Breeze-Lee Foaad's explanation of muscle training in "Popping Dance Tutorial- How to Get Harder Pops!," YouTube video, posted by VersaStyle, November 18, 2021, 9:36, https://www.youtube.com/watch?v=hz1fj6QIhRk. In the video, Breeze-Lee demonstrates the Fresno foundational move.

83. Clemente, "Mr. Wiggles Gives Advice on Popping" (defunct video).

84. Clemente.

85. For aural kinesthesia, see Imani Kai-Johnson, "Music Meant to Make You Move: Considering the Aural Kinesthetic," *Sounding Out!* (blog), June 18, 2012, http://soundstudiesblog.com/2012/06/18/music-meant-to-make-you-move-considering-the-aural-kinesthetic/

86. Crawley, "Otherwise Movements." See polycentrism in the freestyles of She Street (a.k.a. Sheopatra) going down to the floor at the Poppers Picnic in Los Angeles: "Ladies GetDown Cypher @ 5th Popper's Picnic 7/14/12," YouTube video, posted by Jay Tee, July 18, 2012, 8:54, at 0:36 and 6:50, https://www.youtube.com/watch?v=DxnxeBsFEnM

87. Kevin Quashie, *Black Aliveness, or a Poetics of Being* (Durham, NC: Duke University Press, 2021), 15, 21.

88. Quashie, 15.

89. Martha Graham, *Blood Memory* (New York: Doubleday, 1991), 251.

90. Wiggles's mirror writing resonates with feminist theorist Trinh T. Minh-ha's use of mirror writing as a metaphor for writing that subverts Enlightenment transparency-rationalism. Minh-ha, *Woman, Native, Other: Writing Postcoloniality and Feminism* (Bloomington: Indiana University Press, 1989), 5–46.

91. Kevin Quashie, *The Sovereignty of Quiet: Beyond Resistance in Black Culture* (Piscataway, NJ: Rutgers University Press, 2012), 4. Also see Sarah Cervenak, who points out, "black movement is, more often than not, *read* as disruptive physicality, a philosophical problem to be solved as opposed to that which resolves philosophical problems." Cervenak, *Wandering: Philosophical Performances of Racial and Sexual Freedom* (Durham, NC: Duke University Press, 2014), 5 (original emphasis).

92. Quashie, *The Sovereignty of Quiet*, 133, 134.

93. Jon Bayani, interview by author, Union City, California, February 17, 2010. See "Bionic - Teaching Reel," YouTube video, posted by BionicBayani, November 14, 2011, 2:55, https://www.youtube.com/watch?v=dzLvaIkrKeY

94. Denise Ferreira da Silva uses the terms *affectability* and *transparency* to offer a detailed description of modern representation that grounds a political ontology of antiblackness. Silva, *Toward a Global Idea of Race* (Minneapolis: University of Minnesota Press, 2007).

95. Quashie, *The Sovereignty of Quiet*, 134. Manu Vimalassery, Juliana Hu Pegues, and Alyosha Goldstein engage critical indigenous thought to describe colonial unknowing in terms of an epistemological orientation that buttresses certain uses of settler colonial theory. Vimalassery, Pegues, and Goldstein, "Introduction: On Colonial Unknowing," *Theory & Event* 19, no. 4 (2016), https://www.muse.jhu.edu/article/633283

96. Quashie, *The Sovereignty of Quiet*, 119.

97. Denise Ferreira da Silva, "Toward a Black Feminist Poethics: The Quest(ion) of Blackness toward the End of the World," *Black Scholar* 44, no. 2 (2014): 90.

98. Warren, "The Catastrophe," 358.

99. Flooridians Workshop at Massive Monkees: The Beacon, Seattle, February 13, 2019.

100. Warren, "The Catastrophe," 358.

101. Also see Jeff Chang's interview with hip hop concert dance choreographer Rennie Harris about spiritual connections between popping and Japanese butoh performance in Chang, *Total Chaos: The Art and Aesthetics of Hip-Hop* (New York: Basic Civitas Books, 2006), 67–68.

102. Crawley, *Blackpentecostal Breath*, 6.

103. Dana Dorham, interview by author, Berkeley, California, 2015.

104. See James Higgins, "The Robot: The Dance or the Act?," Locker Legends, accessed June 15, 2023, https://2022.lockerlegends.net/the-robot/

105. The Clinkers skits were broadcast on CBS's *The Shields and Yarnell Show* in 1977–78. Shields started out performing at the Hollywood Wax Museum in the late 1960s. Marcel Marceau discovered him there and invited Shields to attend his École Internationale de Mime in Paris, on full scholarship. However, Shields was more interested in the everyday art of mime and left the school, relocating to the San Francisco Bay Area with Yarnell.

106. Pop Tart remembers Shields would call the police on him "all the time" when he was dancing at San Francisco's Pier 39, explaining that Shields moved to the Market Street area to avoid competing with the local dance groups. Lonnie R. Green, interview by author, October 22, 2011.

107. Tommy Washington, interview by author, Berkeley, California, May 2015.

108. See "(BRS) Boogaloo Robot Strut (Bay Area Dance)," YouTube video, posted by dizzrockn, May 5, 2008, 7:46, https://www.youtube.com/watch?v=DuYqpWVAiz4. Richmond Robotter Ralph Plik Plok Montejo (collaborating with dancer Zulu Gremlin) contributed elements of the MTV Video Music Award–nominated choreography for Missy Elliott's video "Lose Control" (2005), which showcases Richmond style.

109. Renée Lesley, interview by author, Richmond, California, 2010.

110. Lesley.

111. Sara Ahmed, *Living a Feminist Life* (Durham, NC: Duke University Press, 2017), 7.

112. Emilio Austin Jr., quoted in Heather Wisner, "From Street to Studio: Hip Hop Comes Inside," *Dance Magazine* 80, no. 9 (2006): 76.

113. bell hooks, "Homeplace (a Site of Resistance)," In *Available Means: An Anthology of Women's Rhetoric(s)*, edited by Joy Ritchie and Kate Ronald (Pittsburgh: University of Pittsburgh Press, 2001), 384, 386.

114. hooks, 388.

115. Deborah Granny Robotroid Delois Johnson, interview by author, East Oakland, California, January 12, 2010.

116. On Richmond's cultural significance, see "Destiny Muhammad on Rosie Lee Tompkins," YouTube video, posted by Berkeley Art Museum & Pacific Film Archive, July 14, 2021, 36:51, https://www.youtube.com/watch?v=ZEtgp5S38aM, for a sonic response to the improvised quilt-making practice of artist Rosie Lee Tompkins (1936–2006), who migrated to Richmond in 1958.

117. Richard Rothstein, *The Color of Law: A Forgotten History of How Our Government Segregated America* (New York: Liveright, 2017), 5.

118. Shirley Ann Wilson Moore, *To Place Our Deeds: The African American Community in Richmond, California, 1910–1963* (Berkeley: University of California Press, 2001).

119. Moore, 4.

120. McKittrick, *Demonic Grounds*, x.

121. Renée Lesley, interview by author, Richmond, California, 2010.

122. Judith Hamera, *Dancing Communities: Performance, Difference, and Connection in the Global City* (New York: Palgrave Macmillan, 2007), 77.

123. Hamera, 67.

124. Raquel Monroe, "'I Don't Want to Do African . . . What about My Technique?': Transforming Dancing Places into Spaces in the Academy," *Journal of Pan African Studies* 4, no. 6 (2011): 45.

125. Hamera, *Dancing Communities*, 75.

126. Aimee Cox, *Shapeshifters: Black Girls and the Choreography of Citizenship* (Durham, NC: Duke University Press, 2015), 27.

127. Cox, 27.

128. Renée Lesley, interview by author, Richmond, California, 2010.

129. Crawley, *Blackpentecostal Breath*, 2–11.

130. Renée Lesley, interview by author, Richmond, California, 2010.

131. Goldman, *I Want to Be Ready*, 46.

132. Crawley, "Otherwise Movements."

133. Cox, *Shapeshifters*, 29 (emphasis added).

134. Monroe, "I Don't Want to Do African . . . What about My Technique?," 45.

135. hooks, "Homeplace," 389.

136. Medea Sirkas formed in San Francisco in 1991, with Fayzo, Boogaloo Dana, and Justice Cleo Supreme. Fayzo traces their lineage to antecedent strutting groups Demons of the Mind, founded by Larry McDonald in 1978, and Live Incorporated. Dennis Infante, "Interview with Medea Sirkas aka Demons of the Mind," *One Cypher* (blog), January 3, 2005, http://www.onecypher.com/2005/01/03/interview-with-medea-sirkas-aka-demons-of-the-mind/

137. Crawley describes "an excessive otherwise of breath . . . 'impure' appendages to words that are no less important for, no less generative of, meaning." Crawley, *Blackpentecostal Breath*, 46.

138. Medea Sirkas, in conversation with author, Berkeley, California, May 5, 2015.

139. Medea Sirkas, dancing for the Robot Project, in collaboration with the author and Dr. Ken Goldberg, University of California, Berkeley, May 2015.

140. Tommy Washington, interview by author, Berkeley, California, May 2015.

141. For an explanation that puts dance in touch with jazz music, see David's Guitar Loft (@davidsguitarloft), "How does Dizzy Gillespie keep time?," Instagram post, February 18, 2023, https://www.instagram.com/reel/Coz1BPqgSh1/. Thanks to d. Sabela grimes for this reference.

142. See Naomi Macalalad Bragin, "Streetdance and Black Aesthetics," in *The Oxford Handbook of Hip Hop Dance Studies*, ed. Mary Fogarty and Imani Kai-Johnson (Oxford: Oxford University Press, 2022), 347–64.

143. See chapter 1, "At Netta's House." For an example of nonverbal vocal percussion in Get Lite cipher dancing of Harlem youth, see "Black Starr vs Kiidd Patt Liive=]," YouTube video, posted by cornbread126bee, April 4, 2008, 9:49, https://www.youtube.com/watch?v=k1UCmpEM-Lg

144. "Justin Bieber's 'Somebody to Love' Video Shoot—Medea Sirkas Behind

the Scenes," YouTube video, posted by Zulu Gremlin, June 24, 2010, 0:28, https://www.youtube.com/watch?v=D7yPIFMvsGk (video now private).

145. Jocelyn Vena, "Justin Bieber 'Somebody to Love' Video Premieres Friday," MTV (website), June 10, 2010, https://www.mtv.com/news/ootl38/justin-bieber-somebody-to-love-video-premieres-friday

146. Tommy Washington and Dana Dorham, in conversation with author, October 12, 2022.

147. See the earlier section "Stop-Motion Dance."

148. Crawley, *Blackpentecostal Breath*, 2–11. For a parallel critique of proprietary whiteness in the context of the dance style Turfing captured on MTV's World of Jenks, see Naomi Macalalad Bragin, "Shot and Captured: Turf Dance, YAK Films, and the Oakland, California, R.I.P. Project," *TDR: The Journal of Performance Studies* 58, no. 2 (2014): 99–114.

149. "Meet Hi-Hat: Celebrity Choreographer and Sears Arrive Air Band Judge," YouTube video, posted by searsarrivelounge, August 4, 2009, 1:50, https://www.youtube.com/watch?v=PEqdvmNOfFU. I was surprised to find out only after I wrote this section and shared it with Fayzo that Hi-Hat was the lead choreographer who, via her prior connection with Zulu Gremlin, brought Medea Sirkas to be in Justin Bieber's video.

150. Hi-Hat also starts out explaining that when she was growing up, one of her inspirations for dance was watching cartoons.

151. Most robot dancers I interviewed would similarly slip into vocal percussion when I asked them to describe the feel of the dance.

152. I also write about the difference between choreography intrinsic to improvisation-based dance vernaculars and choreo-centric dance. See Bragin, "Streetdance and Black Aesthetics."

153. Geneva Smitherman's foundational work on African American English and political activism considers the significance of code-switching as an African American vernacular practice, among students and in classroom pedagogies. Smitherman, *Talkin and Testifyin: The Language of Black America* (1977; Detroit, MI: Wayne State University Press, 1986).

154. Stefano Harney and Fred Moten describe this feel as "Hapticality, or Love," in *The Undercommons: Fugitive Planning and Black Study* (New York: Minor Compositions, 2013), 97–99.

155. Harney and Moten, 61.

156. Silva, "Toward a Black Feminist Poethics," 85; and on the idea of separability within the context of Enlightenment philosophy, see Silva, *Toward a Global Idea of Race*.

157. Sharpe, *In the Wake*.

158. Stuckey, *Slave Culture*.

Chapter 3

1. The epigraphs are quoted from, respectively: Tyrone Proctor, recorded interview by Ohana Creative Video, n.d., 4:58, reposted by Jody Watley, "In Cele-

bration of Tyrone Proctor," Jody Watley (website), June 8, 2020, https://jodywatley.net/2020/06/08/in-celebration-of-tyrone-proctor/; "Afropessimism and Its Others: A Discussion between Hortense J. Spillers and Lewis R. Gordon," YouTube video, posted by Soka University of America, May 24, 2021, 1:23:31, https://www.youtube.com/watch?v=Z-s-Ltuo6NI

2. Tyrone Proctor, dance class at In the Groove Studios, Oakland, California, March 27, 2012.

3. "Waves of Emotions - Axelle Ebony - Dance Film - Whacking," YouTube video, posted by Axelle "Ebony" Munezero, February 6, 2023, 4:08, https://www.youtube.com/watch?v=qLJo-az6qVo.

4. Andrew Frank, Arthur Goff, and Tinker are often collectively referenced as innovators of waacking/punking, both by the 1970s generation and by contemporary dancers. All three dancers appeared on *Soul Train.*

5. "Soul Train Ball & Battle" was held at Uptown Studios in Oakland, California. See "Tyrone 'The Bone' Proctor Shaking His Groove Thang," YouTube video, posted by Funkd Uptv, March 25, 2012, 1:00, https://www.youtube.com/watch?v=b1cuEomvCwo; "Soul Train Ball & Battle: A Tribute to Don Cornelius Oakland, CA 03/24/12," YouTube video, posted by Mooncricket Films, March 25, 2012, 7:23, https://www.youtube.com/watch?v=e9r6SlzQtco

6. See M. Jacqui Alexander and Gina Athena Ulysse, "Groundings on *Rasanblaj* with M. Jacqui Alexander," *emisférica* 12, no. 1 (2021), https://hemisphericinstitute.org/en/emisferica-121-caribbean-rasanblaj/12-1-essays/e-121-essay-alexander-interview-with-gina.html

7. The section epigraphs are from, respectively: Saidiya Hartman, "Venus in Two Acts," *Small Axe: A Caribbean Journal of Criticism* 12, no. 2 (2008): 4; Wu Tsang, interview by Paige K. Bradley, *Artforum*, March 23, 2016, https://www.artforum.com/interviews/wu-tsang-discusses-her-film-debuting-in-hong-kong-at-spring-workshop-58841; Alexis Pauline Gumbs, *Undrowned: Black Feminist Lessons from Marine Mammals* (Chico, CA: AK Press, 2020), 16.

8. I use the asterisk in trans* after Marquis Bey, "The Trans*-ness of Blackness, the Blackness of Trans*-ness," *TSQ: Transgender Studies Quarterly* 4, no. 2 (2017): 284.

9. For an in-depth, community-engaged ethnographic study of Black queer space and place in Los Angeles, see Kai M. Green, "Into the Darkness: A Quare (Re)membering of Los Angeles in a Time of Crises, 1981-Present" (PhD diss., University of Southern California, 2017), which includes interviews with Jewel Thais-Williams, founder of the first black LGBT club, the Catch One, in 1972.

10. Archie Burnett, phone conversation with author, March 14, 2023. Archie remembers traveling to Amsterdam and France in the early 1990s, teaching clubbing movement but not yet referring to the dances by separate style names. Breed of Motion's first iteration included dancers Archie Burnett, Steven Enrique, Benjamin Harris, Javier Izquierdo, Willi Ninja, and Tyrone Proctor.

11. "What Is Waacking? Queer History of Punking, Whacking, Waacking 1970-2003: The Intro," YouTube video, posted by Kumari Suraj, July 3, 2016, 8:40, https://www.youtube.com/watch?v=l62XRkUym2Q

12. Samara Cohen, interview by author, 2013. At the time of the interview, Lockerooo was organizing a party called Waacktopia at Sapphire Lounge in New

York City, with the purpose of cultivating community for waackers to experience the dance within a club environment that centered disco music.

13. Naomi Macalalad Bragin, "Techniques of Black Male Re/Dress: Corporeal Drag and Kinesthetic Politics in the Rebirth of Waacking/Punking'," *Women & Performance: A Journal of Feminist Theory* 24, no. 1 (2014): 61–78.

14. Marlon M. Bailey, *Butch Queens Up in Pumps: Gender, Performance, and Ballroom Culture in Detroit* (Ann Arbor: University of Michigan Press, 2013).

15. See Alexander and Ulysse, "Groundings on *Rasanblaj*."

16. Alexander and Ulysse.

17. See Niko Chike, "Brian 'Footwork' Green and the House Dance Conference," July 2003, Other America Files (website), posted February 25, 2019, https://www.theotheramericafiles.org/2019/02/25/brian

18. The section epigraph is from Tavia Nyong'o, "Punk'd Theory," *Social Text* 23, no. 3/4 (2005): 20.

Located at 4225 Crenshaw Boulevard in Los Angeles's Leimert Park neighborhood, Maverick's Flat opened in 1966 and was commonly known as the "Apollo of the West." In 2000, the club was designated a Los Angeles Historic-Cultural Monument. The building has undergone renovations and changing ownership since 2016, with plans by current owner Nina RoZá to reopen as a private event venue.

19. "Celebration" took place just days after the 2012 Grammy Awards aired, and it joined multiple responses to the Grammys' structural erasure of nonwhite artists. Not only did the Grammys cut thirty-one music categories that year (mostly affecting artists of color), but the In Memoriam slideshow left out both Don Cornelius and Etta James (who had died weeks earlier), despite including Whitney Houston, who died the day before the award ceremony. Aggrieved hosts Questlove and LL Cool J called out this erasure. Jorge Rivas, "Carlos Santana: Grammy Academy Is Racist for Cutting Award Categories," *Colorlines*, August 19, 2011, https://www.colorlines.com/articles/carlos

20. In the 2000s, these early-generation dancers were traveling largely within Europe, Japan, South Korea, Taiwan, and Hong Kong, as well as Canada and the United States. Dancers in Russia and Brazil were also organizing key cultural events. In 2015, Michoacán-born Viktor Manoel toured to Mexico City (see Caitlin Donohue, "Can You Waack?" 48 Hills (website), January 7, 2016, https://48hills.org/2016/01/can-you-whack/). I was not able to confirm instances of dancers traveling to continental Africa, the Middle East, Central America or the Caribbean, to teach formal classes. Among younger generation dancers, Lorena Valenzuela more recently brought her festival, Strike With Force, to Mexico. Kumari Suraj created Bollywaack (a style fusing their Indian cultural heritage with waacking) in 2009, traveling to India to teach, choreograph, and judge. See "What Is Bollywaack?," Kumari Suraj (website), accessed June 15, 2023, https://kumarisuraj.com/bollywaack/

21. Brian Green incorporated waacking/punking into his video choreography for "Free," sung by R & B artist Mýa, for which he won the 2001 American Choreographers Award for Best Hip-Hop Choreography in a Music Video.

22. Kumari Suraj offers a significant online resource on waacking/punking

history, culling together a wide range of photos and video footage of the dance from the 1970s through 2003. See "What Is Waacking? Queer History of Punking, Whacking, Waacking 1970–2003."

23. Jennifer Dunning, "Last Dance: A Studio Tears Up Its Floors," *New York Times*, February 9, 2008. Fazil's closed its doors on February 8, 2008, after seventy-three years in the Hell's Kitchen neighborhood of Manhattan. Gentrification is central to the story of Fazil's demolition.

24. Nelson George, *The Hippest Trip in America: "Soul Train" and the Evolution of Culture and Style* (New York: HarperCollins, 2014), 63.

25. Tyrone would carry to his classes a voluminous collection of burner CDs with his curated playlists of disco tracks for his students to study.

26. Known as an original dancer of waacking/punking, Lonny Kevin Carbajal was born on December 11, 1959, and died on November 13, 1989, both in Los Angeles. He appeared in *Roller Boogie* (1979), *Xanadu* (1980), and *Breakin' 2: Electric Boogaloo* (1984).

27. "Jody Watley - Still a Thrill," YouTube video, posted by Jody Watley, June 16, 2009, 4:41, https://www.youtube.com/watch?v=kg6Dt3pia9g

28. "Grace Jones Do or Die Feat. Viktor (Manoel) and Danny Lugo," YouTube video, posted by AlyssaChloeNYC, January 7, 2012, 0:27, https://www.youtube.com/watch?v=v2-1uUbYFL4

29. See Cathy Cohen, *The Boundaries of Blackness: AIDS and the Breakdown of Black Politics* (Chicago: University of Chicago Press, 1999).

30. Vital to waacking/punking social spaces, as well, are movement stories of Mexican and Central American dancers, their mobility and life possibilities often cutting across US-Mexico borderlands and becoming bound up in geopolitical strategies of social ordering and control. See Kelly Lytle Hernández's excavation of settler colonial history in the Tongva Basin, *City of Inmates: Conquest, Rebellion, and the Rise of Human Caging in Los Angeles, 1771–1965* (Chapel Hill: University of North Carolina Press, 2017).

31. See Essex Hemphill, ed., *Brother to Brother: New Writings by Black Gay Men*, conceived by Joseph Hemphill Beam (Alyson Publications, 1991); Marlon Riggs, *Tongues Untied* (1989), documentary film, 55 min.; Marlon Riggs, *Black Is . . . Black Ain't* (1995), documentary film, 98 min.; and Kenyon Farrow's website, https://kenyonfarrow.com

32. Michel-Rolph Trouillot challenges the idea that silences do not have power to enter history: "presences and absences embodied in sources (artifacts and bodies that turn event into fact) and archives (facts collected, thematized, and processed as documents and monuments) are neither neutral or natural. They are created. As such, they are not mere presences and absences, but mentions or silences of various kinds and degrees." Further, "some peoples and things are absent in history . . . this absence itself is constitutive of the process of historical production." Trouillot, *Silencing the Past: Power and the Production of History* (Boston: Beacon Press, 2015), 48, 49. Dancers challenge one another's accounts to resist freezing hip hop/streetdance history in static, linear, or unidirectional terms. History is as much about people's recounting of what happened as it is the content of historical events themselves.

33. Margarita Reyna, interview by author, February 20, 2014.

34. Tyrone Proctor, interview by author, 2017.

35. Ana Sanchez, "Punkin+Posing=Whacking," panel at Peridance Studios, New York, July 21, 2011. Tavia Nyong'o draws on Toni Morrison's definition of American Africanism to locate punk in a theory of the vernacular, modeling a dialectical approach to queer theories of race and sexuality that blur hard divisions between black and white. Nyong'o studies the "experiential field" indexed by the reappearance of the word *punk* in 1970s British music subcultures and in MTV's practical joke show of the 2000s, *Punk'd*. See Nyong'o, "Punk'd Theory," 22.

36. Sanchez, "Punkin+Posing=Whacking."

37. Nathaniel Mackey, "Other: From Noun to Verb," *Representations* 39 (1992): 51–70.

38. Viktor Manoel, interview by author, 2011.

39. Tyrone Proctor, telephone conversation with author, March 21, 2014.

40. My research refers to Gino's location at 1132 Vine Street, although some online sites mention an earlier location that was open a few years before burning down. Other 1970s nightclubs that suffered major fires were Jewel's Catch One and Total Experience, the latter of which burned down.

41. Margarita also recalled a high school program that bused teenagers from East Los Angeles to and from Gino's on Saturday nights.

42. Billy Goodson, interview by author, January 8, 2021.

43. Viktor Manoel, interview by author, 2011. Michael Angelo succumbed to AIDS in 1996.

44. Hustle was created in the 1970s, primarily within communities of Puerto Rican teenagers living in the South Bronx, a history documented by first-generation dancer Willie Estrada in *The Dancing Gangsters of the South Bronx: Rise of the Latin Hustle* (New York: Latin Empire, 2016). Like waacking/punking, hustle waned in the wake of the AIDS epidemic, with the passing of many gay innovators and the stigma attached to disco music and queer culture. The dance form resurged in 2000s streetdance culture, with practitioners showing a renewed interest in partner dancing that expanded streetdance beyond solo improvised dance styles. Thanks to Abdiel Jacobsen for their help with this citation.

45. José Esteban Muñoz, "The Wildness of the Punk Rock Commons," *South Atlantic Quarterly* 117, no. 3 (2018): 658.

46. Muñoz, 655.

47. Margarita Reyna, interview by author, 2014.

48. Billy Goodson, interview by author, January 8, 2021.

49. Ana Sanchez, "Punking+Posing=Whacking," workshop at Peridance Studios, New York, July 20, 2011.

50. See Bragin, "Techniques of Black Male Re/Dress."

51. Adolfo Quiñones, interview by author, August 28, 2011.

52. Billy Goodson, interview by author, 2020.

53. The epigraph and subsequent Shabba Doo quotations in this section are from Adolfo Quiñones, interview by author, August 28, 2011.

54. Alexander and Ulysse, "Groundings on *Rasanblaj*."

55. Alok Vaid-Menon, *Beyond the Gender Binary* (New York: Penguin Workshop, 2020), 16–17.

56. Vaid-Menon, 25.

57. Kareem Khubchandani, *Ishtyle: Accenting Gay Indian Nightlife* (Ann Arbor: University of Michigan Press, 2020), 3. Khubchandani uses drag performance as an ethnographic research method for making performer-audience power dynamics visible.

58. Billy Goodson, interview by author, January 8, 2021.

59. Stefano Harney and Fred Moten, *The Undercommons: Fugitive Planning and Black Study* (New York: Minor Compositions, 2013), 125–26.

60. Omise'eke Natasha Tinsley, *Ezili's Mirrors: Imagining Black Queer Genders* (Durham, NC: Duke University Press, 2018), 43.

61. The epigraph and subsequent Margarita quotations in this section are from Margarita Reyna, interview by author, February 20, 2014.

62 . Anna Martine Whitehead, "Expressing Life through Loss: On Queens That Fall with a Freak Technique," in *Queer Dance*, ed. Clare Croft (Oxford: Oxford University Press, 2017), 282.

63. Ana Sanchez, "Punking+Posing=Whacking," workshop at Peridance Studios, New York, July 20, 2011; Whitehead, "Expressing Life through Loss," 283 (quoted).

64. Susan Leigh Foster, "Dance and/as Competition in the Privately Owned US Studio," in *The Oxford Handbook of Dance and Politics*, ed. Rebekah J. Kowal, Gerald Siegmund, and Randy Martin (Oxford: Oxford University Press, 2017), 64.

65. Dallace Zeigler, speaking in "Waacking Through Three Generations," YouTube video, posted by himerria, September 15, 2013, 1:52, https://www.youtube.com/watch?v=N6phaHSrZZo

66. Foster, "Dance and/as Competition in the Privately Owned US Studio," 68.

67. The section epigraph is from Fred Brathwaite, speaking in "Warhol, Club Culture, and the Black Celebrity Image," panel conversation moderated by Adrian Loving, YouTube video, posted by the Andy Warhol Museum, November 2, 2022, 1:16:59, https://www.youtube.com/watch?v=xDdSV1GoEXU

68. Katrina Hazzard-Donald, "Dance in Hip Hop Culture," in *Droppin' Science: Critical Essays on Rap Music and Hip Hop Culture*, ed. William Eric Perkins (Philadelphia: Temple University Press, 1996), 225.

69. *Soul Train* dancers touring internationally in the 1970s helped establish Japan as a key location for the global dissemination of early hip hop/streetdance. Waacking/punking continued to be taught at dance studios in Japan during the 1980s and 1990s, as the dance was waning in the United States. Archie Burnett also describes traveling to western Europe in the early 1990s to teach clubbing with Willi Ninja, although they didn't refer to the dance directly by name at that time. Archie Burnett, phone conversation with author, March 14, 2023.

70. Muñoz, "The Wildness of the Punk Rock Commons," 658.

71. For example, Disco Demolition Night was a 1979 event at Chicago's

Comiskey Park (then the home of the White Sox), spearheaded by white rock 'n' roll radio DJ Steve Dahl, who blew up a dumpster filled with disco, funk, and R & B records, ultimately setting off a riot in the crowd. See Daryl Easlea, *Everybody Dance: Chic and the Politics of Disco* (London: Helter Skelter, 2004). Nile Rodgers, founding member of the cross-genre band Chic, was a Black Panther and tied his lyrics to a politicized experience of blackness.

72. Tavia Nyong'o, "I Feel Love: Disco and Its Discontents," *Criticism* 50, no. 1 (2008): 101–12.

73. Nyong'o, 103.

74. Lyric quoted from Too Short, "Burn Rubber," *Married to the Game* (Jive Records, 2003). For an example of how this discourse played out in black political analysis, see Eldridge Cleaver, *Soul On Ice* (1968; New York: Delta Trade Paperbacks, 1999).

75. As waacking/punking and hustle gained visibility in 2000s hip hop/streetdance culture, dancers circulated their living knowledge of early disco music's cultural relationship to hip hop. Thanks to Steffan Clemente for referencing the foundational work of these early hip hop DJs. See "Disco Era: Proto Disco 1," YouTube video, posted by MixMasterMax, December 27, 2008, 9:26, https://www.youtube.com/watch?v=hG327SioTg4

76. For a sonic example that blends rap with house music, a genre that grew from disco, see Azealia Banks, "1991," YouTube video, posted by Azealia Banks, September 2, 2012, 3:30, https://www.youtube.com/watch?v=ooM_9ca8hxE

77. The section epigraphs are from, respectively: "bell hooks - Are You Still a Slave? Liberating the Black Female Body," YouTube video, posted by the New School, May 7, 2014, 1:55:32, https://www.youtube.com/watch?v=rJkohNROvzs; Alok Vaid-Menon, "Femininity Does Not Belong to Cis Women," Alok (website), September 17, 2015, https://www.alokvmenon.com/blog/2015/9/17/femininity-does-not-belong-to-cis-women. On queer nightlife, see Kemi Adeyemi, Kareem Khubchandani, and Ramón H. Rivera-Servera, introduction to *Queer Nightlife*, ed. Kemi Adeyemi, Kareem Khubchandani, and Ramón H. Rivera-Servera (Ann Arbor: University of Michigan Press, 2021), 16.

78. Heather Ferrigan, "Dance, Sisterhood, Love: Martha & Niki Have It All," Stocktown (website), January 19, 2016, http://stocktown.com/dance-sisterhood-love-martha-niki-have-it-al. Also see the documentary film *Martha & Niki* (2015), directed by Tora Mårtens. Martha came to Sweden from Uganda at age thirteen, and Niki was born in Ethiopia and adopted as a baby by her Swedish parents. See "Niki & Martha New Style Winners of Juste Debout 2010," YouTube video, posted by streetstar, January 6, 2011, 3:06, https://www.youtube.com/watch?v=pWJqNWyVNKw

79. *B-girl* in its most culturally specific sense refers to girls who break, but women and girls may use the label more casually to refer to their identification with hip hop culture as a whole, including popping, locking, and other streetdance styles.

80. Joseph Schloss, *Foundation: B-Boys, B-Girls, and Hip-Hop Culture in New York* (New York: Oxford University Press, 2009), 57.

81. Imani Kai-Johnson, "From Blues Women to B-Girls: Performing Badass

Femininity," *Women & Performance: A Journal of Feminist Theory* 24, no. 1 (2014): 19.

82. Kai-Johnson, 25. While she sees aggression and confrontation to be intrinsic to breaking aesthetics, I would also consider how such qualities become emphasized in the context of performance, in this case battling. This is true for other traditionally male-dominated styles like hip hop and popping, which I have found in practice can be imbued with a range of emotional and affective qualities.

83. This and subsequent Waackeisha quotations in this section are from Leah McKesey, interview by author, 2013.

84. Waackeisha's hip hop name is Leah McFly, which she associates with her b-girl/hip hop persona.

85. Audre Lorde, "The Uses of the Erotic: The Erotic as Power" (paper presented at the Fourth Berkshire Conference on the History of Women, Mount Holyoke College, August 25, 1978.

86. Tinsley, *Ezili's Mirrors*, 36.

87. Tinsley, 41.

88. Marcia Ochoa, *Queen for a Day: Transformistas, Beauty Queens, and the Performance of Femininity in Venezuela* (Durham, NC: Duke University Press, 2014) 5 and 2.

89. Kai M. Green and Marquis Bey, "Where Black Feminist Thought and Trans* Feminism Meet: A Conversation," *Souls* 19, no. 4 (2017): 439.

90. Marlon M. Bailey, "Gender/Racial Realness: Theorizing the Gender System in Ballroom Culture," *Feminist Studies* 37, no. 2 (2011): 381-2.

91. Anonymous, interview by author, July 13, 2013.

92. Alexander and Ulysse, "Groundings on *Rasanblaj*."

93. This and subsequent quotations from Reggie in this section are from Reginald Lavince Seale, in conversation with author, May 6, 2013.

94. Darieck Scott, *Extravagant Abjection: Blackness, Power, and Sexuality in the African American Literary Imagination* (New York: New York University Press, 2010), 171. Scott also offers a rejoinder that is helpful to hold in balance: "which is not to say that women cannot manipulate or play with abjection but that where women do so the political ramifications may more easily appear to be a confirmation of the defeat with which abjection works rather than a complication of it" (20).

95. Adolfo Quiñones, interview by author, 2011.

96. Fiona Buckland, *Impossible Dance: Club Culture and Queer World-Making* (Middletown, CT: Wesleyan University Press, 2002), 36.

97. The section epigraph is from Billy Goodson, interview by author, January 18, 2021.

98. Willi Ninja (1961-2006) is founder of the House of Ninja, a legendary innovator and contributor to vogue/Ball culture. Madonna has been critiqued for her failure to acknowledge Willi's heavy influence on her hit 1990 video "Vogue." Willi died of AIDS-related heart failure in New York City at age forty-five. Archie Burnett is a renowned dancer, choreographer, and international teacher of waacking and voguing.

99. "My World Is Empty Without You" is a song written for the Supremes and released by Motown Records in 1965, with lead vocals by Diana Ross and instrumentation by the Funk Brothers and Detroit Symphony Orchestra.

100. The section epigraphs are from, respectively: Karen Barad, "Transmaterialities: Trans*/Matter/Realities and Queer Political Imaginings," *GLQ: A Journal of Lesbian and Gay Studies* 21, no. 2–3 (2015): 387; Archie Burnett, interview by author, August 2, 2011.

101. Tyrone Proctor, recorded interview by Ohana Creative Video, n.d., 4:58, posted to Watley, "In Celebration of Tyrone Proctor."

102. Julian B. Carter, "Sex Time Machine for Touching the Transcestors," *TSQ: Transgender Studies Quarterly* 5, no. 4 (2018): 693.

103. AB Brown, "Relational Generativity in South African Queer Nightlife," in Adeyemi, Khubchandani, and Rivera-Servera, *Queer Nightlife*, 68, 73.

104. Adeyemi, Khubchandani, and Rivera-Servera, introduction to *Queer Nightlife*, 16.

105. Archie Burnett, interview by author, August 2, 2011.

106. Billy Goodson, interview by author, January 18, 2021. Billy was lead dancer and choreographer for Diana Ross, to whom he introduced waacking/punking's innovators. The dancers in order of appearance at Ross's 1979 performance are Andrew Frank, Arthur Goff, Tinker, Billy Starr, Billy Goodson, Andrew Frank, and Lonny Carbajal. See "Diana Ross with Waack Dancers," YouTube video, posted by Markanthony Henry, April 21, 2007, 5:24, http://www.youtube.com/watch?v=etnptlY_4cg

107. David Johnson, interview by author, October 24, 2020.

108. Harney and Moten, *The Undercommons*, 98.

109. Margarita Reyna, interview by author, February 2, 2014.

110. Whitehead, "Expressing Life through Loss," 284.

111. Saidiya Hartman, *The Plot of Her Undoing*, Notes on Feminisms 2 (Feminist Art Coalition, 2020), 5.

112. Billy Goodson, interview by author, January 18, 2021.

Bedtime Story

1. https://www.culturaldc.org/torrents-press-press

2. See Saidiya Hartman, "Venus in Two Acts," *Small Axe: A Caribbean Journal of Criticism* 12, no. 2 (2008): 1–14; Saidiya Hartman, *The Plot of Her Undoing*, Notes on Feminisms 2 (Feminist Art Coalition, 2020).

3. Denise Ferreira da Silva, "Toward a Black Feminist Poethics: The Quest(ion) of Blackness toward the End of the World," *Black Scholar* 44, no. 2 (2014): 81–97.

4. Sylvia Wynter, "Sambos and Minstrels," *Social Text* 1, no. 1 (1979): 149–56.

BIBLIOGRAPHY

Written Texts and Presentations

Abdurraqib, Hanif. *A Little Devil in America: Notes in Praise of Black Performance.* New York: Random House, 2021.

Acham, Christine. *Revolution Televised: Prime Time and the Struggle for Black Power.* Minneapolis: University of Minnesota Press, 2004.

Adams-Louis, Amanda, and Brian Polite, organizers. "Street Dance x Screen Dance: A Visual Call and Response." *Black Portraiture[s] VII: Play and Performance,* Rutgers University, Newark, NJ, February 17, 2022.

Adeyemi, Kemi, Kareem Khubchandani, and Ramón H. Rivera-Servera. Introduction to *Queer Nightlife,* edited by Kemi Adeyemi, Kareem Khubchandani, and Ramón H. Rivera-Servera, 1–18. Ann Arbor: University of Michigan Press, 2021.

Ahmed, Sara. *Living a Feminist Life.* Durham, NC: Duke University Press, 2017.

Alexander, M. Jacqui, and Gina Athena Ulysse. "Groundings on *Rasanblaj* with M. Jacqui Alexander." *emisférica* 12, no. 1 (2021). https://hemisphericinstitute.org/en/emisferica-121-caribbean-rasanblaj/12-1-essays/e-121-essay-alexander-interview-with-gina.html

Arnold, Eric K. "Oakland's Original Boogaloos Speak Out, in Hopes of Reclaiming Their Culture." *Oaklandside,* August 18, 2020. https://oaklandside.org/2020/08/18/oaklands-original-boogaloos-speak-out-in-hopes-of-reclaiming-their-culture/

Bailey, David, and Stuart Hall. "The Vertigo of Displacement: Shifts within Black Documentary Practices." *Ten.8* 2, no. 3 (1992): 14–31.

Bailey, Marlon M. *Butch Queens Up in Pumps: Gender, Performance, and Ballroom Culture in Detroit.* Ann Arbor: University of Michigan Press, 2013.

Bailey, Marlon M. "Gender/Racial Realness: Theorizing the Gender System in Ballroom Culture." *Feminist Studies* 37, no. 2 (2011): 365–86.

Barad, Karen. "Transmaterialities: Trans*/Matter/Realities and Queer Political Imaginings." *GLQ: A Journal of Lesbian and Gay Studies* 21, no. 2–3 (2015): 387–422.

Belmar, Sima. "Behind the Screens: Race, Space, and Place in *Saturday Night Fever.*" In *The Oxford Handbook of Screendance Studies,* edited by Douglas Rosenberg, 461–79. Oxford: Oxford University Press, 2016.

Bey, Marquis. "Black Fugitivity Un/Gendered." *Black Scholar* 49, no. 1 (2019): 55–62.

Bey, Marquis. "The Trans*-ness of Blackness, the Blackness of Trans*-ness." *TSQ: Transgender Studies Quarterly* 4, no. 2 (2017): 275–95.

"Blackness, Aesthetics, and Liquidity." *liquid blackness*, 2014. https://liquidblackness.com/blackness-aesthetics-and-liquidity

Blanco Borelli, Melissa. Introduction to *The Oxford Handbook of Dance and the Popular Screen*, edited by Melissa Blanco Borelli, 1–17. Oxford: Oxford University Press, 2014.

Blanco Borelli, Melissa, and Raquel Monroe, eds. "Screening the Skin: Issues of Race and Nation in Screendance." Special issue, *International Journal of Screendance* 9 (2018).

Blount Danois, Ericka. *Love, Peace, and Soul: Behind the Scenes of America's Favorite Dance Show, Soul Train: Classic Moments*. Milwaukee, WI: Backbeat Books, 2013.

Blount Danois, Ericka. "The Story of the Soul Train Dancers." *Wax Poetics*, no. 57 (2013): 66–70.

Bolden, Tony. "Groove Theory: A Vamp on the Epistemology of Funk." *American Studies* 52, no. 4 (2013): 9–34.

Bolden, Tony. *Groove Theory: The Blues Foundation of Funk*. Jackson: University Press of Mississippi, 2020.

"Boogaloo, Robottin' & Struttin': The Untold Story of the West." Hip Hop Congress (website). Accessed June 15, 2023. https://www.hiphopcongress.com/boogaloo-robottin--struttin.html

Bradley, Rizvana. "Black Cinematic Gesture and the Aesthetics of Contagion." *TDR: The Drama Review* 62, no. 1 (2018): 14–30.

Bragin, Naomi Macalalad. "On the Front Porch: Deborah McCoy and Fresno Streetdance." *Tropics of Meta: Historiography for the Masses* (blog), April 3, 2018. https://tropicsofmeta.com/2018/04/03/on-the-front-porch-deborah-mccoy-and-fresno-streetdance/

Bragin, Naomi Macalalad. "Shot and Captured: Turf Dance, YAK Films, and the Oakland, California, R.I.P. Project." *TDR: The Journal of Performance Studies* 58, no. 2 (2014): 99–114.

Bragin, Naomi Macalalad. "Streetdance and Black Aesthetics." In *The Oxford Handbook of Hip Hop Dance Studies*, edited by Mary Fogarty and Imani Kai-Johnson, 347–64. Oxford: Oxford University Press, 2022.

Bragin, Naomi Macalalad. "Techniques of Black Male Re/Dress: Corporeal Drag and Kinesthetic Politics in the Rebirth of Waacking/Punkin'." *Women & Performance: A Journal of Feminist Theory* 24, no. 1 (2014): 61–78.

Broussard, Albert. *Black San Francisco: The Struggle for Racial Equality in the West, 1900–1954*. Lawrence: University of Kansas Press, 1993.

Brown, AB. "Relational Generativity in South African Queer Nightlife." In *Queer Nightlife*, edited by Kemi Adeyemi, Kareem Khubchandani, and Ramón H. Rivera-Servera, 65–75. Ann Arbor: University of Michigan Press, 2021.

brown, adrienne maree. *Emergent Strategy: Shaping Change, Changing Worlds*. Chico, CA: AK Press, 2017.

Buckland, Fiona. *Impossible Dance: Club Culture and Queer World-Making*. Middletown, CT: Wesleyan University Press, 2002.

Carter, Julian B. "Sex Time Machine for Touching the Transcestors." *TSQ: Transgender Studies Quarterly* 5, no. 4 (2018): 691–706.

Cervenak, Sarah. *Wandering: Philosophical Performances of Racial and Sexual Freedom.* Durham, NC: Duke University Press, 2014.

Chambers-Letson, Joshua. *After the Party: A Manifesto for Queer of Color Life.* New York: New York University Press, 2018.

Chandler, Nahum Dimitri. *X—The Problem of the Negro as a Problem for Thought.* New York: Fordham University Press, 2013.

Chang, Jeff. *Can't Stop Won't Stop: A History of the Hip-Hop Generation.* New York: St. Martin's Press, 2005.

Chang, Jeff. *Total Chaos: The Art and Aesthetics of Hip-Hop.* New York: Basic Civitas Books, 2006.

Chike, Niko. "Brian 'Footwork' Green and the House Dance Conference." July 2003, Other America Files (website), posted February 25, 2019. https://www.theotheramericafiles.org/2019/02/25/brian

Cleaver, Eldridge. *Soul On Ice.* 1968. New York: Delta Trade Paperbacks, 1999.

Clemente, Steffan. "Mr. Wiggles Hip Hop Camp." Mr Wiggles (website). Accessed June 15, 2023. https://wigzee.biz/contact/book%20hip%20hop%20camp/

Clemente, Steffan. "What Are Hip Hop Dances." *Mr Wiggles* (blog). Accessed June 15, 2023. https://wigzee.biz/blog/?post=what-are-hip-hop-dances

Cohen, Cathy. *The Boundaries of Blackness: AIDS and the Breakdown of Black Politics.* Chicago: University of Chicago Press, 1999.

Cook, Dave (Davey D). "LA Loses Its Third Hip Hop Legend in a Month-Skeeter Rabbit." Davey D's Hip Hop Political Palace (forum), May 14, 2006. https://www.tapatalk.com/groups/politicalpalace/la-loses-its-third-hip-hop-legend-in-a-month-skeet-t2170.html

Cook, Dave. "Oakland's Boogaloo Reunion BBQ: A History Lesson in West Coast Street Dance." Davey D's Hip Hop Corner (website), September 22, 2015. https://hiphopandpolitics.com/2015/09/22/Oakland

Cox, Aimee. *Shapeshifters: Black Girls and the Choreography of Citizenship.* Durham, NC: Duke University Press, 2015.

Crawley, Ashon. *Blackpentecostal Breath: The Aesthetics of Possibility.* New York: Fordham University Press, 2016.

Crawley, Ashon. "Otherwise Movements." *New Inquiry*, January 19, 2015. https://thenewinquiry.com/otherwise-movements/

Dance Teacher. "4 Ways d. Sabela grimes is Making the Case for Hip Hop in Higher Ed." August 9, 2018. https://dance-teacher.com/d-sabela-grimes

DeFrantz, Thomas. "The Black Beat Made Visible: Body Power in Hip Hop Dance." In *Of the Presence of the Body: Essays on Dance and Performance Theory*, edited by André Lepecki, 64–81. Middletown, CT: Wesleyan University Press, 2004.

Dixon Gottschild, Brenda. *Digging the Africanist Presence in American Performance: Dance and Other Contexts.* Westport, CT: Greenwood Press, 1996.

Dodds, Sherril. *Dance on Screen: Genres and Media from Hollywood to Experimental Art.* New York: Palgrave Macmillan, 2001.

"Don Campbellock Signature Moves." Don Campbell (website). Accessed June 15, 2023. https://campbellock.dance/about-locking/the-campbellock-aka-locking-moves/

Dunning, Jennifer. "Last Dance: A Studio Tears Up Its Floors." *New York Times*, February 9, 2008.

Easlea, Daryl. *Everybody Dance: Chic and the Politics of Disco*. London: Helter Skelter, 2004.

Ebony. "The 'Outrageous' Waack Dancers." August 1978, 64–68.

Estrada, Willie. *The Dancing Gangsters of the South Bronx: Rise of the Latin Hustle*. New York: Latin Empire, 2016.

Farrow, Kenyon. Website. Accessed June 15, 2023. https://kenyonfarrow.com

Ferrigan, Heather. "Dance, Sisterhood, Love: Martha & Niki Have It All." Stocktown (website), January 19, 2016. http://stocktown.com/dance-sisterhood-love-martha-niki-have-it-all/ (site discontinued).

Fikentscher, Kai. *"You Better Work!": Underground Dance Music in New York City*. Hanover, NH: University Press of New England, 2000.

Forman, Murray, and Mark Anthony Neal, eds. *That's the Joint! The Hip-Hop Studies Reader*. 2004. New York: Routledge. 2012.

Foster, James. "Diary of an Ex-Soul Train Dancer: Q&A with Former Soul Train Dancer Jimmy 'Scoo B Doo' Foster, the Master Locker." Interview by Stephen McMillian. Soul Train (website), August 24, 2011. http://soultrain.com/2011/08/24/diary-of-an-ex-soul-train-dancer-qa-with-former-soul-train-dancer-jimmy-scoo-b-doo-foster-the-master-locker/ (site discontinued).

Foster, Susan Leigh. "Dance and/as Competition in the Privately Owned US Studio." In *The Oxford Handbook of Dance and Politics*, edited by Rebekah J. Kowal, Gerald Siegmund, and Randy Martin, 53–78. Oxford: Oxford University Press, 2017.

Foucault, Michel. *Security, Territory, Population: Lectures at the Collège de France, 1977–1978*. New York: Palgrave Macmillan, 2009.

Freeman, Damita Jo. "Diary of an Ex-Soul Train Dancer Presents: The One and Only Damita Jo Freeman." Interview by Stephen McMillian. *Soul Committed Productions* (blog), August 20, 2012. https://soulcommitted.wordpress.com/2012/09/01/diary

Freeman, Elizabeth, and Tyler Bradway, eds. *Queer Kinship: Race, Sex, Belonging, Form*. Durham, NC: Duke University Press, 2022.

Garza, Alicia. *The Purpose of Power: How We Come Together When We Fall Apart*. New York: One World, 2020.

Gaunt, Kyra D. *The Games Black Girls Play: Learning the Ropes from Double-Dutch to Hip-Hop*. New York: New York University Press, 2006.

George, Nelson. *The Hippest Trip in America: "Soul Train" and the Evolution of Culture and Style*. New York: HarperCollins, 2014.

Ghandi, Leela. *Affective Communities: Anticolonial Thought, Fin-de-Siècle Radicalism, and the Politics of Friendship*. Durham, NC: Duke University Press, 2006.

Glissant, Édouard. *Poetics of Relation*. 1997. Ann Arbor: University of Michigan Press, 2010.

Goldman, Danielle. *I Want to Be Ready: Improvised Dance as a Practice of Freedom.* Ann Arbor: University of Michigan Press, 2010.
Graham, Martha. *Blood Memory.* New York: Doubleday, 1991.
Green, Kai M. "Into the Darkness: A Quare (Re)membering of Los Angeles in a Time of Crises, 1981-Present." PhD diss., University of Southern California, 2017.
Green, Kai M., and Marquis Bey. "Where Black Feminist Thought and Trans* Feminism Meet: A Conversation." *Souls* 19, no. 4 (2017): 438–54.
grimes, d. Sabela. "STREETdance." *Social*Dance*Media: Old Shuffles in a New Paradigm* (blog), August 28, 2008. http://socialdancemedia.blogspot.com/2008/08/streetdance.html
grimes, d. Sabela. "STREETdance[R]." *Social*Dance*Media: Old Shuffles in a New Paradigm* (blog), August 28, 2008. http://socialdancemedia.blogspot.co.uk/2008/08/streetdancer.html
Gumbs, Alexis Pauline. *Undrowned: Black Feminist Lessons from Marine Mammals.* Chico, CA: AK Press, 2020.
Guzman-Sanchez, Thomas. *Underground Dance Masters: Final History of a Forgotten Era.* Santa Barbara, CA: ABC-CLIO, 2012.
Hamera, Judith. *Dancing Communities: Performance, Difference, and Connection in the Global City.* New York: Palgrave Macmillan, 2007.
Harney, Stefano, and Fred Moten. *The Undercommons: Fugitive Planning and Black Study.* New York: Minor Compositions, 2013.
Harris, Laura. "What Happened to the Motley Crew? C.L.R. James, Hélio Oiticica, and the Aesthetic Sociality of Blackness." *Social Text* 30, no. 3 (2012): 49–75.
Hartman, Saidiya. *The Plot of Her Undoing.* Notes on Feminisms 2. Feminist Art Coalition, 2020.
Hartman, Saidiya. *Scenes of Subjection: Terror, Slavery, and Self-Making in Nineteenth-Century America.* New York: Oxford University Press, 1997.
Hartman, Saidiya. "Venus in Two Acts." *Small Axe: A Caribbean Journal of Criticism* 12, no. 2 (2008): 1-14.
Hazzard-Donald, Katrina. "Dance in Hip Hop Culture." In *Droppin' Science: Critical Essays on Rap Music and Hip Hop Culture,* edited by William Eric Perkins, 220–35. Philadelphia: Temple University Press, 1996.
Hazzard-Gordon, Katrina. *Jookin': The Rise of Social Dance Formations in African-American Culture.* Philadelphia: Temple University Press, 1990.
Hemphill, Essex, ed. *Brother to Brother: New Writings by Black Gay Men.* Conceived by Joseph Hemphill Beam. Boston: Alyson, 1991.
Henderson, April K. "Dancing between Islands: Hip Hop and the Samoan Diaspora." In *The Vinyl Ain't Final: Hip Hop and the Globalization of Black Popular Culture,* edited by Dipannita Basu and Sidney J. Lemelle, 180–99. London: Pluto Press, 2006.
Hernández, Kelly Lytle. *City of Inmates: Conquest, Rebellion, and the Rise of Human Caging in Los Angeles, 1771-1965.* Chapel Hill: University of North Carolina Press, 2017.
Heyliger, Sean. "The Jay Payton Show: Oakland's Own Soul Train." *Oakland Public Library* (blog), December 1, 2017. https://oaklandlibrary.org/blogs/post/the-jay-payton-show-oaklands-own-soul-train/

Higgins, James. "The Robot: The Dance or the Act?" Locker Legends. Accessed June 15, 2023. https://2022.lockerlegends.net/the-robot/

hooks, bell. "Homeplace (a Site of Resistance)." In *Available Means: An Anthology of Women's Rhetoric(s)*, edited by Joy Ritchie and Kate Ronald, 383–90. Pittsburgh, PA: University of Pittsburgh Press, 2001.

Horton-Stallings, LaMonda. *Funk the Erotic: Transaesthetics and Black Sexual Cultures*. Chicago: University of Illinois Press, 2015.

Huntington, Carla Stalling. *Hip Hop Dance: Meanings and Messages*. Jefferson, NC: McFarland, 2007.

Hurston. Zora Neale. "Characteristics of Negro Expression." In *The Jazz Cadence of American Culture*, edited by Robert O'Meally, 298–310. New York: Columbia University Press, 1998.

Infante, Dennis. "Interview with Medea Sirkas aka Demons of the Mind." *One Cypher* (blog), January 3, 2005. http://www.onecypher.com/2005/01/03/interview-with-medea-sirkas-aka-demons-of-the-mind/

Jackson, Jonathan David. "Improvisation in African-American Vernacular Dancing." *Dance Research Journal* 33, no. 2 (2001): 40–53.

Jackson, Zakiyyah Iman. *Becoming Human: Matter and Meaning in an Antiblack World*. New York: New York University Press, 2020.

Johnson, Jasmine. "Dear Khary (An Autobiography of Gentrification)." *Gawker*, August 31, 2013. https://gawker.com/dear-khary-an-autobiography-of-gentrification-1227561902

Johnson, Jasmine. "Sorrow's Swing." In *Race and Performance after Repetition*, edited by Soyica Diggs Colbert, Douglas A. Jones Jr., and Shane Vogel, 127–41. Durham, NC: Duke University Press, 2020.

Johnson, Jasmine, and Sean Ossei-Owusu. "'From Fillmore to No More': Black-Owned Business in a Transforming San Francisco." In *Black California Dreamin': The Crises of California's African-American Communities*, edited by Ingrid Banks, Gaye Johnson, George Lipsitz, Ula Taylor, Daniel Widener, and Clyde Woods, 75–92. Santa Barbara: University of California, Santa Barbara, Center for Black Studies Research, 2012.

Jones, Nikki, and Christina Jackson. "'You Just Don't Go Down There': Learning to Avoid the Ghetto in San Francisco." In *The Ghetto: Contemporary Global Issues and Controversies*, edited by Ray Hutchison and Bruce D. Haynes, 215–58. Boulder, CO: Westview Press, 2012.

Judy, Ronald A. T. "On the Politics of Global Language, or Unfungible Local Value." *Boundary 2* 24, no. 2 (1997): 101–43.

Kai-Johnson, Imani. *Dark Matter in Breaking Cyphers: The Life of Africanist Aesthetics in Global Hip Hop*. Oxford: Oxford University Press, 2022.

Kai-Johnson, Imani. "From Blues Women to B-Girls: Performing Badass Femininity." *Women & Performance: A Journal of Feminist Theory* 24, no. 1 (2014): 15–28.

Kai-Johnson, Imani. "Music Meant to Make You Move: Considering the Aural Kinesthetic." *Sounding Out!* (blog), June 18, 2012. http://soundstudiesblog.com/2012/06/18/music-meant-to-make-you-move-considering-the-aural-kinesthetic/

Khubchandani, Kareem. *Ishtyle: Accenting Gay Indian Nightlife*. Ann Arbor: University of Michigan Press, 2020.
King, Jason. "Which Way Is Down? Improvisations on Black Mobility." *Women & Performance: A Journal of Feminist Theory* 14, no. 1 (2004): 25–45.
Kraut, Anthea. *Choreographing the Folk: The Dance Stagings of Zora Neale Hurston*. Minneapolis: University of Minnesota Press, 2008.
Lawrence, Tim. *Love Saves the Day*. Durham, NC: Duke University Press, 2004.
Lepecki, André. *Exhausting Dance: Performance and the Politics of Movement*. New York: Routledge, 2006.
Lorde, Audre. "The Uses of the Erotic: The Erotic as Power." Paper presented at the Fourth Berkshire Conference on the History of Women, Mount Holyoke College, August 25, 1978.
Mackey, Nathaniel. "Other: From Noun to Verb." *Representations* 39 (1992): 51–70.
Mahadeo, Rahsaan. "Funk the Clock: Transgressing Time while Young, Prescient and Black." PhD diss., University of Minnesota, 2019.
Malcolm X with Alex Haley. *The Autobiography of Malcolm X*. New York: Grove Press, 1966.
Malone, Jacqui. *Steppin' on the Blues: The Visible Rhythms of African American Dance*. Chicago: University of Illinois Press, 1996.
Mani, Braj Ranjan. *Debrahmanising History: Dominance and Resistance in Indian Society*. New Delhi: Manohar, 2005.
Mar, Alan D. "The Funk behind Bay Area Street Dance." Master's thesis, San Francisco State University, 2012.
Mauss, Marcel. *Techniques, Technology and Civilisation*. Edited by Nathan Schlanger. New York: Durkheim Press, 2006.
McKittrick, Katherine. *Demonic Grounds: Black Women and the Cartographies of Struggle*. Minneapolis: University of Minnesota Press, 2006.
McKittrick, Katherine. "Rebellion/Invention/Groove." *Small Axe* 20, no. 49 (2016): 79–91.
McQuirter, Marya. "Awkward Moves: Dance Lessons from the 1940s." In *Dancing Many Drums: Excavations in African American Dance*, edited by Thomas F. DeFrantz, 81–103. Madison: University of Wisconsin Press, 2002.
Minh-ha, Trinh T. *Woman, Native, Other: Writing Postcoloniality and Feminism*. Bloomington: Indiana University Press, 1989.
Monroe, Raquel. "'I Don't Want to Do African . . . What about My Technique?': Transforming Dancing Places into Spaces in the Academy." *Journal of Pan African Studies* 4, no. 6 (2011): 38–56.
Moore, Shirley Ann Wilson. *To Place Our Deeds: The African American Community in Richmond, California, 1910–1963*. Berkeley: University of California Press, 2001.
Moten, Fred. *In the Break: The Aesthetics of the Black Radical Tradition*. Minneapolis: University of Minnesota Press, 2003.
Moten, Fred, Theaster Gates, and Adrienne Brown. "Fred Moten, Theaster Gates & Adrienne Brown Live in Conversation." Center for the Study of Race, Politics and Culture, University of Chicago, online, May 20, 2020.

Muñoz, José Esteban. "The Wildness of the Punk Rock Commons." *South Atlantic Quarterly* 117, no. 3 (2018): 653–58.
Ngai, Sianne. *Ugly Feelings*. Cambridge, MA: Harvard University Press, 2005.
Nyong'o, Tavia. "I Feel Love: Disco and Its Discontents." *Criticism* 50, no. 1 (2008): 101–12.
Nyong'o, Tavia. "Punk'd Theory." *Social Text* 23, no. 3/4 (2005): 19–34.
Ochoa, Marcia. Queen for a Day: Transformistas, Beauty Queens, and the Performance of Femininity in Venezuela. Durham, NC: Duke University Press, 2014.
Osumare, Halifu. *The Africanist Aesthetic in Global Hip-Hop: Power Moves*. New York: Palgrave Macmillan, 2007.
Osumare, Halifu. *The Hiplife in Ghana: West African Indigenization of Hip-Hop*. New York: Palgrave Macmillan, 2012.
Pabon, Jorge. "Physical Graffiti: The History of Hip-Hop Dance." In *Total Chaos: The Art and Aesthetics of Hip-Hop*, edited by Jeff Chang, 18–26. New York: Basic Civitas, 2006.
Perillo, J. Lorenzo. *Choreographing in Color: Filipinos, Hip-Hop, and the Cultural Politics of Euphemism*. Oxford: Oxford University Press, 2020.
Perkins, William Eric, ed. *Droppin' Science: Critical Essays on Rap Music and Hip Hop Culture*. Philadelphia: Temple University Press, 1996.
Pond, Steven F. "'Chameleon' Meets *Soul Train*: Herbie, James, Michael, Damita Jo, and Jazz-Funk." *American Studies* 52, no. 4 (2013): 125–40.
Puar, Jasbir. "'I Would Rather Be a Cyborg Than a Goddess': Becoming-Intersectional in Assemblage Theory." *Philosophia* 2, no. 1 (2012): 49–66.
Quashie, Kevin. *Black Aliveness, or a Poetics of Being*. Durham, NC: Duke University Press, 2021.
Quashie, Kevin. *The Sovereignty of Quiet: Beyond Resistance in Black Culture*. Piscataway, NJ: Rutgers University Press, 2012.
Raengo, Alessandra, and Lauren McLeod Cramer. "Editors' Notes." *liquid blackness* 5, no. 1 (2021): 1–3.
Ralph, Laurence. "Love, Peace, and Soul." *Transition* 108 (2012): 19–31.
Read, Jo. "Cadences of Choreomusicality: Investigating the Relationship between Sound and Movement in Staged Performances of Popping and Animation in the United Kingdom." PhD diss., De Montfort University, 2017.
Rivas, Jorge. "Carlos Santana: Grammy Academy Is Racist for Cutting Award Categories." *Colorlines*, August 19, 2011. https://www.colorlines.com/articles/carlos
Rose, Tricia. *Black Noise: Rap Music and Black Culture in Contemporary America*. Middletown, CT: Wesleyan University Press, 1994.
Rosenberg, Douglas, ed. *The Oxford Handbook of Screendance Studies*. Oxford: Oxford University Press, 2016.
Rosenberg, Douglas. *Screendance: Inscribing the Ephemeral Image*. Oxford: Oxford University Press, 2012.
Rothstein, Richard. *The Color of Law: A Forgotten History of How Our Government Segregated America*. New York: Liveright, 2017.

Rutledge, Gregory E. "Futurist Fiction & Fantasy: The *Racial* Establishment." *Callaloo* 24, no. 1 (2001): 236–52.
Salkind, Micah E. *Do You Remember House? Chicago's Queer of Color Undergrounds*. New York: Oxford University Press, 2019.
"San Francisco Strutter Lonnie 'Poptart' Green." Strutter's Room (website). Accessed June 15, 2023. http://www.thestruttersroom.com/about/
Schloss, Joseph. *Foundation: B-Boys, B-Girls, and Hip-Hop Culture in New York*. New York: Oxford University Press, 2009.
Scott, Anna. "It's All in the Timing: The Latest Moves, James Brown's Grooves, and the Seventies Race-Consciousness Movement in Salvador, Bahia-Brazil." In *Soul: Black Power, Politics, and Pleasure*, edited by Monique Guillory and Richard C. Green, 9–22. New York: New York University Press, 1998.
Scott, Darieck. *Extravagant Abjection: Blackness, Power, and Sexuality in the African American Literary Imagination*. New York: New York University Press, 2010.
Scott, Johnie. "The NEA." *Artforum*, Summer 2017. https://www.artforum.com/print/201706/the-nea-68668
Segal, Lewis. "Jeff Kutash's Street-Style Dancing." *Los Angeles Times*, August 31, 1986.
Shange, Savannah. "'This Is Not a Protest': Managing Dissent in Racialized San Francisco." In *Black California Dreamin': The Crises of California's African-American Communities*, edited by Ingrid Banks, Gaye Johnson, George Lipsitz, Ula Taylor, Daniel Widener, and Clyde Woods, 93–106. Santa Barbara: University of California, Santa Barbara, Center for Black Studies Research, 2012.
Sharpe, Christina. *In the Wake: On Blackness and Being*. Durham, NC: Duke University Press, 2016.
Silva, Denise Ferreira da. "1 (life) ÷ 0 (blackness) = ∞ − ∞ or ∞ / ∞: On Matter beyond the Equation of Value." *E-Flux* 79 (2017). https://www.e-flux.com/journal/79/94686/
Silva, Denise Ferreira da. "Toward a Black Feminist Poethics: The Quest(ion) of Blackness toward the End of the World." *Black Scholar* 44, no. 2 (2014): 81–97.
Silva, Denise Ferreira da. *Toward a Global Idea of Race*. Minneapolis: University of Minnesota Press, 2007.
Slusser, Sean. "Defying Gravity, Breakin' Boundaries: The Rise of Fresno's Climax Crew." In *Dispatches from the Straight Outta Fresno Archives*, by Valley Public History Initiative: Preserving Our Stories, n.p. Oakland: California Humanities, 2018. https://calhum.org/wp-content/uploads/2018/04/FSU_SOF_booklet_low-res.pdf
Slusser, Sean. "Straight Outta Fresno: How the Popping Dance Movement Empowered Youth of Color." KCET, November 17, 2016. https://www.kcet.org/shows/artbound/straight-outta-fresno-how-the-popping-dance-movement-empowered-youth-of-color
Smitherman, Geneva. *Talkin and Testifyin: The Language of Black America*. 1977. Detroit, MI: Wayne State University Press, 1986.

Snead, James A. "On Repetition in Black Culture." *Black American Literature Forum* 15, no. 4 (1981): 146–54.
Stuckey, Sterling. *Slave Culture: Nationalist Theory and the Foundations of Black America*. 1987. Oxford: Oxford University Press, 2013.
Stuckey, Sterling. "Through the Prism of Folklore: The Black Ethos in Slavery." *Massachusetts Review* 9, no. 3 (1968): 417–37.
Tate, Greg. *Everything but the Burden: What White People Are Taking from Black Culture*. New York: Broadway Books, 2003.
Thompson, Ahmir Khalib. *Soul Train: The Music, Dance, and Style of a Generation*. New York: Harper Design, 2013.
Thompson, Katrina Dyonne. *Ring Shout, Wheel About: The Racial Politics of Music and Dance in North American Slavery*. Urbana: University of Illinois Press, 2014.
Thompson, Robert Farris. "Hip Hop 101." In *Droppin' Science: Critical Essays on Rap and Music in Hip Hop Culture*, edited by William Eric Perkins, 211–19. Philadelphia: Temple University Press, 1996.
Tinsley, Omise'eke Natasha. *Ezili's Mirrors: Imagining Black Queer Genders*. Durham, NC: Duke University Press, 2018.
Trouillot, Michel-Rolph. *Silencing the Past: Power and the Production of History*. Boston: Beacon Press, 2015.
Tsang, Wu. Interview by Paige K. Bradley. *Artforum*, March 23, 2016. https://www.artforum.com/interviews/wu-tsang-discusses-her-film-debuting-in-hong-kong-at-spring-workshop-58841
Vaid-Menon, Alok. *Beyond the Gender Binary*. New York: Penguin Workshop, 2020.
Vaid-Menon, Alok. "Femininity Does Not Belong to Cis Women." Alok (website), September 17, 2015. https://www.alokvmenon.com/blog/2015/9/17/femininity-does-not-belong-to-cis-women
Vena, Jocelyn. "Justin Bieber 'Somebody to Love' Video Premieres Friday." MTV (website), June 10, 2010. https://www.mtv.com/news/ootl38/justin-bieber-somebody-to-love-video-premieres-friday
Vimalassery, Manu, Juliana Hu Pegues, and Alyosha Goldstein. "Introduction: On Colonial Unknowing." *Theory & Event* 19, no. 4 (2016). https://www.muse.jhu.edu/article/633283
Vincent, Rickey. *Funk: The Music, the People, and the Rhythm of the One*. New York: St. Martin's Griffin, 1996.
Warren, Calvin. "The Catastrophe: Black Feminist Poethics, (Anti)Form, and Mathematical Nihilism." *Qui Parle* 28, no. 2 (2019): 353–72.
Watley, Jody. "In Celebration of Tyrone Proctor." Jody Watley (website), June 8, 2020. https://jodywatley.net/2020/06/08/in-celebration-of-tyrone-proctor/
"What Is Bollywaack?" Kumari Suraj (website), accessed June 15, 2023. https://kumarisuraj.com/bollywaack/
"What Is the Campbellock a.k.a. Locking." Don Campbell (website). Accessed June 15, 2023. https://campbellock.dance/about-locking/what-is-the-campbellock-aka-locking/
Whitehead, Anna Martine. "Expressing Life through Loss: On Queens That Fall

with a Freak Technique." In *Queer Dance*, edited by Clare Croft, 281–90. Oxford: Oxford University Press, 2017.

Whittaker, Nicholas. "Case Sensitive: Why We Shouldn't Capitalize 'Black.'" *Drift*, no. 5 (September 17, 2021). https://www.thedriftmag.com/case-sensitive/

Wisner, Heather. "From Street to Studio: Hip Hop Comes Inside." *Dance Magazine* 80, no. 9 (2006): 74–76.

Wynter, Sylvia. "Black Metamorphosis: New Natives in a New World." Unpublished manuscript, c. 1970s.

Wynter, Sylvia. "Rethinking 'Aesthetics': Notes towards a Deciphering Practice." In *Ex-iles: Essays on Caribbean Cinema*, edited by Mbye Cham, 237–79. Trenton, NJ: Africa World Press, 1992.

Wynter, Sylvia. "Sambos and Minstrels." *Social Text* 1, no. 1 (1979): 149–56.

Yogis, Jaimal. "What Happened to Black San Francisco?" *San Francisco Magazine*, January 18, 2008. https://sanfran.com/what-happened-black-san-francisco (article removed from site).

You, Haili. "Defining Rhythm: Aspects of an Anthropology of Rhythm." *Culture, Medicine and Psychiatry* 18 (1994): 361–84.

Multimedia

"Afropessimism and Its Others: A Discussion between Hortense J. Spillers and Lewis R. Gordon." YouTube video, posted by Soka University of America, May 24, 2021, 1:23:31. https://www.youtube.com/watch?v=Z-s-Ltuo6NI

"All Judges Demo." YouTube video, posted by Boog Studio TV, January 27, 2019, 10:13. https://www.youtube.com/watch?v=kGhDpX8aQE

"Animation Dance Style Tutorial (JRock) Advanced and for Beginners." YouTube video, posted by Styles upon Styles, October 16, 2018, 7:53. https://www.youtube.com/watch?v=oV-soLRxMRU

"Animation Exhibition Battle // .stance // Highlight the Style." YouTube video, posted by stance, September 12, 2019, 28:25. https://www.youtube.com/watch?v=gXJ46GaSysU

"bell hooks - Are You Still a Slave? Liberating the Black Female Body." YouTube video, posted by the New School, May 7, 2014, 1:55:32. https://www.youtube.com/watch?v=rJkohNROvzs

"Bionic - Teaching Reel." YouTube video, posted by BionicBayani, November 14, 2011, 2:55. https://www.youtube.com/watch?v=dzLvaIkrKeY

"Black Starr vs Kiidd Patt Liive=]." YouTube video, posted by cornbread126bee, April 4, 2008, 9:49. https://www.youtube.com/watch?v=k1UCmpEM-Lg

"Boogaloo: The Greatest Story Never Told (Official Trailer)." One Cypher (website), posted October 8, 2021, 3:15. http://www.onecypher.com/2021/10/08/boogaloo

"Boogaloo Dana from Medea Sirkas Demonstrating Robot/Animatronics." YouTube short, posted by medeasirkas-legacytv808, April 21, 2022. https://youtube.com/shorts/kRpdqJhXIfo

"(BRS) Boogaloo Robot Strut (Bay Area Dance)." YouTube video, posted by dizzrockn, May 5, 2008, 7:46. https://www.youtube.com/watch?v=DuYqpWVAiz4

"Destiny Muhammad on Rosie Lee Tompkins." YouTube video, posted by Berkeley Art Museum & Pacific Film Archive, July 14, 2021, 36:51. https://www.youtube.com/watch?v=ZEtgp5S38aM

"Diana Ross with Waack Dancers." YouTube video, posted by Markanthony Henry, April 21, 2007, 5:24. http://www.youtube.com/watch?v=etnptlY_4cg

"Don 'Campbellock' Campbell on the History of 'Locking' at HHI 2015." YouTube video, posted by PacificRimVideoPress, August 9, 2015, 3:34. https://www.youtube.com/watch?v=qROnQORvHHc

"Don Campbellock Explains the Origin of 'Locking.'" YouTube video, posted by John Carluccio, March 31, 2020, 2:00. https://www.youtube.com/watch?v=5KhsfDg3oNw

"The Fillmore Strut by OG Harry Berry of SF." YouTube video, posted by dizzrockn, April 16, 2008, 4:20. https://www.youtube.com/watch?v=myD4MWmewuI

"Grace Jones Do or Die Feat. Viktor (Manoel) and Danny Lugo." YouTube video, posted by AlyssaChloeNYC, January 7, 2012, 0:27. https://www.youtube.com/watch?v=v2-1uUbYFL4

"Granny & Robotroid Inc - 1977." YouTube video, posted by SkillzOne, February 15, 2016, 2:00. https://www.youtube.com/watch?v=Ka2qHrizK6A

"Harlem of the West: The San Francisco Fillmore Jazz Era." Conversation with Elizabeth Pepin Silva and Lewis Watts. YouTube video, posted by California Historical Society, February 16, 2021, 1:55:07. https://www.youtube.com/watch?v=M2Ku1d78csU

"HER-story 'Damita Jo Freeman' Soul Train Dancer Receives an Appreciation Award." YouTube video, posted by God Bless Hip Hop, September 11, 2013, 11:34. https://www.youtube.com/watch?v=EKObcjkon_A

"Justin Bieber's 'Somebody to Love' Video Shoot—Medea Sirkas Behind the Scenes." YouTube video, posted by Zulu Gremlin, June 24, 2010, 0:28. https://www.youtube.com/watch?v=D7yPIFMvsGk (video now private).

"Jody Watley - Still a Thrill." YouTube video, posted by Jody Watley, June 16, 2009, 4:41. https://www.youtube.com/watch?v=kg6Dt3pia9g

Kelley, Avery, dir. *Soul Train Soul Change*. Short film posted to Vimeo by Lynne O'Hara, June 10, 2020, 9:59. https://vimeo.com/427723480

"Ladies GetDown Cypher @ 5th Popper's Picnic 7/14/12." YouTube video, posted by Jay Tee, July 18, 2012, 8:54. https://www.youtube.com/watch?v=DxnxeBsFEnM

"Legendary Dance Crew Medea Sirkas Break Down the History of the Culture and Demonstrate Live." YouTube video, posted by Sway's Universe, November 11, 2018, 20:38. https://www.youtube.com/watch?v=z_4AVyqihmI

Mårtens, Tora, dir. *Martha & Niki*. 2015. Documentary film, 92 min.

"Master Locker Jimmy 'Scoo B Doo' Foster Interview (Guest Host Lil B)." YouTube video, posted by Funkd Uptv, August 15, 2011, 26:09. https://www.youtube.com/watch?v=YnG1gcNOsOM

"Meet Hi-Hat: Celebrity Choreographer and Sears Arrive Air Band Judge." YouTube video, posted by searsarrivelounge, August 4, 2009, 1:50. https://www.youtube.com/watch?v=PEqdvmNOfFU
"Niki & Martha New Style Winners of Juste Debout 2010." YouTube video, posted by streetstar, January 6, 2011, 3:06. https://www.youtube.com/watch?v=pWJqNWyVNKw
"Official Tyrone P Waacking & Soul Train Tribute by 'The Chapter' Mtl." YouTube video, posted by the Chapter Waacking, August 29, 2020, 11:12. https://www.youtube.com/watch?v=GaUHZGnTzhw
Okumura, Kozo, dir. *Far East Coast Is in da House: Street Dancers in Japan*. Michigan State University, 1998. Documentary film, 32 min.
"Pandora Marie Female Popper Popping Freestyle Robot Dancer x Mechanical Monday." YouTube video, posted by Pandora Marie, December 4, 2017, 3:16. https://www.youtube.com/watch?v=rDDAHc9848A
"Part 1: Homeless Man-Diamond D 'Red' Original Oakland Boogaloo Popper 52 Years Old." YouTube video, posted by Mooncricket, October 5, 2011, 4:55. https://www.youtube.com/watch?v=fsoAF5yo-aM
"Poppers Picnic #7 2014 Pop Tart & Harry Berry aka Frisco." YouTube video, posted by Chineserobot, July 13, 2014, 2:47. https://www.youtube.com/watch?v=vPiGso6j_hc
"Popping Dance Tutorial- How to Get Harder Pops!" YouTube video, posted by Versa-Style, November 18, 2021, 9:36. https://www.youtube.com/watch?v=hz1fj6QIhRk
Riggs, Marlon, dir. *Black Is . . . Black Ain't*. 1995. Documentary film, 98 min.
Riggs, Marlon, dir. *Tongues Untied*. 1989. Documentary film, 55 min.
"Robotter's Room (Featurette #4) [HD] - The Solo Robotter's / Richmond Robottin History." YouTube video, posted by Ralph Montejo, August 26, 2013, 5:13. https://www.youtube.com/watch?v=cW2Dsew7XqQ
"Rufus Thomas - 'Breakdown' & 'Funky Chicken' Live @ Wattstax 1973." YouTube video, posted by ianwoodsman, November 25, 2011, 9:45. https://www.youtube.com/watch?v=KCFyKRtlLOI
Sanders, Sam. "The Legacy of 'Soul Train.'" *It's Been A Minute*. NPR, October 17, 2021. MP3 audio, 36:02. https://www.npr.org/2021/10/15/1046380826/
Sanders, Sam, Anjuli Sastry Krbechek, Liam McBain, and Jordana Hochman. "There Was Nothing Like 'Soul Train' on TV. There's Never Been Anything Like It Since." *It's Been a Minute*. NPR, September 28, 2021. MP3 audio, 36:00. https://www.npr.org/2021/09/14/1037118049/
"Scarecrow Riley Moore." YouTube video, posted by Robonati, November 12, 2009, 0:32. https://www.youtube.com/watch?v=mmsqYBsomyw
Sotirova, Ina, dir. *Check Your Body at the Door*. 2011. Documentary film, 60 min.
"Soul Train Ball & Battle: A Tribute to Don Cornelius Oakland, CA 03/24/12." YouTube video, posted by Mooncricket Films, March 25, 2012, 7:23. https://www.youtube.com/watch?v=e9r6SlzQtco
Stuart, Mel, dir. *Wattstax*. Columbia Pictures, 1973. Documentary film, 103 min.
Talbot, Joe, dir. *The Last Black Man in San Francisco*. Plan B Entertainment, 2019. Film, 120 min.

"Talk: Nick Cave and Friends, with Linda Johnson Rice, Damita Jo Freeman, and Nona Hendryx." Moderated by Naomi Beckwith. Facebook Live video, posted by Museum of Contemporary Art Chicago, November 17, 2020, 1:08:09. https://www.facebook.com/43871522761/videos/1225021567876301

"Tyrone 'The Bone' Proctor Shaking His Groove Thang." YouTube video, posted by Funkd Uptv, March 25, 2012, 1:00. https://www.youtube.com/watch?v=b1cuEomvCwo

"Warhol, Club Culture, and the Black Celebrity Image." Panel conversation moderated by Adrian Loving. YouTube video, posted by the Andy Warhol Museum, November 2, 2022, 1:16:59. https://www.youtube.com/watch?v=xDdSV1GoEXU

"Waves of Emotions - Axelle Ebony - Dance Film - Whacking." YouTube video, posted by Axelle "Ebony" Munezero, February 6, 2023, 4:08. https://www.youtube.com/watch?v=qLJo-az6qVo

"What Is Waacking? Queer History of Punking, Whacking, Waacking 1970–2003: The Intro." YouTube video, posted by Kumari Suraj, July 3, 2016, 8:40. https://www.youtube.com/watch?v=l62XRkUym2Q

"When I Move / You Move: The Conversation #2 'Hip-Hop' Dance in Seattle Perspectives in Black." YouTube video, posted by Dani Tirrell, August 25, 2020, 1:58:17. https://www.youtube.com/watch?v=iQTmJyIa9no

Wilkerson, Spencer, dir. *If Cities Could Dance*. Season 4, episode 2, "Boogaloo: The Dance That Defined Oakland's Culture," 8:33. Aired January 15, 2021, on KQED.

INDEX

Italicized page numbers refer to figures.

Printed and bound by CPI Group (UK) Ltd, Croydon, CR0 4YY

09/06/2025

14686106-0001